QUMRAN AND THE BIBLE

*Studying the Jewish and Christian Scriptures
in Light of the Dead Sea Scrolls*

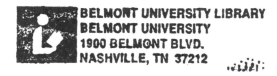

Nóra Dávid and Armin Lange (Eds.)

QUMRAN AND THE BIBLE

Studying the Jewish and Christian Scriptures in Light of the Dead Sea Scrolls

PEETERS

LEUVEN — PARIS — WALPOLE, MA

2010

A catalogue record for this book is available from the Library of Congress.

© 2010 — Peeters, Bondgenotenlaan 153, B-3000 Leuven

ISBN 978-90-429-2455-0
D/2010/0602/134

PREFACE

On October 28th, 2008, the University of Vienna awarded Emanuel Tov its honorary doctorate in recognition of a life dedicated to the study of the Dead Sea Scrolls and the textual histories of the Hebrew and Greek Bibles. As the diploma of Emanuel's honorary doctorate puts it:

> qui eximia opera scientific et de historia textuum biblicorum sive Hebraice sive Graece conscriptorum illustranda et de libris prope asphaltitum lacum repertis summa diligentia examinandis edendisque optime meritus est

The work of Emanuel Tov on the textual histories of the Hebrew and Greek Bibles has changed our perception of how the texts of these Bibles came to be. It is because of his work that their textual plurality is well known. He has revolutionized our perception of how the Hebrew and Greek Bibles came to be what they are today. This alone would be a good reason to award an honorary doctorate. But Emanuel's editions of manuscripts from various sites at the Dead Sea as well as his editorial work as Editor-in-Chief of the Dead Sea Scrolls publication project has even more far reaching consequences. The Dead Sea Scrolls and Emanuel Tov's research and editorial work on them changed and will continue to change our understanding not only of the textual histories of the Hebrew and Greek Bibles but also the religious, cultural, literary, and political histories of Ancient Judaism and Early Christianity.

To better illuminate the impact of Emanuel Tov's work on the various fields of Biblical, Jewish, and Christian studies, the University of Vienna decided to accompany the traditional awards ceremony with a small symposium on "Qumran and the Bible." The proceedings of this symposium as well contributions by Emanuel Tov, Lika Tov, and Armin Lange are published in the present volume.

It is a pleasant obligation for us to express our gratitude and thanks to all those who made the honorary doctorate of Emanuel Tov and the Vienna symposium on "Qumran and the Bible" possible and helped to organize them. Foremost among them are Vienna University's rector, Prof. Dr. Georg Winckler and the Dean of the Faculty for Historical and Cultural Studies Prof. Dr. Michael Viktor Schwarz, but also Monika Beringer-Ermer, Cornelia Blum, Dara Fischer, Nikolaus Ortner, Margarethe

Rössl, and Matthias Weigold. Another word of gratitude is due to the lec-
turers of our symposium, Prof. Dr. Heinz-Josef Fabry, Prof. Dr. Florentino
García Martínez, and Prof. Loren T. Stuckenbruck for their presentations
and contributions to this volume as well as to Guy Feldman from the Israeli
Embassy in Vienna and Emanuel Tov himself for their speeches during the
awards ceremony. Further words of thanks are due to Prof. Dr. Kristin De
Troyer for accepting the volume into her series Contributions to Biblical
Exegesis and Theology and to Paul and Patrick Peeters for publishing
and producing it. Last but not least we would like to acknowledge the
help of Michael Segal, Marlene Schiffman, and Bennie H. Reynolds, who
polished the English of the contributions of Florentino García Martínez,
Armin Lange, and Lika Tov.

It is a special pleasure to the editors of this volume that both Emanuel
and Lika Tov agreed to contribute to it. This volume begins with a contribution by Emanuel Tov ("Some Academic Memoirs"). In a way, Emanuel
also tells in this article how the story of our volume itself began. His essay
is a reminiscence on his academic life, on his work as Editor-in-Chief
of the Dead Scrolls publication project, and on his life-long academic
engagement with the texts of the Hebrew and Greek Bibles as well as
with the Dead Sea Scrolls. Emanuel Tov begins these memoirs with his
high school years and ends with the completion of the DJD series. In
between, Tov provides the reader with a wealth of information going far
beyond personal experiences.

By now Lika Tov's art on the Dead Sea Scrolls is well known inside
and outside of Dead Sea Scrolls studies. In her contribution ("Some
Dead Sea Scrolls Fragments as a Source of Inspiration for My Art"),
Lika tells the story of her Dead Sea Scrolls art and how she developed her
unique artistic understanding of the Scrolls. Not to give away too much,
it should just be mentioned that Lika's especially trained eye for forms
developed a new perspective on Dead Sea Scrolls fragments during
Emanuel's work as editor in chief of the Dead Sea Scrolls publication
project. Next to all that is precious in a marriage, Lika and Emanuel Tov
gave the world not only a scholarly but also an artistic treasure.

Armin Lange ("The Textual Plurality of Jewish Scriptures in the Second
Temple Period in Light of the Dead Sea Scrolls") engages with the
textual history of the Hebrew Bible and shows how the work of Emanuel
Tov provides a tool that allows for analysis of the textual plurality of
the Jewish scriptures in the Second Temple period. Scribal corruption,
redactional reworkings, harmonistic editing, abbreviation, compilation,
and recension are causes of textual plurality. The proto-Masoretic standard

text stands not at the beginning of the textual histories of the Jewish Scriptures, but developed late in the Second Temple period. First efforts towards such a standard text can be observed in the second half of the first cent. B.C.E.

Based on the example of the Book of Joshua, Florentino García Martínez asks in his contribution ("The Dead Sea Scrolls and the Book of Joshua") how the Dead Sea Scrolls can help to better understand the books of the Hebrew Bible. Three editions of the Book of Joshua and one or two rewritings of this book exist in different copies next to each other and without distinction in the Qumran collection. Joshua quotations from the Dead Sea Scrolls prove a rewritten composition of Joshua can attain the same or even higher authority than Joshua. Furthermore, a complete quotation of Psalm 122 in the *Apocryphon of Joshua* shows that the book of Psalms can be considered as a conglomerate of raw materials that can be plundered for new literary constructions. All of this points to the inadequacy of the category "Bible" for the study of the Second Temple period.

Heinz-Josef Fabry ("Die Rezeption biblischer Texte in frühjüdischer Zeit im Licht der Qumrantexte") studies the various forms of interpretive literature in the Qumran library. Fabry shows that 1) Qumran literature participates in a broad hermeneutical tradition which goes back to a time before the final stages of the biblical books were reached and that 2) the biblical manuscripts from the Qumran library apply the same interpretative techniques in their variant readings as the interpretative literature from the Qumran library does itself. Fabry sees the continuous Pesher at the beginning of Qumran hermeneutics. Its actualizing readings developed later on into midrashic interpretation. In the end, these Midrashim did not even need to quote a lemma any more. Both commentator and reader were able to correlate a given interpretation to its interpreted base text without quotation. Qumran hermeneutics attest to the existence of an interpretative *inspiratio continua* which only ended with the closure of the Hebrew canon.

Loren Stuckenbruck ("The Dead Sea Scrolls and the New Testament") asks for the relevance of Qumran for the understanding of the New Testament. The Dead Sea Scrolls illuminate the multilingual world in which the early Christians cultivated their identity. Some of the diversity of early Christianity reflects the diversity of Second Temple Judaism. Parallels between the Dead Sea Scrolls and early Christian literature point to cross-currents of tradition. Such parallels need to be explored in the broader contexts of Second Temple Judaism, the Greco-Roman, and the ancient

Near Eastern worlds. Parallels between the Dead Sea Scrolls and the New Testament help to explore "*perspectives* conveyed by the litera-ture on religious life, cosmology, time and theological anthropology where a tradition-historical stimulus for reinvigorating the discipline can be found."[1]

The editors, Vienna May 2010

---

[1] Stuckenbruck, 171.

TABLE OF CONTENTS

SOME ACADEMIC MEMOIRS

Emanuel Tov

1. Beginnings and High School Years

I have always resisted the suggestion to write my memoirs and it remains a strange idea, not unusual, but simply strange. But now I have no choice, encouraged as I have been by the editor of this volume. The honor shown me makes the writing of a short version of my memoirs a worthy enterprise.

From which point should one start writing one's memoirs? From the day I was born or beforehand, from my elementary or high school years, or from my youth in general? Luckily, I received some instructions, namely that I should provide background information concerning my work on the Septuagint and the Dead Sea Scrolls (DSS). We can thus skip the first so many years of my life.

My interest in these topics started formally with the beginning of my study at the Hebrew University at the age of 20, but the seeds of these interests were sown at an earlier age. As a child, I first wanted to become a physician, but that wish dissipated rather quickly when I realized that I could not stand the sight of blood. I do not remember the full list of professions that I subsequently wanted to embrace, but among them were archeology (as was the desire of my wife to be, Lika), classics, and sociology. With the latter purpose in mind, I traveled once from Amsterdam to Groningen in my penultimate school year to speak with Prof. J. E. Ellemers of Groningen University, a famous sociologist specializing in the sociology of the *kibbutz*. I do not remember the details of that conversation, but I did not continue with those aspirations. I do know that much later, in the summer of 2003, I addressed the academic community of Groningen University on the occasion of being conferred with the Ubbo Emmius medal by that university. In my speech, I referred to my consultation with Prof. Ellemers in the distant past, some forty-five years earlier. I spoke of him in vague terms, fearing that he may no longer be among us. Great was my surprise when Prof. Ellemers introduced himself to me during the ensuing reception.

In my school years, I was attracted to ancient literatures, greatly enjoying the study of Greek and Latin at the classical gymnasium in Amsterdam,[1] the city of my birth in 1941. I liked the world of the classics, and I was in love with the Latin and Greek languages. I liked to master new fields of knowledge that for us, as children, were a *tabula rasa* when embarking on them. We learned the Latin and Greek paradigms, compared the two languages, and accepted from our teachers the view that the study of the verbal systems of the Latin and Greek languages[2] would be instrumental in developing our logic. Further, if you have these language systems in your mind, we were told, it is easier to learn other languages even if, like Arabic, they differ completely from the classical languages. At school, I loved to follow the logic of Plato, to walk around the battlefields of Troy with Homer and to follow Odysseus in his travels. I also liked translating (always from the source language to Dutch) the poetry of Virgil and the terse style of Tacitus' *Histories*. Tacitus did not use a single superfluous word and, prone to efficiency myself, that is how I had always wanted to express my own thoughts in other languages. Not in Latin, because we never spoke or wrote in that language, which was a constant complaint of our teachers, referring to our less-knowledgeable generation. They themselves mastered these proficiencies, but were not instructed to pass them on to us. The small group of pupils in our *gymnasium alpha* (in my case, a subdivision of the Spinoza Lyceum) excelled in all these topics, and we were probably raised as little scholars. Indeed, two persons continued in classical languages at Amsterdam University, while others took up the study of other languages; some turned to other free professions.

In many ways, at the university I stayed close to the love of my school years, but added a new dimension to it, that of the study of the Hebrew language. While in high school, alongside my study of classical and modern languages, I took up the study of Hebrew from age 13 onwards. At that age,

[1] We specialized in the *humaniora*, especially the classics and modern languages and literatures. At age 11, I myself chose the type of school I wanted to attend from the age of 12 onwards. The social elite went to a "gymnasium," while the next group went to a "lyceum," where one could choose in grade 2 whether to follow the gymnasium direction or the more general HBS direction. At a later stage, one could choose the *alpha* direction, which involved the specialization in languages and classics, or the *beta* direction with a specialization in the sciences. In the *alpha* direction, which I chose, we only had a token continued education in the sciences; and in the *beta* direction the continued study of the classics was minimal.

[2] In our final year, we studied nine hours of Greek (Plato, Herodotus, Homer) and an equal number of hours of Latin (Ovidius, Virgil, and Tacitus) together with modern languages (Dutch, English, French, and German).

I became a Jewish "man" (*bar-mitzvah*), and Rabbi Benedikt influenced me to take up Hebrew. The auto-didactic system of learning Hebrew at the private *Talmud Torah* school of Mr. Mundzstuck very much resembled that of the learning procedures followed at my high school.[3] The self-study of Hebrew involved the learning of loose-leaf instruction pages, with accompanying paradigms and exercises. Mr. Mundzstuck would move from student to student and older students sometimes helped younger ones. Twice a week, I set out on the 20-minute bicycle ride to this Hebrew school, a rather dilapidated two-room facility on the second floor of the Swammerdam Street synagogue. The study of Hebrew was based on love and self-determination. Most students were religious and were sent by their parents, while I was not religious and not sent by anyone, and therefore probably enjoyed the learning of Hebrew more than others. This was more or less the pattern of my life until the time I finished high school at the age of 17 and a half.

Throughout my high school years I was a member, later a leader, and subsequently *the* leader of a Jewish Zionistic youth movement (*Habonim*, "the builders") in the Netherlands, and that activity involved further learning of Jewish history, the history of Israel, etc. Upon finishing my high school, this study took place in Jerusalem, where I was sent by my movement in 1959–1960, at the "Institute for Youth Leaders from Abroad." At that institute I continued to study Hebrew and took my first classes in Hebrew Bible. Not having been brought up in a religious environment, I had never studied Bible. It was there that I decided to enroll later in the Department of Bible at the Hebrew University. At an earlier stage, while still at high school, I had wanted to study classical literatures at the university, and I enrolled for one year at Amsterdam University (1960–1961), but due to my work responsibilities as the leader of the youth movement, I did not study much, and the enrollment was little more than a formality.

In the meantime, I advanced my study of the Hebrew Bible at a low-key level. I took private courses in reading Ezekiel with an Israeli student who happened to be studying in Amsterdam, and I also taught Hebrew.

---

[3] The learning procedure ("Dalton System") followed at my high school involved both frontal teaching (two-thirds of the time) and the preparation of special assignments completed at school (one-third of the time). This system suited self-disciplined pupils, while others were lost. Each teacher gave us a number of assignments and during designated times we could finish these tasks in the classrooms of the teacher of that subject, under his or her guidance. During these hours, pupils wandered from class to class in order to complete this special type of homework.

In addition, I studied the book of Joshua and wrote educational programs for re-enacting the conquest of Canaan with children aged 9–11 who came to the summer camps of *Habonim*.

2. University Studies

Soon, I was able to combine my two fields of interest. When I immigrated to Israel in 1961 and enrolled in the Bible Department at the Hebrew University, I found out that I could not study merely one subject, so I added Greek to the study of Bible. In my mind, Bible was my main topic for the B.A., but for the university they were equal.

During my study, some topics were easier than others, but I received good grades in them all. I was able to skip the preparatory studies in the Greek language due to my previous studies at high school in Amsterdam, and jumped immediately to the departmental courses. In the Department of Greek, my main interests were closest to those of Prof. Baruch Lifschitz who taught epigraphy, Hellenistic authors, and some tragedies. I could not help noticing that his notes were written in French, while he taught in Hebrew. He must have felt what I was to feel also in my own teaching that for those of us born abroad it takes longer to read Hebrew pages than it does for native Israelis.

For Prof. Lifschitz, we had to prepare readings from some fifteen classical authors for proficiency examinations, and for each of these we had to read major sections and show expertise in an oral exam. I prepared most of these texts together with Judith, the daughter of my Bible professor, Isac Leo Seeligmann. Judith reminded me recently that I once said to Prof. Lifschitz that I read Herodotus like the *Yediot Aharonot* newspaper. At the end of my study, I had to take a B.A. examination, for which I chose Homer as my field of specialization. Together with Judith, I read all the books of the Ilias and Odyssey, greatly enjoying this reading experience. While at high school, I had to translate Greek into Dutch, but I now had to translate Greek into Hebrew, which took some time to get used to. Raanana (later Prof.) Meridor taught Greek syntax to a small group of 6–7 students, and this was the backbone of our language studies. With unequaled determination and thoroughness, she wrote her corrections in red in our Greek writing exercises.

During the first two years, some of my studies in Bible were a little more difficult for me than those in Greek because I was disadvantaged in comparison with my native-Israeli fellow students. They had learned Tanakh at elementary and high school, and some of them knew great parts of the Bible by heart. On the other hand, my own high school studies probably prepared me better than them for a critical and philological reading of the text, since my fellow students, religious and secular, often explained the Biblical Hebrew in accord with the meaning of the words in modern Hebrew.

When I started to study, at the beginning of the 1960s, there was great interest in the study of the Bible in Israel, where that literature was and is conceived as national literature that has cultural, historical, and even political significance for the country. Each year, some 100 new students flocked to the department, focusing on Bible as one of their two "majors". When I arrived at the department, Prof. Seeligmann was the only professor, along with several lecturers. He taught the major courses on Bible, each year focusing on one literary genre (wisdom literature, prophecy, historiography, etc.). All the B.A. students took part in these courses, some 250 of them in Mazer Lecture Room 1. They were the centerpiece of the study in the department because of Seeligmann's high intellectual standards, wide knowledge, and acumen. These courses were the talk of the day also because of Seeligmann's peculiar character. He used to write Hebrew backwards on the blackboard, and often finished a session in the middle of a sentence, keeping sharply to time, and continued from exactly that point in the sentence the week thereafter. In a class of some 250 students, he often addressed students personally, a source of embarrassment for some.

In my second year of B.A. studies, I was allowed to participate in Seeligmann's M.A. course on the Septuagint (LXX). These weekly meetings became the highlight of my studies, and I followed these courses for four years. It is there that I learned my methodological approach towards the LXX, and my own LXX classes delivered over the course of forty years (from which sabbaticals need to be deducted) followed the pattern of my teacher's system. I provide little introduction to the LXX (students had to fill in the background information themselves), and the focus of the course was an intimate knowledge of a single biblical book in the LXX. Such a book was not exhausted, since we did not succeed in reading more than 4–5 chapters. The analysis in the class was very thorough, much more than that covered by the professional literature on any given book. There are very few commentaries on the LXX, and in Seeligmann's day there were even fewer; the analysis in the class is much more profound than in the few LXX commentaries that have been written in the meantime. From Seeligmann I learned the core of the philological approach, which involves the intimate study of all the details relating to the LXX.

At the first stage, this involves the understanding of the meaning, text, grammar and background of the LXX of a given book, its exegesis and the reconstruction of elements in its parent text, then the same regarding the Hebrew book, its ancient versions, and the Qumran Hebrew manuscripts. As a consequence the Alexandrian-Greek translators came to life in his class. At a second stage, the details in the LXX are compared with those in the MT (Masoretic Text), conclusions are drawn and preferences on the readings of the MT or the LXX are expressed. Seeligmann was a master in the methodological background of such reasoning, using the whole gamut of his expertise in all these areas, and many more. He frequently drew on his vast knowledge of biblical exegesis, classical Greek and ancient cultures. He excelled in assuming stages in the transmission of the Greek and Hebrew texts that have now been lost. The technical process of assuming scribal errors was always in his mind, but he was prone to assuming theological developments either in the translator's mind or in the Hebrew readings in earlier stages in the development of the text.[4]

My interest in the texts and versions of the Bible was further kindled and developed by Prof. Shemaryahu Talmon, with whom I served as an assistant for several years. He included the newly discovered Qumran scrolls in the study of the text more often than other scholars, and he also was an expert on the Samaritan (Hebrew) version of the Torah. He developed a literary approach to textual criticism, and he had the gift of outlining the overall development of all the ancient versions. With his brilliant ideas on these and other topics (I recall especially his seminar on the Oracles against the Foreign Nations), he enthused the whole class and whetted their appetite for further independent study.

I learned much from the analyses of Profs. Haran and Loewenstamm and enjoyed their critical acumen. I vividly remember the courses given by Prof. Meir Weiss. His thoroughness, candor, and intellectual integrity had no equal. To give just one example, it took him four academic hours to analyze with the class the first verse of the book of Job. He could convincingly present a specific view of a *crux* in the text, and then, with a good sense of humor, he would proceed to oppose that view even more convincingly.

Having studied with these professors at an early stage in my education opened the way for classes with Prof. M. H. Goshen-Gottstein in my

---

[4] For an excellent example, see Seeligmann's study "δεῖξαι αὐτῷ φῶς," *Tarbiz* 27 (1958): 127–41 (Heb.).

M.A. studies. I would not have been ready for his approach at an earlier stage in my study. First of all, I did not know enough but, equally important, I would not have been ready to absorb his demanding requests and his irony. Goshen left a profound impression on me in his courses on Syriac and Aramaic, biblical philology in general, and the history of Semitic scholarship.

I continued to be influenced by Prof. Goshen within the framework of the Hebrew University Bible Project (HUBP), a project that aimed at producing a critical edition of the Bible. In order to produce such an edition based on the text of the Aleppo Codex, specialists collected data within the project relating to the ancient witnesses. I learned much from the cooperation with Profs. Talmon and Rabin in our joint editing of the Jeremiah volume.[5] At an earlier stage, I was involved in the formulation of the principles of editing and of the description of the individual translation phenomena. Sarah Ory, David (later Prof.) Weissert and I discussed the principles among us and later with Prof. Goshen. Goshen's organizational skills and insights were the key to the success of this operation. I learned much from the formulation of these principles as is visible in my book on the LXX.[6]

3. Beginnings of an Academic Career

While still an M.A. student, I did limited teaching. I gave a course that we called *Bibliographia*, which offered an introduction to all the tools a student needs to master such as the *Biblia Hebraica*, dictionaries, bibliographical tools, etc. The teaching of this, my first course entailed much preparation and called on considerable mental resources. In the beginning, after lectures, I was worn out and literally had to rest for three hours. I was especially impressed by the fact that older people, in one case a man in his mid-forties, took a 25-year-old teacher, still a student, seriously.

My academic career started upon my return from Harvard University, where I had expanded my education in the Department of Near Eastern Languages and Literatures as it was then called (see below, §7). I served as an "assistant," the lowest teaching level, both at the Hebrew University and at the developing Haifa University, hoping that continued employment would come from one of these places. The next appointments followed at the Hebrew University, first as instructor, then as senior lecturer, asso-

---

[5] *The Hebrew University Bible. The Book of Jeremiah* (Jerusalem: Magnes Press, 1997).
[6] *The Text-Critical Use of the Septuagint in Biblical Research* (2d rev. and enl. ed.; Jerusalem Biblical Studies 8; Jerusalem: Simor, 1997).

ciate professor and professor, all received at a fairly young age, something that would be more difficult today. For each appointment, I had to submit a list of publications that were evaluated by experts at the Hebrew University and elsewhere. The criteria were stringent, but are even stricter today. My appointment was in the Department of Bible, where I taught the introductory course (twice), exegesis of specific books, and a number of courses on the LXX, Qumran, and textual criticism.

4. Textual Criticism of the Hebrew Bible

The deliberations within the HUBP helped me to crystallize my own views on many aspects of the text-critical procedure, though not on all stages of that procedure. The culmination of that procedure is the evaluation of the textual evidence, which is the expression of a view on the question as to which of two or more readings is the better one. In this area, I could not learn from the HUBP for the simple reason that that project does not engage in textual comparison. I developed my views in that area at an abstract level, and subsequently wrote a theoretical paper on this area,[7] which formed the basis for a chapter in my Hebrew handbook on textual criticism.[8] Looking back at the way in which that book developed, at first in Hebrew, then in other languages, I advanced my thinking by systematically writing *Vorstudien* on the various areas of textual criticism. My principle was and, remains, if you don't know an area well, write a paper on it! Of course, there were experts in several areas of textual criticism who mastered those fields better than me, such as Prof. Yeivin on the Masorah and Prof. Maori on the Peshitta, etc. My first inclination was to ask them to write chapters in my book, but I then realized that I would have to explain to them at length my guiding principles and they might have disagreed with them. Realizing the difficult procedure involved, I decided that it would be more meaningful for me, and ultimately also for the readers, to present my own views on all aspects of textual criticism. The editions of *TCHB* developed in this sequence: Hebrew, English (first edition), German,[9] English (second edition),[10] and

---

[7] "Criteria for Evaluating Textual Readings: The Limitations of Textual Rules," *HTR* 75 (1982): 429–48.

[8] *Textual Criticism of the Bible: An Introduction* (Heb.; Jerusalem: Bialik Institute, 1989).

[9] *Der Text der Hebräischen Bibel: Handbuch der Textkritik* (trans. H.-J. Fabry; Stuttgart: Kohlhammer, 1997).

[10] *Textual Criticism of the Hebrew Bible* (2d rev. ed.; Minneapolis and Assen: Fortress Press and Royal Van Gorcum, 2001) [below: *TCHB*].

Russian.[11] Technical limitations prevented the second English edition from being a full-fledged revision; in making changes, I was limited to the borders of each printed page since the edition was printed from camera-ready pages. If I wanted to add something important on a given page I had to omit something else on that or the next page.[12]

My thinking on textual criticism is influenced by the reading in detail of many manuscripts and ancient translations, and less so by abstract theories. I always had in mind the many different texts of the Bible that were circulating, for example at Qumran. All these manuscripts differed from one another, but within that plurality one may recognize some groups (families). I brought some stability to the description of this plurality, I hope, by providing a statistical description of the different types of Qumran scrolls.[13] Further, I suggested that the scriptural Judean Desert scrolls (except for those from Qumran) reflect the Jerusalem Temple text that was later to become the MT, while the Qumran scrolls reflected many different text forms.[14]

My studies on the LXX and, more recently, on 4QReworked Pentateuch[15] led me to new thoughts regarding the development of the final stages of the authoring of the biblical books and the first stages of their transmission. The reconstructed Hebrew texts underlying the LXX of 1 Samuel, Jeremiah, and Ezekiel show that the formulation of these books developed stage by stage, and this reconstructed development makes it difficult to posit a single original text of these books. In my view, there was not one original text, but a series of "original texts."

---

[11] *Tekstologiya Vetchoga Zaveta* (trans. K. Burmistrov and G. Jastrebov; Moscow: Biblisko-Bagaslovski Institut Sv. Apostola Andrjeya [St. Andrews Theological Seminary], 2001).

[12] On the other hand, the third edition of my *TCHB* will not be bound by technical considerations. The new edition, which is now [2009] in its planning stages, will be completely novel in many ways. I will be free to completely deviate from the previous editions by adding and omitting long sections and even chapters. I will allow myself to shorten the complicated chapter 3 on the original text, to expand the discussion of textual criticism and exegesis and/or theology, to greatly expand the chapter on text editions, to add chapters or segments on "a didactic approach to textual criticism," and computer-assisted research of textual criticism, etc.

[13] For the latest formulation, see my collected papers: *Hebrew Bible, Greek Bible, and Qumran – Collected Essays* (TSAJ 121; Tübingen: Mohr Siebeck, 2008), 128–54.

[14] See Tov, *Hebrew Bible, Greek Bible, and Qumran*, 171–88.

[15] I published that text together with S. A. White as: "4QReworked Pentateuch[b-e] and 4QTemple?" in H. Attridge et al., in consultation with J. VanderKam, *Qumran Cave 4.VIII, Parabiblical Texts, Part 1* (DJD XIII; Oxford: Clarendon, 1994), 187–351, 459–63. Ten years afterwards, I realized that these texts do not reflect a non-biblical rewritten composition, but biblical texts that included many exegetical elements.

5. The CATSS Project and Septuagint Lexicography

Those who consult the CATSS database comparing the LXX and MT
will be surprised to find out that it originated in LXX lexicography.
Its beginnings were in the summer of 1974 when John W. Wevers and
I were strolling alongside the walls of the Old City of Jerusalem. I was
then 33 years old, and John knew my work on the LXX. I had just completed my dissertation on the LXX of Jeremiah and was about to leave
for my first research leave, now called a "post-doc," at Oxford without
a specific research assignment or project. Prof. Goshen had linked me up
with a well-known New Testament scholar, George D. Kilpatrick, with
whom I was to take some courses and to discuss my ideas on LXX
research. The plans were to take an unexpected turn when John Wevers
convinced me to embark on the creation of a LXX lexicon. John was the
president of the newly established IOSCS (International Organization for
Septuagint and Cognate Studies), and in that capacity he considered it
his task to develop new research tools. I accepted the challenge and was
expected to advance my thinking at Oxford, which was an ideal place for
this purpose. Among other things, I consulted with Prof. Peter Glare who
was in the middle of the revision of the large Liddell and Scott lexicon
of the Greek language. I vividly recall him sitting in his room in the
Ashmolean Museum (or another office in St. Giles) surrounded by large
wooden boxes containing many compartments filled with small entry-
slips. I also consulted with other lexicographers and I read general books
and studies on lexicography. Only a few studies on LXX lexicography
existed, although there were many studies on individual words or seman-
tic fields, some even book length. I collected the bibliographical data in a
little brochure,[16] and compiled card indexes of individual words.[17] I also
developed my views on the special nature of LXX words and LXX
lexicography deriving from the unnatural character of these words in the
Greek language as reflections of their Hebrew counterparts.[18] I summarized my views in a document sent to Professors Wevers, Goshen, and
Hanhart, who then reacted. I also published my thoughts in 1976.[19]

---

[16] *A Classified Bibliography of Lexical and Grammatical Studies on the Language of the
Septuagint and Its Revisions* (3d ed.; Jerusalem: Academon, 1982).

[17] In December 2008, I discarded these index cards since their contents are now all covered
by J. Lust, E. Eynikel, and K. Hauspie, *A Greek-English Lexicon of the Septuagint, I–II*
(Stuttgart: Deutsche Bibelgesellschaft, 1992, 1996).

[18] See my study contained in *The Greek and Hebrew Bible – Collected Essays on the
Septuagint* (VTSup 72; Leiden: Brill, 1999), 109–28.

[19] See Tov, *The Greek and Hebrew Bible*, 95–108.

Two developments led me away from my plan to create a LXX lexicon:

1) I became increasingly aware of our lack of knowledge in the area of papyrology relating to the LXX. These were not only my own personal shortcomings, but also those of my colleagues. In order to present an adequate lexicographical description of the LXX words, we need to be able to present the contemporary vocabulary, possibly from the same locale as that of the translators, definitely that of Egypt. The older lexicon of Moulton-Milligan[20] provided some references, but presently much more material is available. In the 1980s, such evidence was available in scattered publications that I found difficult to keep track of. During a research stay at Macquarie University, Sydney in 1989, I realized how much more these scholars (Edwin Judge, John Lee, Greg Horsley) knew than me about the papyri, and even they could not fully cope with the material. Their project was meant to find parallels for New Testament words,[21] but much of the evidence they had gathered could also be used for LXX lexicography. All this happened before the computer age made vast quantities of papyri accessible on line,[22] and at the time I was frustrated that major papyrological sources were not easily available.

2) The budding lexicon project created an important by-product to which most of my attention was directed. In 1980, before spending a year at the Department of Religious Studies at the University of Pennsylvania, I asked my host, R. A. (Bob) Kraft, whether he would be willing to join forces in creating Stage 1 of the lexicon project, viz., a computerized comparison of the words of the MT and LXX. I had become increasingly aware that the meaning of many LXX words is determined by that of their Hebrew counterpart so that the awareness of Greek-Hebrew equivalents would provide important background information for LXX lexicography. For example, the use of *eirene* runs parallel to that of *shalom*, which it represents in almost all of its occurrences, that of *diatheke* runs parallel to that of *berit*, etc. In order to provide this background material for the lexicon, I planned an electronic tool presenting the words of MT and LXX in parallel columns. The concept of such a word-by-word comparison stemmed from the

---

[20] J. P. H. Moulton and G. Milligan, *The Vocabulary of the Greek Testament Illustrated from the Papyri and Other Non-Literary Sources* (London: Hodder and Stoughton, 1930).

[21] See: *New Documents Illustrating Early Christianity*, vols. 1–9 (North Ryde, N.S.W.: The Ancient History Documentary Research Centre, Macquarie University, 1981–2002).

[22] Perseus Digital Library: http://www.perseus.tufts.edu/hopper/.

days of my work in the HUBP. Bob Kraft was far ahead of me in everything relating to computers, and it was he who developed the ideas for the electronic creation of the database (along with the project's programmer, the late J. Abercrombie), while I developed the concept of comparing the details in the Hebrew and Greek texts. For this purpose we needed to write a grant proposal and Bob had the gift of providing a detailed description of a project that did not yet exist – something I learned from him – and together we turned to the NEH. We received major funding ($300,000), most of which went into the buying of an Ibycus computer system and overhead costs to the University of Pennsylvania. From 1981 onwards, we started to create a large electronic database that automatically created the equivalences between the LXX and MT, lexeme by lexeme (such as W/B/BYT/Y = KAI\ E)N TW=I OI)/KWI AU)TOU=), to be corrected manually. The manual correction of the computer results,[23] together with the addition of notes on translation technique (all in "col. a") and the creation of the reconstructed Hebrew source of the LXX ("col. b") was my responsibility, while Bob started to insert variants for the Greek texts. My part of the job was executed mainly in Jerusalem with a team of five assistants and a programmer, funded by the Israel Academy of Sciences. The result was a database of Greek-Hebrew equivalents to be joined by separate Greek and Hebrew morphological lexica for all the text words enabling the search of any word or form in the Hebrew and Greek Bible.

This database, named CATSS (Computer Assisted Tools for Septuagint Studies) was meant to be Stage 1 of the lexicon project. It was used by several scholars, most notably by Lust-Eynikel-Hauspie in their brief lexicon of the LXX.[24] Otherwise, the text was not easily accessible to other scholars because of its uneasy ASCII transcription format as exemplified in the previous paragraph.

A major step forward for the CATSS project took place when our data were made accessible within the Accordance program for the Macintosh, and later for the P.C. with screen emulation. Because of the advanced search possibilities enabled by Accordance,[25] this program now provides sophisticated software for the research on MT, LXX, and a comparison

---

[23] That is, the determining of the exact equivalence of the Greek and Hebrew words, based on insights in translation technique, exegesis, and textual relations.

[24] See n. 17. For other studies based on the CATSS database and for a more detailed description of the project, see Tov, *The Greek and Hebrew Bible*, 31–51.

[25] For details, see http://www.accordancebible.com/

of the two texts. The CATSS project provides data for the comparison of all LXX texts for which a Hebrew/Aramaic parallel text is either available or has been reconstructed (Psalm 151, Baruch, Sirach). I am very proud of this tool, although I realize that many details need to be improved. F. Polak of Tel Aviv University prepared a revised version of CATSS named "Tov-Polak." This database is now available (Accordance, Bible Works, Logos), and is being constantly improved. I now use the program much more than paper sources when preparing for my LXX classes, and in recent years I have even been able to prepare my classes on my laptop while in an airplane.

6. Septuagint Research

My LXX research was advanced by my appointment as Grinfield lecturer on the Septuagint at Oxford University. That university holds on to all kinds of scholarships and fellowships that would have been diverted at other universities to more urgent needs, but not so at Oxford. This two-year appointment is for one week of three lectures. One needs to apply for this position, but as I had never heard of its existence, I was encouraged by Oxford University to apply and, upon acceptance, successfully completed a tenureship of two years in 1980–1982. Subsequently, the university extended this appointment for two additional terms of two years (1982–1986). I used this opportunity to advance my ideas on the Greek Minor Prophets Scroll from Naḥal Ḥever, inner-translational relations and the contribution of the LXX to the literary analysis of Hebrew Scripture. Fifteen to twenty persons, not including my driver,[26] attended the lectures. As the Grinfield lecturer, my name was once mentioned in the Manchester Evening News of 1 April as a member of the Oxford Eight in the Oxford and Cambridge Boat Race, a rowing competition, when the journalist searched for the most obscure names of appointments at Oxford.

My studies on the LXX focused first on inner-translational developments and gradually moved to the relevance of this translation for the study of the Bible. My initial publications dealt with that translation's early revisions that were intended to approximate the Greek text to the Hebrew text current in Israel from the first century B.C.E. until the second

---

[26] There is a story, no doubt apocryphal, about a well-known Oxford professor who gave his first lecture in the Grinfield series in the 1950s or 1960s with one person in attendance. At the end of the lecture, when the lecturer abundantly thanked that person for his interest and commitment, he replied: "Don't bother, Sir, I'm your driver."

century C.E. For that purpose, I established principles for the criteria defining and characterizing the revisions. My preoccupation with matters of translation technique and the reconstruction of the Hebrew parent text of the LXX were influenced by the practical work in the HUBP described in §2.

Subsequently, the focus of my interest moved to the relevance of the LXX for biblical scholarship, both for textual and literary criticism. In several books, the LXX reflects a Hebrew basis that needs to be taken into consideration in the exegesis of those books, both when the Hebrew parent text of the LXX presumably preceded the MT (Joshua, 1 Samuel 16–18, Jeremiah, Ezekiel, etc.) and when it contains an exegetical layer reacting to the forerunner of the MT (1 Kings, Esther, and Daniel). In all these books, it would be advantageous for the exegete of the Hebrew books to take the Greek translation into consideration. A precondition for this procedure is that the analysis of the translation technique as described in §5 will have established that the LXX is a good source for establishing the text that lay in front of the translator.

7. Qumran Scrolls

Most of my publications until 1990 pertained to textual criticism, especially the LXX. A second line of investigation began with my deeper involvement with the Dead Sea scrolls from 1990 onwards. Prior to that time, I also was much involved with the scrolls, but not in an official way. I might say that I was already interested in the scrolls at age 14 when I bought a little monograph in Dutch in the AO (Algemene Ontwikkeling [general knowledge]) series by A. S. van der Woude (1955), which I still have. In the following year (1956), when in England, I bought John Allegro's introduction to the Dead Sea Scrolls. Only later, from 1961 onwards, upon my enrollment in the Bible Department at the Hebrew University was I able to take courses in that area. I studied the paleography of the scrolls with N. Avigad, the ideas of the scrolls with D. Flusser, the language of the Isaiah Scroll with Y. Kutscher, and exegesis and textual criticism in the scrolls with S. Talmon. I was to receive more serious and practical instruction in the scrolls during my two years of study at Harvard University (1967–1969). I studied there with Prof. John Strugnell who was to be appointed as editor-in-chief of the Dead Sea Scrolls Publication Project in 1984, but also before that time he was one of the leading members of the Cave 4 team. I took John's course on the scrolls, which included the writing of seminar papers on one of the texts that had been

assigned to our teacher. Students who knew little about the scrolls before
their participation in the course wrote seminar papers on the basis of
the PAM photographs, while another member of the seminar critiqued
the paper. The level of these discussions was extremely high and we all
enjoyed John's enthusiastic guidance.

This course, as well as a private tutorial with Prof. F. M. Cross,
prepared me well for the task of editor-in-chief that I did not yet know
about. With Cross, I read the unpublished 4QSam[b] scroll (published, after
much delay, in 2005) in a private tutorial. I still treasure Cross's careful
hand-written transcription of the scroll, his notes and my own preparations for that tutorial. In due course, F. M. Cross was to accept some of
my suggestions for readings and analysis. The tutorial was given in the
library building (Widener I) in a greatly inspiring study.[27] Cross served
as the second advisor of my dissertation on the LXX of Jeremiah and
Baruch, together with S. Talmon, which was accepted by the Hebrew
University in 1974.[28]

Upon my return to Israel in 1969, after my Harvard years, I wrote
studies on various topics in the area of textual criticism. The study of
the scrolls was to regain a central place in my work when in 1985 I was
asked by Père Benoit, editor-in-chief of the Dead Sea Scrolls Publication
Project, to publish the extensive remains of the Greek Minor Prophets scroll
from Naḥal Ḥever in a separate volume in the *DJD* series. The request
came from Benoit, but originated with D. Barthélemy who had already
published a preliminary edition of most of the fragments in his epoch-
making monograph *Les devanciers d'Aquila.*[29] My work entailed five years

---

[27] FMC tells the story that one day he spread out on the ground of that room the revised pages
of his *The Ancient Library of Qumran*. Great was his surprise when he found out that the
cleaning lady had discarded those pages, thus "killing" the idea of a revised edition.

[28] When I went to Harvard in 1967, I was to write the mentioned dissertation on Jeremiah,
as agreed upon with Prof. S. Talmon, but that did not prevent F. M. Cross from suggesting other topics to me. I recall how he pulled out a yellow sheet of paper from the
bottom right drawer of his desk and started reading out to me a list of dissertation topics.
They all pertained to areas in textual criticism that were worthy of further investigation in light of recent developments in research. For example, with the publication of
Barthélemy's studies on Aquila and Theodotion, F. M. Cross thought that the time was
ripe for a dissertation about Symmachus, which ultimately was written at Oxford University by Alison Salvesen. In any event, I politely declined and told F. M. Cross that
I wished to adhere to my chosen dissertation topic about the LXX of Jeremiah.

[29] D. Barthélemy, *Les devanciers d'Aquila* (VTSup 10; Leiden: Brill, 1963). That monograph totally changed the perceptions of many aspects of LXX research, as it described
the Naḥal Ḥever scroll as an early revision of Greek Scripture (named *kaige*-Theodotion),
segments of which were transmitted as "Theodotion" and even as "LXX". The text
published by Barthélemy hardly deserved the name "edition," and the philological work
towards such an edition still needed to be executed.

of analyzing the readings of the manuscripts, providing philological details, and preparing a commentary on the nature of the revision of Greek Scripture included in this scroll. I was much helped by R. A. Kraft who was to write the codicological description of this manuscript and who critically reviewed everything I wrote when I taught for a year at the University of Pennsylvania as his guest in 1985–1986. Most instrumental in advancing this edition was a seminar on this scroll that Bob and I offered to the students.

This volume, including a detailed computer-assisted reconstruction of the scroll, prepared with Kraft's guidance, was the first manuscript in the *DJD* series to be presented electronically to OUP. The computer version went through various stages, from the University of Pennsylvania's Ibycus system to my PC, and then to OUP's system, so that careful proofreading was needed at every stage.

In retrospect, another preparation for my work as editor-in-chief was my first experience with the publication of Hebrew scrolls beyond my Harvard seminar papers. In 1987, Gene Ulrich, chief editor of the Cave 4 biblical volumes, asked me to prepare the Jeremiah texts for publication.[30] In the course of that work, I learned much about fragments, reconstruction, PAM photographs, electronic submission of text editions, the ever-misleading scales of photographs, etc. Gene and his staff edited my editions in an exemplary way.

From 1990 onwards, my involvement with the scrolls would be more extensive. In the year 1989–1990, Moshe Weinfeld and I convened a research group on Qumran studies at the Institute for Advanced Studies at the Hebrew University, which was very intensive and beneficial for the research of us all.

In the course of my study of the scrolls, I focused much on the Qumran scribes. In 2004, I published a detailed monograph on these scribes, suggesting that the study of scribal habits allows us to obtain a better understanding of the scrolls and scribes.[31] This monograph describes the technical aspects of all the Judean Desert texts, such as the measurements of the sheets, columns and margins, the beginnings and ends of scrolls, systems of correcting mistakes, orthography systems, and scribes. My division of the Qumran scrolls into two groups distinguished by external

---

[30] In his cover letter, Gene stressed that the texts would be taken away from me if I did not finish my task within three years. I stayed within those boundaries, but the volume was not published until 2000 (*DJD* XVI).

[31] *Scribal Practices and Approaches Reflected in the Texts Found in the Judean Desert* (STDJ 54; Leiden: Brill, 2004).

features was first proposed in a study I published in 1986[32] and further elaborated in my book *Scribal Practices* (2004).

8. Editor-in-Chief

In the course of 1990, the Israel Antiquities Authority (IAA) dethroned Strugnell as editor-in-chief and in the late summer I was asked to replace him. The timing was not very good for me as I was about to leave in September for a year's participation at the Netherlands Institute for Advanced Studies (NIAS). The IAA was looking for an Israeli scholar to reorganize the work and enlarge the team so as to speed up the publication of the scrolls, which was lagging behind greatly.[33] It was not ideal to start this assignment during the period of tension surrounding John Strugnell, but I accepted the call because of a feeling of responsibility.[34] I knew I had the oversight committee of the IAA behind me (Professors J. Greenfield and S. Talmon as well as M. Broshi), but I presumed that the general press would be critical of the publication team during the first years, which indeed turned out to be the case.

I was to work with the IAA and its Dead Sea Scrolls oversight committee; as time went on and we became better acquainted, I built up confidence and when results were forthcoming, I was given more freedom. Ayala Sussmann, the IAA contact person for this purpose, with whom I was to work on a daily basis, was especially helpful.

I was actually appointed not only by the IAA, but also by the International Publication Team. Since these were the scholars with whom I had

---

[32] One group of texts is written in a special spelling (forms like *ki'*), morphology (e.g., *malkehemah, me'odah*), and scribal habits (writing the divine name in the old Hebrew script, erasing elements with lines and dots above and below words and letters, placing dots in the margins guiding the drawing of the lines). The great majority of the Qumran sectarian scrolls belong to this group; hence my suggestion that these scrolls were written by sectarian scribes, possibly at Qumran. These scribes copied biblical as well as non-biblical scrolls, altogether one-third of the Qumran scrolls, while the other scrolls were brought to Qumran from outside.

[33] In the first forty years of the publication efforts, only eight *DJD* volumes had been published, the last of which, described above, was my own (*DJD* VIII).

[34] There were no real negotiations with the IAA, since neither they nor I myself were able to define the job. I only had two conditions: that I would be able to run the operation from my university office and not from the Rockefeller Museum, and that my teaching load would be reduced to one-half by having the IAA pay the Hebrew University one-half of my salary. Amir Drori, the director of the IAA, was very determined to get the job finished, and he therefore saw to it that the latter condition was met, even during the most difficult financial times for the IAA, when workers were laid off.

to work, I stipulated to the IAA that the members of the team would appoint me as editor-in-chief as well.[35]

The first year of our work was one of general organizational activity. While at NIAS, I prepared myself for the job in different ways. In my mind, the most important aspects were the establishment of a financial support system for the publication efforts, organization of the team, and standardization of the publication conventions. I vaguely knew that my predecessor received an annual contribution from the Oxford Centre for Hebrew and Jewish Studies for various aspects of the production. That support, ultimately coming from an "anonymous" source in England, continued to be given to us as well.[36] I anticipated that this money would not suffice, since we needed funds for an increasing number of goals: computers and printers for the production, assistance for team members who could not secure such help from their own sources, and an occasional trip to Jerusalem for team members who needed to see "their" fragments. Dr. Weston Fields suggested to me in 1990 that we start a fundraising agency precisely for that purpose, the Dead Sea Scrolls Foundation (DSSF). He was to be the managing director who would do the active search for funds, and I was to be the director of the DSSF, whose task it would be to oversee the operation together with the boards of directors and advisors.[37]

The second task I set myself in 1990 was the enlargement, reorganization and stabilization of the team. I had no authority to make any changes in

---

[35] In turn, some of the team members stipulated that the operation would be run by a triumvirate consisting of Émile Puech, Gene Ulrich, and myself, with the understanding that I would be responsible for the daily activities. This suggestion was accepted, and it worked. Gene Ulrich, serving as chief editor of the biblical manuscripts, was a source of support and advice throughout all these years. I also had a good working relationship with Émile Puech.

[36] Every year I reported to the director of the Oxford Centre and to the "anonymous" donor, usually together with Prof. Alan Crown, administrator of the Qumran project of the Oxford Centre. The donor wanted to know how the money had been spent and what the plans were for the future. Newly published volumes were always rushed to the Oxford Centre and the donor. The money, given to us through the IAA, was spent on the salaries of my secretary/producer of the project and that of the other workers.

[37] The two boards of the DSSF met annually at the meeting of the Society of Biblical Literature (Sundays and Mondays between 7 and 8.30 a.m.). The fundraising was successful, and we raised reasonably large sums of money that were immediately spent on the aforementioned needs. Although most of the work was executed by Dr. Fields, this task became too heavy for me alongside my responsibilities as editor-in-chief, and we therefore asked Prof. S. Paul, my colleague in the Bible Department of the Hebrew University, to accept the position in 2000. He has continued to execute this task with great loyalty and insight.

personnel myself, and everything went through the oversight committee of the IAA, to which I made my recommendations. These assignments were made on the basis of an inventory of the available fragments that I started to compile with the aid of S. Pfann and that was published in conjunction with the microfiche edition of all the fragments.[38] The principle was to assign to scholars texts that could realistically be completed by them within a few years.[39] Unfortunately, this process was not painless. We were not able to come to an understanding with Milik, not even when others and I had called on him in Paris. Milik had in fact ceased to actively prepare manuscripts for publication in the *DJD* series, and even though he had prepared for publication several manuscripts of partial publications, for example the Tobit fragments, he did not complete these assignments, and they had to be re-assigned. F. M. Cross readily agreed to limit his efforts to certain biblical texts, which he did, in fact, finish fifteen years later.[40] Strugnell was happy to continue working on 4QInstruction. I had asked my Harvard classmate, Daniel Harrington, likewise a student of John Strugnell, to work alongside him and this cooperation worked out very well, resulting in the publication of the lengthy volume XXXIV in 1999.[41]

As part of these organizational activities, a large number of scroll fragments were assigned or reassigned to scholars who would prepare them for publication within a reasonable amount of time.[42] The oversight committee imposed no limitations on who could receive an assignment; the decisions depended purely on whether we considered the scholars to be up to the task, with no regard to their country of origin, religion, institutional affiliation or stage in their academic career.[43] Many new

---

[38] *The Dead Sea Scrolls on Microfiche: A Comprehensive Facsimile Edition of the Texts from the Judean Desert*, with a *Companion Volume* (Leiden: Brill/IDC, 1993).

[39] It was soon realized that the texts that had been assigned to J. T. Milik and F. M. Cross could never be finished within a decade, probably not even within a century. The oversight committee of the IAA thus decided to leave these scholars with a reasonable workload and to redistribute the remainder of their assignments to other scholars.

[40] The major publication was to be F. M. Cross, D. W. Parry, R. Saley, E. Ulrich, *Qumran Cave 4.XII: 1–2 Samuel* (DJD XVII; Oxford: Clarendon, 2005).

[41] J. Strugnell, D. J. Harrington, S.J., and T. Elgvin, in consultation with J. A. Fitzmyer, S.J., *Qumran Cave 4.XXIV: 4QInstruction (Musar leMevîn): 4Q415 ff.* (DJD XXXIV; Oxford: Clarendon, 1999).

[42] I always reminded and prodded the editors, mostly in a friendly way, but some had to be reminded by official letters sent by Amir Drori or myself. A few editors returned their assignments, for reassignment to others. At the end of the day, all editors were grateful that they were reminded and prodded, even the ones who received official letters. Many realized that without a push, friendly or not, they would never have reached the end of their publication.

[43] By 1990, nineteen scholars had completed their assignments and twenty-six of the earlier editors remained on the team. With the appointment of fifty-three new scholars,

team members were Israelis, who had previously been barred from the publication enterprise.

From the beginning of our enterprise, I took care of the standardization of the publication conventions. I discussed these issues in March 1991 with the team members who participated in the Madrid Qumran conference. The details of this, my first, organizational activity with the team were written up and circulated among the team members.

At the same time, I had to decide in which electronic format the editions would be prepared. The computerized preparations of the volumes, including the standardization of the details relating to the publication, turned out to be one of the key elements in the success of our enterprise.[44] Our office worked in different ways with the various editors. One author continued to submit hand-written pages, numbering in the hundreds, until the very end of the publication process. Others submitted their texts in PC format, which required a good amount of formatting by us, especially since the Hebrew needed to be retyped, left to right! However, most editors presented us with Macintosh-formatted files, which made it very easy for us to adapt to our *DJD* style.[45]

the overall number of editors who worked on the project totaled ninety-eight. Some of the new editors focused almost exclusively on the texts from the Judean Desert, but since there is no clearly defined discipline of Scrolls research, most scholars came from a variety of backgrounds, focusing on either the textual criticism or exegesis of Hebrew Scripture, intertestamental literature, Apocrypha, Septuagint, or New Testament.

[44] At that time, I had less experience than Gene Ulrich, and therefore I simply followed his lead. Gene convinced me to use the Macintosh platform, which we did to our great satisfaction. Then, and in my view still today in 2009, Macintosh provided overall the best and most user-friendly platform for the preparation of our volumes, using a program that could be handled well by experienced computer users and novices alike. It was clear to me that the only chance of completing the publication was to prepare the camera-ready pages ourselves. It worked so beautifully that even with the passing of the years, when more advanced versions than Microsoft Word 5.1 became available, I decided not to employ them; "if it works, stick with it," and for the coordination of an international project a step forward is sometimes a step backwards. Our standardization allowed the editors to submit their work electronically, and, indeed, during the last years of the project almost every editor prepared the first drafts on his or her own Mac.

[45] As our own systems improved, and our confidence in E-mail grew, we increasingly used that medium for receiving and returning files. We were at the height of our expertise in the preparation of vol. XVII (Samuel) and the files of that edition must have crossed in cyberspace hundreds of time before they were actually published. Our system was to indicate with colors the different editorial activities: Red for elements omitted, green for elements added or changed, and blue for remarks. In this way, we interacted beautifully with our editors without the necessity to send long lists of corrections and changes referring to page so and so. We never had any problem with details going wrong when sent via E-mail, except for, perhaps, in the beginning.

The publication process of the Qumran scrolls has taken some time, possibly a little too long but, in actual fact, not overly long for forty volumes,[46] together with all the inventories and supporting publications, such as the Brill microfiche edition (see n. 38). Nevertheless, had the initial team in the 1950s consisted of twenty, thirty, or even fifty scholars, and not just of nine, the publication *could* have been completed some time ago.[47]

By the time I became editor-in-chief, the fragments had been cleaned, sorted, photographed, as well as identified and partially inventoried. The claim has often been made that this important work was completed in the mid-1950s, but the identification, photographing, and inventorying continued to take much of our time and energy. Initial identifications and the grouping of fragments turned out to be very helpful, but opinions changed and regrouping and re-identification became necessary in several instances.

We also had to give names to the compositions. The story of the name giving warrants a novel in its own right. Once included in the official edition, a name can no longer be changed. Some of these names are utterly subjective; for example, we are still haunted by the so-called 'Wiles of the Wicked Woman' (4Q184), so named by John Allegro. According to many, even the name 'Temple Scroll' is a misnomer, and in my view, 11QPsalms[a] is *not* a biblical scroll.

I was involved also in Carbon-14 examinations of some twenty documents.[48] The choice of the manuscripts and the sampling of the few square millimeters of the documents was a painstaking and instructive process. I will never forget the tears in the eyes of Lena, the conservator at the

---

[46] John Strugnell used to remind us that the preparation of the *DJD* series did not take as long as the publication of similar corpora. The greater part of the Cairo Genizah fragments is still awaiting redemption after more than a century. By the same token, the Greek Oxyrhynchus papyri are far from being published after one century. The British Academy has voted to support this enterprise for a second century. Strugnell made the point that the publication of one volume in the papyrus collections of Rylands, Berlin, Tebtunis, Michigan, and Oxyrhynchus took an average of 7.2 years.

[47] If more funds had been available from the beginning, greater progress could have been made, but I don't think that insufficient financial support was the major reason for the delay. The major reasons for the delay were probably the limited size of the initial team, lack of organization of the publication procedure, a lack of experience, and certain prejudices. Even if de Vaux had had the benefit of ample funds, computers, and E-mail, the volumes would not have rolled off the press, since the organization lacked the necessary insights. All the same, *we* would not have succeeded in our task without the valuable input of our predecessors, especially John Strugnell and Józef Milik, the master of masters.

[48] See A. J. T. Jull, D. J. Donahue, M. Broshi, and E. Tov, "Radiocarbon Dating of Scrolls and Linen Fragments from the Judean Desert," *Radiocarbon* 37 (1995): 11–19.

Rockefeller Museum, when she had to cut out a few square millimeters of surface for these Carbon-14 tests.

Beyond the preparatory activities for the publication and organization of the team, the editor-in-chief organized the assignments, provided scholars with photographs through the good services of the IAA, and guided his colleagues as much as he could. I was in touch with all the editors on a constant basis[49] and that's why, at the peak of our activities, I met with 20–30 colleagues at the yearly SBL meetings as well as at other conferences.[50] As my own experience and confidence grew, I was increasingly able to advise the editors with regard to their difficult task in preparing text editions.[51] Obviously, they all knew their fragments better than me. But I advised as to how to present the fragments; I also remarked on the style of writing, length of the commentary, introductory remarks, preparation of the plates, etc.

In 1990, we were thinking in terms of the complete *DJD* series containing 30 volumes, but eighteen years later, at the completion of the

[49] Editors of editions, more than other scholars, work in isolation without much feedback, and they therefore need the interaction with others. Rather than waiting for the completed manuscripts, I therefore asked for parts, enabling us to make progress on the edition, and thus providing the editor with the necessary interaction. We often aided editors in organizing their thoughts, both before they submitted their manuscripts and afterwards. In this way, several mistakes were caught at the eleventh hour by a member of our staff, even at the preparation stage of the concordances of the individual volumes.

[50] If some colleagues praised my persistence and even tact, the flipside of that virtue was being a *nudnik*, constantly inquiring into the progress being made on editions. When I went to scholarly meetings, as a traveling agent for the project, I always came home with manuscripts or proofs.

[51] It really is not easy to prepare a *DJD* edition because a heavy burden of responsibility lies on the shoulders of each editor. It would take a long time before the texts would be re-edited, if at all. The editors felt the burden of responsibility knowing that their understanding of the fragments would guide scholarship for a long time. The editors realized this responsibility in deciphering the fragments, making connections between the fragments assigned to them as well as other fragments already published and yet to be published. For example, is the fragment to be published a biblical fragment or a fragment of a biblical commentary? Editors naturally wanted to ensure that they offered the best and most trustworthy proposal for all aspects of their editions. Most of all, they feared the idea that on the day after the release of the volume a colleague would read a few key letters in the fragment differently, or that someone would reach a better understanding of the fragment. Because of this fear, some editors delayed handing in their texts. In some cases, I had to be stern and disallow further alterations after we went through successive series of corrections. On one occasion, an editor gave me the final manuscript with tears in his eyes. I remember that on another occasion an editor sent in corrections when the camera-ready manuscript had already gone off to OUP. In one case, I sent corrections to OUP when they already had the camera-ready copy, but immediately realized that this is a recipe for disaster (the correction was inserted, but something else went wrong).

project, we ended up with 40 large-sized volumes or 12,947 pages and 1,394 plates. We prepared thirty-two of these volumes in Jerusalem and Notre Dame, in addition to a Concordance volume.[52] Two enterprises, not connected to the *DJD* series, involved the publication of all the scrolls in a six-volume popular edition based on *DJD* and other sources, the *DSSR*,[53] and an electronic edition of the same, *DSSEL*.[54]

During the first six years, I was very ably assisted in Jerusalem by Claire Pfann, and during the following fourteen years by Janice Karnis. They both served as my secretary, production manager, main copy-editor, and main typist. They developed the system of editing, nomenclature, computer encoding, and printing. I was lucky to have such good helpers. While I was very proficient in all these areas myself, and became very experienced in computers, they were better, and that's an ideal situation.[55]

A large project like this succeeded due to the assistance of many persons, foremost among them being our colleagues at Notre Dame University in the USA: Gene Ulrich, chief editor of the biblical volumes, all produced at that university (after 1992), and Jim VanderKam, who served as the consulting editor of many volumes, often together with M. Brady.

We prepared camera-ready printouts of all the pages of the *DJD* editions, and the publisher, Oxford University Press, reproduced our manuscripts photo-mechanically. You could say that we carried out all the functions traditionally taken care of by publishers (copy-editing, printing, proof-reading). Our publisher multiplied the pages we produced, redid the title pages, and produced the plates. These aspects are no small contribution to the editorial process, and OUP performed these tasks very well. The editions had a beautiful and uniform appearance, the bindings were very professional, and the plates were usually excellent. In several cases, the

---

[52] M. G. Abegg, Jr., *The Dead Sea Scrolls Concordance, Vol. 1. The Non-biblical Texts from Qumran* (Leiden: Brill, 2003).

[53] D. W. Parry and E. Tov, *The Dead Sea Scrolls Reader, Parts 1–6* (Leiden: Brill, 2004–2005).

[54] E. Tov, ed., *The Dead Sea Scrolls Electronic Library,* Brigham Young University, Revised Edition 2006, part of the *Dead Sea Scrolls Electronic Reference Library* of E. J. Brill Publishers (Leiden: Brill, 2006) <All the texts and images of the non-biblical Dead Sea Scrolls, in the original languages and in translation, with morphological analysis and search programs>.

[55] Over the course of the years, we had several people working for the project in the room adjacent to my own at the Hebrew University. Eva Ben David and Valerie Zakovitch served for the longest period. Others were Nehemia Gordon, Simi Chavel, Shmuel Ben Or, and Miriam Berg. We were also assisted by several volunteers: Sarah Presant, Søren Holst, Ingrid Hjelm, as well as some proofreaders.

plates had more contrast than the photographic material we submitted. That is, by manipulating every single photograph, the firm that handled the plates for OUP (in Oxford, in the region of Oxford, and for the last three volumes, in India!) was able to improve the contrast of the photographic images. At times, OUP caught some of our mistakes at the last moment, such as discrepancies between the table of contents and the actual pages, and at times they introduced new mistakes by printing different details on the book jacket than those appearing on the title page, or by imprinting the wrong details on the spine of the book.

On the whole, OUP contributed much to our enterprise by way of the high quality of their products, but this cooperation also involved much investment on my part in maintaining good communication with the various departments at OUP. Had I not done this, the production would have been delayed. The production was not uneventful. One time, the delivery of the proofs was delayed by a week because there was snow in or around Oxford, and the truck needed to be repaired. On another occasion, the camera-ready manuscripts of two complete volumes were lost at OUP's printers. There were mishaps in the production of two sets of plates caused by the printer using too much ink, resulting in several overly dark plates. But these were isolated instances. During the whole period I worked with the same editorial assistant (Jenny Wagstaffe), with whom we have excellent relations.

Politics. Soon enough, I realized that the job that I was to perform was not only scholarly and editorial, for which tasks I was prepared, but also political in all senses of the word. The political aspects of guiding the project pertained to the relations between the project and the outside world, including publishers, possible donors, journalists, and universities. I was also involved in two news conferences, at the beginning and the end of the project, and once I had to appear before a committee of the Israeli parliament.

I became aware of these political aspects already in the fall of 1991. I was painting the outside of my house, when my wife handed me the phone. Jim Sanders from Claremont was on the other end of the line describing a situation that I understood only partially since I had not yet had time to go through the papers left by John Strugnell. In short, Sanders said that the photographs of the scrolls that had been deposited in the Huntington Library in Pasadena, CA had been opened up to the public.[56]

---

[56] This action was related to the heart of a public controversy surrounding the scrolls. From the beginning of the publication activities in 1950, access to the photographs of the scrolls had been limited to the very few members of the publication team. Over the

The director of the Huntington Library, William A. Moffett, sidestepped earlier arrangements by announcing that anyone entering the library would be allowed to see the photographs. The actions of the Huntington Library and the subsequent publication of a *Facsimile Edition* of all the scroll fragments[57] probably had only marginal influence on the publication, that is, scholars hardly, if ever, used the documents "freed" by the Huntington Library or the *Facsimile Edition*. However, most of the influence may have been at the psychological level.[58]

When was the project begun and completed? On both ends, there was a lack of clarity. I was appointed in August 1990, and while based at NIAS (see above), made many preparatory steps between then and September 1991, but began the real work after that date. I therefore sometimes said that we started in 1990 and sometimes that we got underway in 1991.

It is much more difficult to say when the project ended. There were actually several acts of closing the project; while some parties were interested in having the project closed officially, others wanted to have it prolonged. In the fall of 2001, the great majority of our work had been completed, and we were not sure how long it would take to complete the remainder. The IAA arranged for a press conference in the New York Public Library, in which the completion of the project was announced.[59]

years, major criticism was voiced against this monopoly of the international team, which, it was claimed, harmed the progress of research, and gave the members of the team an unfair advantage over outsiders. The originals and photographs were located in Jerusalem, but it was a comforting feeling to know that one set of photographs was found in a safe place in the USA. These photographs had never been used and, in accord with the agreements, they were not to be used.

[57] H. Eisenman and J. M. Robinson, *A Facsimile Edition of the Dead Sea Scrolls* (Washington, D.C.: Biblical Archaeology Society, 1991). These two actions were considered a major victory for those fighting the monopoly of the International Team. H. Shanks was behind the publication of the photographs of the scrolls that was considered illegal by the International Team.

[58] Scholars involved realized that the quality of the images in that edition is so substandard that they cannot be used for any research. For me, the edition served a practical purpose since I was able to use it as one of the bookkeeping resources in the project. In my office copy of the *Facsimile Edition*, we denoted the PAM number, museum plate, name, and place of publication of every fragment and in this way were able to continue the work of identification. In recent years, we lent our copy to E. J. C. Tigchelaar who was able to make some further discoveries of unpublished fragments, although he also had his own sources.

[59] At that point, two other series had also been completed. Several volumes of texts had appeared in the *Judean Desert Series*: Y. Yadin, *The Finds from the Bar Kochba Period in the Cave of the Letters* (JDS 1; Jerusalem: IES, 1963); N. Lewis, *The Documents from the Bar-Kochba Period in the Cave of Letters: Greek Papyri* (JDS 2; Jerusalem: IES, Institute of Archaeology, Hebrew University, Shrine of the Book, Israel Museum, 1989). The Masada series was also completed: Y. Yadin and J. Naveh, *Masada I. The*

The press was not well represented, but the New York Times was there as well as some other leading newspapers. Amir Drori and I spoke, and later, while watching television in my hotel room, I saw my name appearing on the banner of CNN. This was a brief moment of glory, but the work continued. We announced that all the scrolls were published, and that work was continuing on three additional volumes. That announcement was nevertheless correct, since the few texts that were to be included in *DJD* volumes had already appeared elsewhere, though not with the same level of perfection as in *DJD*.

From New York I continued to Denver, CO, where the SBL meeting was to take place. We were to make a similar announcement at the SBL and, in fact, Esther Chazon, chairperson of the Qumran unit, had arranged for a plenary session at the congress where I was to speak. At the beginning of the session, I was pleasantly surprised when my chairman, Jim VanderKam, presented me with a small *Festschrift*, an issue of *Dead Sea Discoveries* (*DSD*). I was completely taken by surprise. There followed some moments of emotion and silence from my side, but the show had to go on. Reacting to my speech,[60] some people said that they never knew me to be a stand-up comedian.

After these public events, work on *DJD* continued, and in fact one volume was added to our enterprise that had not been planned previously, vol. XL presenting a re-edition of 1QH[a]. While not much was left for publication in *DJD*, there was an interest in including some *re-editions* of older volumes, but most of these plans did not get off the ground, or advanced very slowly. Earlier attempts to pull together a supplement volume with corrections by the original editors did not get off the ground because of lack of interest by the editors. It therefore became increasingly clear to me that I needed to announce an official closing date for our publication enterprise. It would not be good for the series to linger on indefinitely, because the public needs an official statement that our mission has been completed. The first date planned for this

Aramaic and Hebrew Ostraca and Jar Inscriptions (Jerusalem: IES and Hebrew University of Jerusalem, 1989); H. M. Cotton and J. Geiger, *Masada II, The Yigal Yadin Excavations 1963–1965, Final Reports: The Latin and Greek Documents* (Jerusalem: IES, 1989); S. Talmon and Y. Yadin, *Masada VI, The Yigal Yadin Excavations 1963–1965, Final Reports* (Jerusalem: IES and Hebrew University of Jerusalem, 1999). Furthermore, most cave 1 texts had appeared in stand-alone editions.
[60] The speech was published in a catalogue of the Grand Rapids Dead Sea Scrolls exhibit: "Celebrating the Completion of the Publication of the Dead Sea Scrolls," in *The Dead Sea Scrolls* (ed. E. Middlebrook Herron; Grand Rapids: Public Museum and Eerdmans, 2003), 33–45.

closing act was February 2008, the second was July 2008, but the actual announcement came on 1 February 2009. The announcement went to my fellow editors, OUP, IAA, the Hebrew University and our financial supporters (in historical sequence: the Oxford Centre for Hebrew and Jewish Studies and the DSSF). In my letter, I wrote to my fellow editors that I had been longing for some time to carry the title "the former editor-in-chief".

As I write these lines in May 2009, I am no longer editor-in-chief, but as happens with large projects such as ours, it is difficult to indicate an exact date for closing a project.[61] My revised inventory of all the fragments from the Judean Desert, now completed, is to be published by Brill Publishers in 2010.[62]

There is no morale from embarking on and completing a large project. I started the project because of a feeling of responsibility, and I simply did the work because it needed to be done. The first few years were the most difficult because I needed to establish myself among my peers and the authorities, and I needed to build up experience and confidence when speaking with my fellow editors. In those years, I sometimes regretted taking on such an enormous task. I was not working two half-jobs (one-half on the scrolls and one-half as a professor), but I was actually working one-and-a-half jobs since the editorial work alone involved a full job.[63] Of course, I had my free moments, but I was thinking all the time about work going on at the office.

I learned an enormous amount at the scholarly level. When working with my colleagues, I learned about their texts. When reading manuscripts, proofs, and plates of others, I made it a point to think also about scribal aspects of the texts. I have been interested in the Qumran scribes for a long time, and while working with colleagues I started to make notes for myself, to be worked out later. These notes enriched my monograph *Scribal Practices*.

Dealing with my colleagues, the editors, was probably the most difficult aspect of my work. Some scholars worked very speedily; one editor, for example, finished 80 pages of text in one year. Natural procrastinators are the weak spot of any project. Intuitively, I have tried to adapt

---

61 The very last volume, a re-edition of 1QIsa[a,b], never published in *DJD*, is scheduled to be released in the fall of 2010. The printing of the volume in February 2010 (in China) was found to be substandard and had to be redone.

62 *Revised Lists of the Texts from the Judaean Desert* (ed. E. Tov; Leiden: Brill, 2010).

63 From 2001 onwards, when my working load in the project became less heavy, I worked on a voluntary basis in addition to a full teaching load at the Hebrew University.

myself to each person's *modus operandi* by being sweeter to some, harsher to others, and occasionally trying both approaches. I have always tried to convince colleagues that there's life after *DJD*, but have not always succeeded in this. So, in the course of working with colleagues, you also learn a lot about personalities. I made many friends. And it is unavoidable that as well as making new friends you also create a few non-friends.

I also learned how to deal with the press. Although some journalists are better than others, they all ask the same questions, and their main information comes from popular books written *against* the scrolls,[64] not *about* the scrolls. In fact, if a journalist did *not* ask me which fragments were confiscated and burned by the Vatican, I would be surprised. I would be equally surprised if a journalist did not ask me where Jesus of Nazareth is mentioned in the scrolls, why the monks of Qumran had some ladies buried in their cemetery, and when we intend to finish the translation (they never used the word 'publication') of the scrolls.

While the first years were difficult, when the first volumes started rolling off the press, I drew satisfaction from our work. It did not become less difficult, but the satisfaction was a good antidote for the tribulations.

Towards the end of my tenure, there were several honors that came my way. It was extremely rewarding to be given a *Festschrift*.[65] Fifty-four colleagues wrote valuable studies. I read them all, and then reacted. At a different level, I now know what it feels like to be awarded an honorary doctorate, from the University of Vienna, home of Armin Lange.[66] At again a different level, there were prizes that came as welcome surprises.[67]

---

[64] Especially M. Baigent and R. Leigh, *The Dead Sea Scrolls Deception* (London: Arrow, 1991); iidem, *Die Verschlusssache Jesus—Die Qumranrollen und die Wahrheit, über das frühe Christentum* (Munich: Droemar Knaur, 1991).

[65] *Emanuel, Studies in Hebrew Bible, Septuagint, and Dead Sea Scrolls in Honor of Emanuel Tov* (eds. S. M. Paul, R. A. Kraft, L. H. Schiffman, and W. W. Fields, with the assistance of E. Ben-David; VTSup 94; Leiden: Brill, 2003).

[66] In an extremely impressive ceremony, before the dignitaries of that university, all in traditional dress, I gave a semi-scholarly lecture with a PowerPoint presentation on the Scribes of Qumran (in English) and I described my feelings and work (in German). At that time I was also given a surprise Vrennese birthday present: *From Qumran to Aleppo: it Discussion with Emanuel Tov about the Textual History of Jewish Scriptures in Honor of his 65th Birthday* (ed. A. Lange, M. Weigold and J. Zsengellér; FRLANT 230; Göttingen: Vandenhoeck & Ruprecht, 2009).

[67] The Humboldt Research Prize (suggested by Professors Lichtenberg and Hengel) in the years 1999-2004, the Emet Prize for Bible Studies received from the prime minister of Israel, Ariel Sharon, in 2004, the Ubbo Emmius Medal given by Groningen University in 2003, and the Israel Prize for Bible Studies, received in April 2009 from the heads of state of Israel.

SOME DEAD SEA SCROLLS FRAGMENTS
AS A SOURCE OF INSPIRATION
FOR MY ART

Lika TOV, Jerusalem

While looking at Dead Sea Scrolls fragments you may realize that the writing on them did not change in the course of time, except for textual damages such as faded ink or darkened leather which blackened out the ink. With special photographic techniques this could often be corrected and the original characters were made visible again.

The shapes of the individual Dead Sea Scrolls however did undergo changes. Some broke or fell apart, leaving many small pieces of parchment, leather and papyrus in the caves where they had been put for storage about two millenia ago. Even in the Judean desert the weather was not always dry enough to keep the parchments of the Dead Sea Scrolls in perfect condition. Due to exposure to humidity the parchment scrolls wrinkled, distorting the writing and the outline. Moist papyrus has a tendency to crumble at the edges while drying. Animals and bad human handling also damaged the scrolls and hence altered their shape. For example: insects may have lived in scrolls, mice nibbled on pieces of fragments, snakes soiled them, etc. Each fragment therefore has a unique shape.

As an illustrator, graphic artist and printmaker I use, among others, Israeli and Biblical themes. Many of the book jackets I designed needed Hebrew lettering for titles and I either drew those letters by hand or calligraphed them. At that time I did not like the existing typefaces, so I designed my own. In a way I felt that the texts on the scroll fragments had been written by colleagues, just much earlier, in antiquity.

In 1993, after a DJD volume had been published, the proofs of the plates were discarded. I received those xeroxes as a pile of scrap paper (size A3) to be used for sketching on the unprinted side. Besides using the white side of my new sketching paper, I noticed the black and white images on the used side. The fragments depicted there had sometimes such surprisingly recognizable shapes, that they stimulated my imagination, as in a Rohrshach-test. From that time on I started to collect such pages with pictures of Dead Sea Scrolls fragments.

Some years later, after more volumes of DJD were published, my new "old fragments" collection had grown. Furthermore, the photographic proofs of fragments from the Greek Minor Prophets Scroll from Naḥal Ḥever (published in 1987) were in my possession as well. I decided that time had come to try to put on paper what I saw in the Dead Sea Scrolls fragments.

As one watches clouds and sees images in them, I studied the shapes of the fragments that looked special to me. From the first moment when I saw a particular page of my collection, I drew lines between the fragments in my mind. I did not want to draw these lines for real though yet, since I thought that I might change my mind. But after seeing that same page several times more, it became clear to me that I had no choice but to add those lines. It took me some time to overcome my hesitation and to finally complete the ancient fragments by adding those missing lines. As if the fragments had been waiting for this touch, the image of a young woman seemed to come to life immediately. Was this Miriam dancing? (Figure 1a and b)

There were more pages with fragments waiting for my pen, to be changed right away from dull fragments to having exciting appearances. Each of those fragments seemed to have a hidden message about what their real meaning was – even without connection to their text, just as an image. I felt that it was my special assignment as an artist to add those few lines that apparently were meant to be there. It would open the eyes to the visual aspects of the fragments and what they might reveal. Of no less importance were the spaces in between fragments, for these negative shapes became positive by adding the right lines (Figure 2).

Browsing through my new 'Rohrshach-test' fragment collection, I had no idea yet what exactly to do with it, but I knew that I would try to integrate the fragments in my printing art. The technique I work with is called "collagraph." This is a collage of paper cuts, glued on a cardboard backing. Lines and text are impressed with a sharp object or just with a firmly pressed pen. From this plate, which is inked and treated like an etching or an engraving, the print can be made on an etching press. The special advantages to this technique are the free form outlines and the fact that all colors can be printed at once.

In 1996, I attempted for the first time to reconstruct a whole scroll by combining copies of several continuing pages from a DJD volume. On every page is the image of one column with an extra centimeter of the previous and the next column on each side. By overlapping, gluing, and cutting them I succeeded in getting a precise copy of the original. In this way, I got an impression of what the whole scroll had actually looked like when it was opened for the first time. I made such a reconstruction of the "Psalms Scroll" (11QPs[a]) that is almost completely preserved and on whose parchment the text was beautifully written. The tetragrammata, i.e. occurrences of the name of God, were very clearly visible, written in paleo-Hebrew characters יהוה.

I rolled the reconstructed scroll up, guided by the pattern of its damaged bottom line that was less deteriorated towards the end of the scroll, from where I had to start. In each circumvention one can match up the first damaged part with the next similar one and find out how many circumventions the original scroll had, when rolled up, before being opened. Thinking about the persons who had written the scrolls 2000 years ago, I drew some scribes busy with their writing. Afterwards, I cut them out and glued them together with a few smaller fragments onto a part of the "Psalms Scroll" as the backdrop, calling it: "They Wrote the Dead Sea Scrolls." This piece became my first collagraph inspired by a scroll fragment (Figure 3a and b).

A few months later I was asked to try my hand at making a print of another scroll. This print was going to be on the subject of the "Copper Scroll" for a congress to be held in Manchester a year later. If I could create something interesting, it would be used as an illustration for the conference's proceedings volume.[1]

After the Copper Scroll was discovered, its brittle columns had been carefully separated with the use of precision dentist's surgical saws and cutters. By gluing and pasting xerox copies of these parts in the right order, I remade them into the shape of a whole scroll. However, seeing how long it became, I decided to do this only for the first three columns of the Copper Scroll.

The Copper Scroll includes a list of all kinds of treasures hidden in different locations around Jerusalem and in the rest of Israel. The script of this account is similar to that written on buildings and sarcophagi. Scratching or incising its characters into the copper of the Copper Scroll must have been an arduous task. After having scratched a few sentences in the cardboard that I use for making a printing plate, my hand started to hurt. I am sure that the scribes of the Copper Scroll encountered this very same problem. After I finished the collagraph, I studied the different handwritings that I encountered in the twelve columns of the Copper

---

[1] George J. Brooke and Philip R. Davies, eds., *Copper Scroll Studies* (JSPSup 40; London: Sheffield Academic Press, 2002).

Scroll and wrote a short article about my findings. It was published together with the other papers of the Manchester Congress.[2] In my finished picture you can see images of persons hiding treasures or looking for them and finding them. Some identifiable locations that are mentioned in the text of the Copper Scroll I depicted also in this print (Figure 4).

Some pieces of inscribed parchment looked to me like animals, waiting to become part of an illustration. In this case they looked like kissing sheep. Around them I drew some more sheep and goats as well as a shepherd playing a flute. The scene is situated in the Judean Desert next to a cave. This piece I named "Judean Desert Pastorale" (Figure 5a and b).

Another fragment had the appearance of a rooster. I took the whole page with fragments of which this rooster was in the center and drew in the open space a hen and little chicks. The other, smaller fragments, I also made into chicks, adding legs and beaks. For the outline I used an earthenware utensil, found at the site of Qumran. This print I gave the title: "From Leather to Feather" – I could also have called it: "Qumran Chicken Soup" (Figure 6a and b).

One scroll when rolled up deteriorated from its upper left side and its lower right side towards the middle. When unrolled, it had a zigzag pattern. Together with drawings of real snakes that live in the Judean Desert, I turned it into a harmonious desert scene (Figure 7).

There are still some animals that I discovered among the fragments for me to put in their visual surroundings, but they will have to wait. I am sure that more creatures are hiding in the Scrolls and I will eventually find them.

The shape of the top part of a fragment caught my eye since it was similar to a lid covering one of the famous scrolls jars found at Qumran. The architecture of the Shrine of the Book in the Israel Museum in Jerusalem is based on this shape. Therefore I turned the outline of this striking building into a frame for the fragment in question. The fragment fits well inside it. To complete the picture and illustrate the fragment's text I added some Essenes who are thanking the Lord, to the picture. This became the print called "Essene Scene" (Figure 8a and b).

The "Thanksgiving Scroll" (1QH^a) had suffered much from the appetite of hungry insects. They had eaten through many of its layers. When

---

[2] Lika Tov, "Some Palaeographic Observations Regarding the Cover Art," in Brooke and Davies, *Copper Scroll Studies*, 288-90.

unrolled a series of holes in this scroll shaped like Hebrew letter ד (*dalet*) could be seen. From one such part of the "Thanksgiving Scroll" I produced a print. Its text was not so clear because of the many wrinkles in the material. The few words in larger type on the left side of the fragment mean: "I thank you Lord for saving my soul" (the reason for the name of this scroll). Instead of lines with text I put images of small rejoicing human figures on top of faded areas of the fragment. The hole I left untouched (Figure 9).

With these descriptions I hope to have given some insight as to how my collagraphs developed. In this special world of fragments, it is a growing process from my first impressions until the final work of art. Until now I have made more than 30 different collagraphs based on the shapes of Dead Sea Scrolls fragments and their textual contents. Besides interesting looking fragments from Qumran, I have also used in my art copies of actual documents found in other caves, such as a parchment *mezuzah*, a *ketubah*, a receipt for dates and some Bar Kokhbah letters. Archeological sites and finds, such as potsherds from Masada (the famous name tags), Jewish coins, locations in the Judean Desert, and caves from around the Dead Sea area became part of my oeuvre.

I would never have been able to create these new visions of the Dead Sea Scrolls without their Editor-in-Chief who, from the beginning of his vast task, unknowingly provided me with the most important ingredients for making original Dead Sea Scrolls art.

Figure 1a   PAM 43.296
Courtesy of the Israel Antiquities
Authority

Figure 1b   PAM 43.296
Copyright of drawings Lika Tov

254. 4QCommentary on Genesis C
PAM 43.233; Mus. Inv. 113

Figure 2   PAM 43.233
Courtesy of the Israel Antiquities Authority
Copyright of drawings Lika Tov

Figure 3a   They Wrote the Dead Sea Scrolls   © Lika Tov

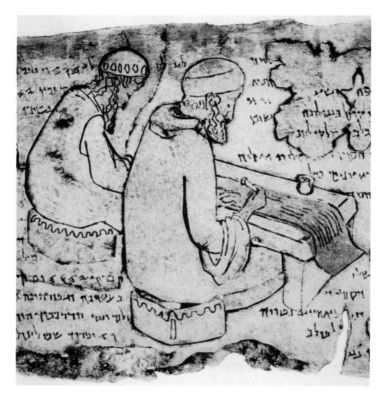

Figure 3b   They Wrote the Dead Sea Scrolls (detail)
                                                   © Lika Tov

Figure 4   Searching for the Treasures of the Copper Scroll

Figure 5a   PAM 43.521
Courtesy of the Israel Antiquities Authority

Figure 5b   Judean Desert Pastorale   © Lika Tov

Figure 6a   PAM 42.012 (detail)
Courtesy of the Israel Antiquities Authority

Figure 6b   From Leather to Feather
© Lika Tov

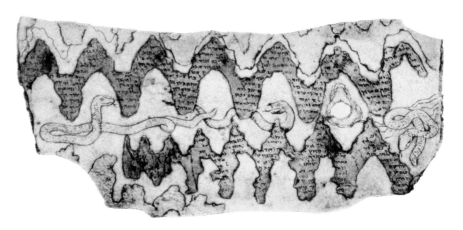

Figure 7   Zigzagging through the Judean Desert   © Lika Tov

Figure 8a   PAM 43.530 and 43.532
Courtesy of the Israel Antiquities Authority

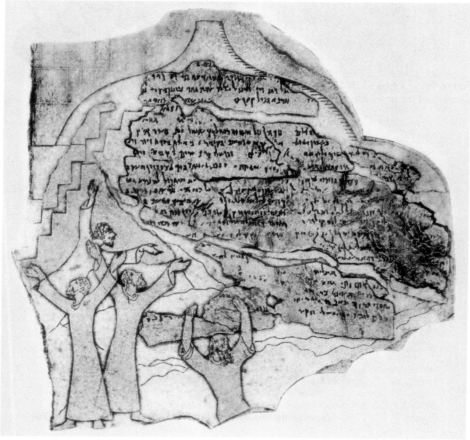

Figure 8b   Essene Scene   © Lika Tov

Figure 9   The Thanksgiving Scroll   © Lika Tov

THE TEXTUAL PLURALITY OF JEWISH SCRIPTURES IN THE SECOND TEMPLE PERIOD IN LIGHT OF THE DEAD SEA SCROLLS

Armin LANGE, University of Vienna*

When the University of Vienna awarded Emanuel Tov its honorary doctorate on October 28th 2008, it was my honor to deliver the *laudatio*. This task was at the same time easy and difficult. There was no lack of praiseworthy material to choose from. But it was quite difficult to decide what not to mention. Instead of simply contributing my *laudatio* to this volume, I decided to engage with questions of textual criticism and the Dead Sea Scrolls because Emanuel was fascinated with textual criticism in general and the Septuagint in particular since the beginnings of his scholarly career.[1] Early on, Emanuel's text-critical research pointed his interest to one of the Dead Sea Scrolls,[2] of which he produced later the *editio princeps*, i.e. 8HevXII gr.[3] Only a few years after his PhD was published, Emanuel began to work on the biblical Dead Sea Scrolls more extensively.[4] Ever since, the Septuagint and the biblical Dead Sea Scrolls

---

* As often in scholarship this article was more of a team effort than might be suspected. I am obliged to my assistant, Dr. Nóra Dávid, for copyediting my article and bringing it into a consistent form. My former student from UNC-Chapel Hill, Dr. Bennie H. Reynolds, stylized my English and improved it to its current readable form. I would not want to miss the opportunity to express my gratitude to both Dr. Dávid and Dr. Reynolds.

[1] Cf. e.g. "Pap. Giessen 13, 19, 22, 26: A Revision of the LXX?" *RB* 78 (1971): 355–83; "L'incidence de la critique textuelle sur la critique littéraire dans le livre de Jérémie," *RB* 79 (1972): 189–99; *The Septuagint Translation of Jeremiah and Baruch: A Discussion of an Early Revision of Jeremiah 29–52 and Baruch 1:1–3:8* (HSM 8; Missoula, Mont.: Scholars Press, 1976).

[2] "Transliterations of Hebrew Words in the Greek Versions of the Old Testament: A Further Characteristic of the *kaige*-Th. Revision?" *Textus* 8 (1973): 78–92.

[3] *The Greek Minor Prophets Scroll from Naḥal Ḥever (8HevXIIgr) (The Seiyal Collection I)* (DJD VIII; Oxford: Clarendon, 1990).

[4] "The Textual Character of the Leviticus Scroll from Qumran Cave 11," *Shnaton* 3 (1978): 238–44 (Heb. with Eng. summ.); "The Relationship between the Textual Witnesses of the Old Testament in the Light of the Scrolls from the Judean Desert," *Beth Miqra* 77 (1979): 161–70 (Heb.); "The Textual Affiliations of 4QSamᵃ," *JSOT* 14 (1979): 37–53.

have represented the two main foci of his research. Through his seminal textbook on the *Textual Criticism of the Hebrew Bible*, his theories are present in almost every classroom today. A common thematic thread between Emanuel's work on the Septuagint and the biblical Dead Sea Scrolls are his studies on the changes scribes applied to the biblical texts. In this article, I would hence like to engage with how the Dead Sea Scrolls changed our ideas about the textual history of the Hebrew Bible during the Second Temple period and how the textual plurality attested by the biblical Dead Sea Scrolls emerged. After a survey of the Dead Sea Scrolls evidence and its most important interpretations, I ask how the proto-Masoretic standard text of the Hebrew Bible developed. I also inquire about the factors that led to the textual plurality of the Second Temple Period – a plurality that belies our conception of the fixed place of the Masoretic Text. In the end of this article I draw some conclusions.

1 The Qumran Library and the Textual Plurality of Jewish Scriptures

Before the work of Emanuel Tov, two basic theories of the textual history of the Hebrew Bible were developed in response to the manuscripts of biblical books that were discovered in the Qumran library, i.e. the local text theory of W. F. Albright and F. M. Cross and the group specific text theory of S. Talmon. Both theories correlate the three principal medieval versions of the Hebrew Bible, i.e. the Masoretic Text, the Septuagint, and the Samaritan Pentateuch, with the Qumran manuscripts. In the beginning of text-critical research on the Dead Sea Scrolls, W. F. Albright[5] and F. M. Cross[6] developed the local text theory. It claims that the three principal medieval witnesses (MT, LXX, and SP) evolved out of a shared *Urtext* and were affiliated with three different geographical regions in antiquity: Judea (Cross speaks of Palestine), Mesopotamia, and Egypt. In Judea, the Samaritan text and its pre-Samaritan forerunner(s) as attested in the Qumran library developed out of this shared *Urtext*. When in the sixth century B.C.E. Jewish exiles took the shared *Urtext* with them to Babylon, the consonantal text of the Masoretic

---

[5] W. F. Albright, "New Light on the Early Recensions of the Hebrew Bible," *BASOR* 140 (1955): 27–33.

[6] E.g., F. M. Cross, "The History of the Biblical Text in Light of the Discoveries in the Judaean Desert," *HTR* 57 (1964): 281–99; idem, "The Contribution of the Qumrân Discoveries to the Study of the Biblical Text," *IEJ* 16 (1966): 81–95; "The Evolution of a Theory of Local Texts," in *Qumran and the History of the Biblical Text* (eds. F. M. Cross and S. Talmon; Cambridge, Mass.: Harvard University Press, 1975), 306–20.

Text evolved out of it in Mesopotamia. Since the fourth century B.C.E., a third text-type evolved in Egyptian Judaism, which became the *Vorlage* of the Septuagint. By way of returnees to Judea both the Egyptian and the Mesopotamian text types would have influenced the Palestinian one eventually.

Against the local text theory, S. Talmon[7] envisions a time of textual instability and plurality at the early stages of the textual history of the Hebrew Bible. This textual plurality is attested both by the various versions of the Hebrew Bible and by the biblical manuscripts from the Qumran library. Out of this textual plurality, the socio-religious groups which developed at the end of the Second Temple period choose individual texts, which in turn developed into group specific texts. In this way, MT, LXX, and SP became affiliated with Judaism, Christianity, and the Samaritans respectively. Talmon describes this process as follows:

> "primal traditions which varied among themselves to a limited degree progressively lost their lease on life and ultimately crystallized in a restricted number of *Gruppentexte*";[8] "... a great number ... of Qumran variants in biblical scrolls and in Bible quotations resulted from insufficiently controlled copying and/or sometimes represent diverging *Vorlagen*. But I would also maintain that an undetermined percentage of these *variae lectiones* derive from the impact of ongoing literary processes of intra–biblical nature."[9] "In other words, the extant evidence imposes on us the conclusion that from the very first stage of its manuscript transmission, the Old Testament text was known in a variety of traditions which differed from each other to a greater or lesser degree. As a result of undirected, and possibly in part also of controlled, processes of elimination, the majority of these variations went out of use. The remaining traditions achieved by and by the status of a *textus receptus* within the socio-religious communities which perpetuated them. These standardized texts were preserved for us in the major versions of the Hebrew Bible and its translations."[10]

Today both the local text theory and Talmon's theory of textual chaos and group specific texts have been largely replaced by the works of

---

[7] S. Talmon, "Aspects of the Textual Transmission of the Bible in Light of Qumran Manuscripts," *Textus* 4 (1964): 95-132; "A Textual Study of the Bible – A New Outlook," in *Qumran and the History of the Biblical Text* (eds. F. M. Cross and S. Talmon; Cambridge, Mass.: Harvard University Press, 1975), 321-400; "The Old Testament Text," in *The Cambridge History of the Bible*, vol. 1: *From the Beginnings to Jerome* (eds. P. R. Ackroyd and C. F. Evans; Cambridge: Cambridge University Press, 1970), 159–99.

[8] Talmon, "Textual Study," 327.

[9] Talmon, "Textual Study," 380.

[10] Talmon, "Old Testament Text," 198–99.

E. Tov and E. C. Ulrich. While Tov developed a grid which allows for classifying each textual witness from the Second Temple period, Ulrich's work is not so much concerned with relating the textual plurality of the Second Temple period to the Hebrew Bible's three principal medieval text traditions, but to study how this textual plurality developed.[11] Ulrich even rejects the use of terms like proto-Masoretic for the characterization of textual witnesses from the Second Temple period as anachronistic.[12] Ulrich assumes that for the Second Temple period, the Septuagint, Josephus Flavius, the quotations and allusions of the New Testament, as well as "the manuscripts of the Scriptures found at Qumran are representative of the Jewish Scriptures generally."[13] Textual plurality would be the result of multiple editions of individual Jewish scriptures existing next to each other.

> If accurate, that would mean that the growth of the individual biblical books developed through repeated creative new editions over time …

---

[11] E. C. Ulrich, "Horizons of Old Testament Textual Research at the Thirtieth Anniversary of Qumran Cave 4," *CBQ* 46 (1984): 613–36; *The Dead Sea Scrolls and the Origins of the Bible: Studies in the Dead Sea Scrolls and Related Literature* (Studies in the Dead Sea Scrolls and Related Literature; Grand Rapids and Leiden: Eerdmans and Brill, 1999; this volume collects most of Ulrich's earlier articles on the question); "The Dead Sea Scrolls and the Biblical Text," in *The Dead Sea Scrolls after Fifty Years: A Comprehensive Assessment.* Vol. 1 (eds. P. W. Flint and J. C. VanderKam; Leiden: Brill, 1998), 79-100; "The Scrolls and the Study of the Hebrew Bible," in *The Dead Sea Scrolls at Fifty: Proceedings of the 1997 Society of Biblical Literature Qumran Section Meetings* (eds. R. A. Kugler and E. M. Schuller (SBLEJL15; Atlanta: Society of Biblical Literature, 1999), 31-41; "The Dead Sea Scrolls and the Hebrew Scriptural Texts," in *The Bible and the Dead Sea Scrolls,* vol. 1: *The Hebrew Bible and Qumran* (ed. J. H. Charlesworth; N. Richland Hills, Tex.: BIBAL Press, 2000), 105-33; "The Qumran Biblical Scrolls—the Scriptures of Late Second Temple Judaism," in *The Dead Sea Scrolls in their Historical Context* (eds. T. H. Lim et al.; Edinburgh: T&T Clark, 2000), 67-87; "The Qumran Scrolls and the Biblical Text," in *The Dead Sea Scrolls Fifty Years after Their Discovery: Proceedings of the Jerusalem Congress, July 20-25, 1997* (eds. L. H. Schiffman et al.; Jerusalem: Israel Exploration Society, 2000), 51-59; "The Text of the Hebrew Scriptures at the Time of Hillel and Jesus," in *Congress Volume, Basel, 2001* (ed. André Lemaire; VTSup 92; Leiden: Brill, 2002), 85-108; "Our Sharper Focus on the Bible and Theology Thanks to the Dead Sea Scrolls," *CBQ* 66 (2004): 1-24; "Qumran Witness to the Developmental Growth of the Prophetic Books," in *With Wisdom as a Robe: Qumran and Other Jewish Studies in Honour of Ida Fröhlich* (eds. K. D. Dobos and M. Kőszeghy; Hebrew Bible Monographs 121; Sheffield: Sheffield Phoenix Press, 2009), 263-74.

[12] "Two Perspectives on Two Pentateuchal Manuscripts from Masada," in *Emanuel: Studies in Hebrew Bible, Septuagint, and Dead Sea Scrolls in Honor of Emanuel Tov* (eds. S. M. Paul, R. A. Kraft, L. H. Schiffman, and W. W. Fields; VTSup 94; Leiden: Brill, 2003), 453–64.

[13] Ulrich, "Qumran Biblical Scrolls," 87.

this process was constitutive of the biblical books from start to end ... the process was still in effect throughout the Second Temple period ... and came to an abrupt halt as the result of radically new and different outside factors. The Scriptures did not "achieve final form" due to a natural and internal process, due to a maturation process, or due to "the fullness of time", but they suffered an abrupt freezing due to the double threat of loss: the threat of loss of their lives, land, and culture to the Romans, and the threat of loss of their ancient identity as "Israel" to the Christians, the growing majority of whom were gentile rather than Jewish.[14]

While Ulrich focuses on explaining how the textual plurality of the Jewish scriptures in the Second Temple period developed, Tov's approach is more descriptive and uses the medieval textual traditions as a grid to analyze the evidence from the Second Temple period. It is very influential beyond the constraints of Dead Sea Scrolls studies because of his textbook, *Textual Criticism of the Hebrew Bible*.[15] Tov reached the major breakthrough that led to the development of his new system while studying 11QpaleoLev[a] – a manuscript that was still unpublished when Tov's article on it appeared in 1979. Because 11QpaleoLev[a] shares readings with MT, SP, as well as LXX, it cannot be characterized as a forerunner of any of the medieval versions. Tov therefore describes 11QpaleoLev[a] in his 1979 article as "independent."[16] As a consequence of this characterization of 11QpaleoLev[a], Tov added another category of texts to the three main medieval text traditions of MT, SP, and LXX. Later on, he described this category as non-aligned texts.[17] According to Tov, there are hence four different categories of texts attested in the library of Qumran:

- nonaligned manuscripts which cannot be aligned with either the Masoretic Text, or the Samaritan Pentateuch, or the Septuagint,

---

[14] Ulrich, "Qumran Biblical Scrolls," 86–87.

[15] ביקורת נוסח המקרא: מבוא פרקי (2d ed.; Jerusalem: Bialik Institute, 1997), 62-94; *Textual Criticism of the Hebrew Bible* (2d rev. ed.; Minneapolis, Minn., and Assen: Fortress Press and van Gorcum, 2001), 80-117.

[16] E. Tov, "The Textual Character of the Leviticus Scroll from Qumran Cave 11," *Shnaton* 3 (1978–1979): 238–44, xxiii (Heb.). In the Hebrew text of his article, Tov uses the terms "אי־תלות" ("independence," 240) and "גירסאות יחודיות" ("singular readings," 244).

[17] In the Hebrew edition of his textbook, Tov uses the phrase "טקסטים שאינם קרובים בלעדית לאחד הטקסטים האחרים" ("texts which are not exclusively close to any other text," המקרא נוסח ביקורת, 92-93).

- pre-Samaritan manuscripts whose text agrees with the text of the medieval Samaritan Pentateuch but lack its ideological variant readings
- manuscripts whose text is close to the Hebrew *Vorlage* of the Septuagint
- proto-Masoretic manuscripts whose text agrees with the consonantal text of the medieval Masoretic text.

Until 2001, Tov viewed those biblical manuscripts from Qumran, which were copied in the characteristic plene-orthography known from 1QIsa[a] and many sectarian manuscripts, as a fifth category of biblical manuscripts.[18] After 2001, Tov revised this hypothesis and now no longer views the so-called Qumran orthography as a textual category of biblical manuscripts.[19]

Tov developed his system in a series of articles and adjusted his appreciation of the evidence in each article to the progressing publication of manuscripts of biblical books from the Qumran library.[20]

---

[18] See for example Tov, *Textual Criticism* (1st edition), 114-15.

[19] See Tov, *Textual Criticism* (2d edition), 114-15; idem, "The Biblical Texts from the Judaean Desert—An Overview and Analysis of the Published Texts," in *The Bible as Book—The Hebrew Bible and the Judaean Desert Discoveries* (eds. E. D. Herbert and E. Tov; London and New Castle: British Library and Oak Knoll Press in association with The Scriptorium: Center for Christian Antiquities, 2002), 139–66, 153-54; idem, *Scribal Practices and Approaches Reflected in the Texts Found in the Judean Desert* (STDJ 54; Leiden: Brill, 2004), 261-73.

[20] E. Tov, "The Relationship between the Textual Witnesses of the Old Testament in the Light of the Scrolls from the Judean Desert," *Beth Miqra* 77 (1979): 161–70 (Heb.); "A Modern Textual Outlook Based on the Qumran Scrolls," *HUCA* 53 (1982): 11–27; "Hebrew Biblical Manuscripts from the Judaean Desert: Their Contribution to Textual Criticism," *JJS* 39 (1988): 1–37; "The Significance of the Texts from the Judean Desert for the History of the Text of the Hebrew Bible: A New Synthesis," in *Qumran between the Old and the New Testament* (eds. F. H. Cryer and Th. L. Thompson; Copenhagen International Seminar 6; JSOTSup 290; Sheffield: Sheffield Academic Press, 1998), 277–309; "Die biblischen Handschriften aus der Wüste Juda – Eine neue Synthese, in *Die Textfunde vom Toten Meer und der Text der hebräischen Bibel* (eds. U. Dahmen, A. Lange, and H. Lichtenberger; Neukirchen-Vluyn, Neukirchener Verlag, 2000), 1–34; "The Biblical Texts from the Judaean Desert," passim; "The Biblical Text in Ancient Synagogues in Light of Judean Desert Finds," *Meghillot* 1 (2003): 185–201, viii–ix (Heb.); "The Text of the Hebrew/Aramaic and Greek Bible Used in the Ancient Synagogues," in *The Ancient Synagogue: From Its Origins until 200 C.E.—Papers Presented at an International Conference at Lund University October 14–17, 2001* (eds. B. Olsson and M. Zetterholm; ConBNT 39; Stockholm: Almqvist & Wiksell International, 2003), 237–59; "The Nature of the Masoretic Text in Light of the Scrolls from the Judean Desert and Rabbinic Literature," *Shnaton* 16 (2004): 119–34, x–xi (Heb).

	1992	1997	1998	2000	2001
Non-aligned	10%	25%	25%	35%	35%
Pre-SP	5%	5%	5%	5%	5%
Vorlage of LXX	5%	5%	5%	5%	5%
Proto-MT	60%	40%	40%	35%	35%
Qumranorthography	20%	25%	25%	20%	20%

2002	Pentateuch	Prophets and Ketubim
Non-aligned	37.0%	53.0%
Pre-SP	6.5%	
Vorlage of LXX	4.5%	3.0%
Proto-MT	52.0%	44.0%

In his last survey article on the biblical manuscripts from Qumran, Tov provides for the first time a complete list of how he classifies which manuscript. His classifications are as follows.[21]

56 non-aligned manuscripts: 4QGen^k (4Q10), 2QExod^a (2Q2), 4QExod^b (4Q13), 4QExod^d (4Q15), 4QExod^e (4Q16), 4QExod–Lev^f (4Q17), 11QpaleoLev^a (11Q1), 4QDeut^b (4Q29), 4QDeut^c (4Q30), 4QDeut^h (4Q35), 4QDeut^j (4Q37), 4QDeut^{k1} (4Q38), 4QDeut^{k2} (4Q38a), 4QDeut^m (4Q40), 4QDeut^n (4Q41), 5QDeut (5Q1), 4QJosh^a (4Q47), 4QJudg^a (4Q49), 4QSam^a (4Q51), 4QSam^c (4Q53), 6QpapKgs (6Q4), 1QIsa^a, 4QIsa^c (4Q57), 4QIsa^k (4Q64), 2QJer (2Q13), 4QEzek^a (4Q73), 4QXII^a (4Q76), 4QXII^c (4Q78), 4QXII^d (4Q79), 4QXII^e (4Q80), 4QXII^g (4Q82), 4QPs^a (4Q83), 4QPs^b (4Q84), 4QPs^d (4Q86), 4QPs^e (4Q87), 4QPs^f (4Q88), 4QPs^k (4Q92), 4QPs^l (4Q93), 4QPs^n (4Q95), 4QPs^q (4Q98), 4QPs^x (4Q98g), 11QPs^a (11Q5), 11QPs^b (11Q6), 11QPs^c (11Q7), 11QPs^d (11Q8), 4QQoh^a (4Q109), 4QDan^a (4Q112), 4QDan^b (4Q113), 4QDan^c (4Q114), 4QDan^d (4Q115), 6QpapDan (6Q7), 4QCant^a (4Q106), 4QCant^b (4Q107), 6QCant (6Q6), 4QLam (4Q111), 4QChron (4Q118).

Five pre-Samaritan Manuscripts: 4QpaleoExod^m (4Q22), 4QExod-Lev^f (4Q17), 4QLev^d (4Q26, maybe), 4QNum^b (4Q27), 4QDeut^n (4Q41, secondary).

---

[21] Tov, "The Biblical Texts from the Judaean Desert," 154–57.

Seven manuscripts which are close to the Hebrew Vorlage of the Septuagint: 4QExod[b] (4Q13) (secondarily), 4QLev[d] (4Q26), 4QNum[b] (4Q27 secondarily), 4QDeut[q] (4Q44), 4QSam[a] (4Q52; secondarily), 4QJer[b] (4Q71), 4QJer[d] (4Q72a).

57 proto-Masoretic manuscripts: 4QGen–Exod[a] (4Q1), 4QGen[b] (4Q2); 4QGen[c] (4Q3), 4QGen[d] (4Q4), 4QGen[e] (4Q5), 4QGen[f] (4Q6), 4QGen[g] (4Q7), 4QGen[j] (4Q9), 4QpaleoGen–Exod[l] (4Q11), 1QEx (1Q2), 4QEx[c] (4Q14), 1QpaleoLev–Num[a] (1Q3; Tov calls this manuscript 1QpaleoLev), 4QLev[b] (4Q24), 4QLev[c] (4Q25), 4QLev[e] (4Q26a), 4QLev–Num[a] (4Q23), 1QDeut[b] (1Q5), 4QDeut[d] (4Q31), 4QDeut[e] (4Q32), 4QDeut[f] (4Q33), 4QDeut[g] (4Q34), 4QDeut[i] (4Q36), 4QDeut[o] (4Q42), 4QpaläoDeut[r] (4Q45), 4QJos[b] (4Q48), 1QSam (1Q7), 4QSam[b] (4Q52), 4QKgs (4Q54), 1QIsa[b] (1Q8), 4QIsa[a] (4Q55), 4QIsa[b] (4Q56), 4QIsa[d] (4Q58), 4QIsa[e] (4Q59), 4QIsa[f] (4Q60), 4QIsa[g] (4Q61), 4QIsa[h] (4Q62), 4QIsa[m] (4Q66), 4QIsa[o] (4Q68), 4QJer[a] (4Q70), 4QJer[c] (4Q72), 4QEzek[b] (4Q74), 11QEzek (11Q4), 4QXII[b] (4Q77), 4QXII[f] (4Q81), 4QPs[c] (4Q85), 4QPs[g] (4Q89), 4QPs[m] (4Q94), 4QJob[a] (4Q99), 4QpaläoJob[c] (4Q101), 4QProv[a] (4Q102), 4QProv[b] (4Q103), 2QRuth[a] (2Q16), 2QRuth[b] (2Q17), 4QRuth[a] (4Q104), 4QRuth[b] (4Q105), 1QDan[a] (1Q71; Tov calls this manuscript 1QDan), 4QEzra[a] (4Q117).

In later publications, Tov has revised his model once more to our developing understanding of the biblical Dead Sea Scrolls. In conversation with F. M. Cross,[22] Tov prefers now the term proto-Rabbinic as opposed to the term proto-Masoretic to designate those manuscripts which are close to the consonantal text of the later Masoretic manuscripts. Tov furthermore distinguishes now between an inner circle and an outer circle of proto-Rabbinic manuscripts.[23]

> (a) The texts found at sites other than Qumran belong to the same family as the medieval Masoretic texts. This tradition is also reflected in biblical quotations in rabbinic literature, as well as most of the Targumim. These scrolls are therefore considered the inner circle of the

---

[22] See F. M. Cross, "Some Notes on a Generation of Qumran Studies," in *The Madrid Qumran Congress: Proceedings of the International Congress on the Dead Sea Scrolls, Madrid 18-21 March 1991* (eds. J. Trebolle Barrera and L. Vegas Montaner; 2 vols.; STDJ 11; Leiden: Brill, 1992), 1:1-14, 6-11; idem, "The Fixation of the Text of the Hebrew Bible," in idem, *From Epic to Canon: History and Literature in Ancient Israel* (Baltimore: John Hopkins University Press, 1998), 205-18.

[23] Tov, "The Biblical Text in Ancient Synagogues in Light of Judean Desert Finds," ix; cf. idem, "The Text of the Hebrew/Aramaic and Greek Bible," passim; idem, "The Nature of the Masoretic Text," passim.

proto-MT and proto-rabbinic tradition, further underscored by the evidence of the tefillin. These scrolls reflect the practices for writing scriptural scrolls as described at a later stage in rabbinic literature; (b) Similar texts from Qumran deviate from the medieval tradition in some details. They are less precise, and they do not conform with the technical details of rabbinic instructions for writing scriptural scrolls. These scrolls belong to the second circle of proto-MT scrolls.

Tov specifies which manuscripts belong to his inner and outer circles of the proto-rabbinic text as follows.

The Inner Circle of proto-Masoretic manuscripts in the Qumran library according to Tov:[24] 4QGen[b] (4Q2), 4QProv[b] (4Q103).

The Inner Circle of proto-Masoretic manuscripts at the other sites around the Dead Sea according to Tov: MasGen (Mas1), MasLev[a] (Mas1a), MasLev[b] (Mas1b), MasDeut (Mas1c), MasEzek (Mas1d), MasPs[a] (Mas1e; 1039-160), MasPs[b] (Mas1f; 1103-1742), SdeirGen (Sdeir1), 34SeNum (34Se2), 5/6ḤevNum[a] (5/6Ḥev1a), XḤev/SeNum[b] (XḤev/Se2), XḤevSeDeut (XḤevSe3), 5/6ḤevPs (5/6Ḥev1b), MurGen (Mur1), MurExod (Mur1), MurNum (Mur1), MurDeut (Mur2), MurIsa (Mur3), MurXII (Mur88), XJosh (MS Schøyen 2713), XJudges, XBiblical Text (X5).

The Outer Circle of proto-Masoretic manuscripts according to Tov:[25] 4QGen-Exod[a] (4Q1), 4QpaläoGen–Exod[l] (4Q11), 4QGen[r] (sic), 1QExod (1Q2), 4QExod[c] (4Q14), 4QJosh[b] (4Q48), 1QSam (1Q7), 4QSam[b] (4Q52), 4QKgs (4Q54), 1QIsa[b] (1Q8), 4QJer[a] (4Q70), 4QJer[c] (4Q72), 4QEzek[b] (4Q74), 11QEzek (11Q4), 4QXII[b] (4Q77), 4QXII[f] (4Q81), 4QPs[c] (4Q85), 4QPs[g] (4Q89), 4QPs[m] (4Q94), 4QJob[a] (4Q99), 4QpaleoJob[c] (4Q101), 4QProv[a] (4Q102), 4QProv[b] (4Q103), 1QDan[a] (1Q71; Tov calls this manuscript 1QDan), 4QEzra (4Q117). Furthermore, for reasons of statistic probability Tov allocates the following manuscripts to his outer proto-Masoretic circle as well: 4QGen[c] (4Q3), 4QGen[d] (4Q4), 4QGen[e] (4Q5), 4QGen[f] (4Q6), 4QGen[g] (4Q7), 4QGen[j] (4Q9), 1QExod (1Q2;

---

[24] In my own work on the manuscripts of biblical books from the Qumran library, I designate this category proto-Masoretic (see, *Handbuch der Textfunde vom Toten Meer*, vol. 1: *Die Handschriften biblischer Bücher von Qumran und den anderen Fundorten* [Tübingen: Mohr Siebeck, 2009], 16, and below, 53-54). Only in his article "The Nature of the Masoretic Text" (122-23 with note 18), does Tov specify which manuscripts he attributes to the inner and outer circle of proto-Rabbinic manuscripts. These manuscripts are included in the above lists as well.

[25] In my own work on the manuscripts of Biblical books from Qumran I designate this category as semi-Masoretic (*Handbuch*, 16, and below 53-54).

sic Tov lists the manuscript two times), 1QpaleoLev–Num^a (1Q3; Tov
calls this manuscript1QpaleoLev), 4QLev^b (4Q24), 4QLev^c (4Q25),
4QLev^e (4Q26a), 4QLev–Num^a (4Q23), 1QDeut^b (1Q5), 4QDeut^d (4Q31),
4QDeut^e (4Q32), 4QDeut^f (4Q33), 4QDeut^g (4Q34), 4QDeutⁱ (4Q36),
4QDeut^o (4Q42), 4QpaleoDeut^r (4Q45), 4QIsa^a (4Q55), 4QIsa^b (4Q56),
4QIsa^d (4Q58), 4QIsa^e (4Q59), 4QIsa^f (4Q60), 4QIsa^g (4Q61), 4QIsa^h
(4Q62), 4QIsa^m (4Q66), 4QIsa^o (4Q68), 2QRuth^a (2Q16), 2QRuth^b
(2Q17), 4QRuth^a (4Q104), 4QRuth^b (4Q105).

As said before, the great strength of Tov's work is that it provides a grid for the analysis of textual evidence from Qumran. By necessity this grid needs to be based on the three medieval textual traditions. One of the most revolutionary results of his research is the recognition of the textual plurality of the books of the Hebrew Bible in the Second Temple period. Although Tov never wrote a systematic study as to how this textual plurality developed, his contributions to individual biblical books and manuscripts show that he understands textual plurality mainly as the result of scribal changes. The Masoretic Text would preserve the text of early mastercopies in the Jerusalem temple. The textual plurality of the Qumran library is due to manuscript traditions which were not regularly cross referenced to these mastercopies.[26] But especially in the case of the major disagreements preserved in the Septuagint, Tov concedes the possibility of early Hebrew manuscript traditions which precede the proto-Masoretic text.[27]

[26] "The Dead Sea Scrolls and the Textual History of the Masoretic Bible," in *The Dead Sea Scrolls and the Hebrew Bible* (eds. K. De Troyer, A. Lange, and S. Tzoref; Göttingen: Vandenhoeck & Ruprecht, in preparation); cf. also "Some Thoughts about the Diffusion of Biblical Manuscripts in Antiquity," in *The Dead Sea Scrolls: Transmission of Traditions and Production of Texts* (eds. S. Metso et al.; STDJ 92; Leiden: Brill, 2010, forthcoming).

[27] See e.g., "The Nature of Large-Scale Differences between the LXX and MT S T V, Compared with Similar Evidence in Other Sources," in *The Earliest Text of the Hebrew Bible: The Relationship between the Masoretic Text and the Hebrew Base of the Septuagint Reconsidered* (ed. A. Schenker; SBLSCS 52; Atlanta: Scholars Press, 2003), 121-44; "The Septuagint as a Source for the Literary Analysis of Hebrew Scripture," in *Exploring the Origins of the Bible: Canon Formation in Historical, Literary, and Theological Perspectives* (eds. C. A. Evans and E. Tov; Acadia Studies in Bible and Theology; Grand Rapids, Mich.: Baker Academic, 2008), 31-56; "The Many Forms of Hebrew Scripture: Reflections in Light of the LXX and 4QReworked Pentateuch," in *From Qumran to Aleppo: A Discussion with Emanuel Tov about the Textual History of Jewish Scriptures in Honor of his 65th Birthday* (eds. A. Lange, M. Weigold and J. Zsengellér; FRLANT 230; Göttingen: Vandenhoeck & Ruprecht, 2009), 11-28.

Thus, Tov's position disagrees significantly with the one of E. C. Ulrich (see above) who regards the textual plurality of the Second Temple period as a result of the parallel existence of different editions, reworkings, or redactions of a given book at the same time. The difference between the two positions lies not so much in the question as to whether in some cases the changes made by scribes to a text amounts to a redaction – Tov himself has described this phenomenon repeatedly[28] – but whether these redactions can be traced back to one (proto-Masoretic) *Urtext* or whether they are an unbroken continuation of the redactions of biblical books as identified by higher criticism. The latter would imply that there was no *Urtext* at all. Furthermore, Ulrich would describe even small scale changes as redactional layers while Tov seems to reserve this characterization for large scale differences.

Tov's typological-text grid has variously been questioned in the recent past.[29] What Tov described until 2002 as proto-Masoretic includes manuscripts of different character. Some of them are extremely close to the text of MT with less than 2% deviation while others differ significantly more.[30] When this difference became more apparent, Tov responded to his critics by distinguishing between an inner and an outer circle of proto-Rabbinic manuscripts (see above). To avoid the impression of group-specific texts[31] and to warrant a stringent terminology, in the following arguments, I describe manuscripts which deviate less than 2%

---

[28] See most prominently *The Text-Critical Use of the Septuagint in Biblical Research* (1st ed.; Jerusalem Biblical Studies 3; Jerusalem: Simor Ltd., 1981), 260-66; ibid., (2d rev. and enlarged ed.; Jerusalem: Simor Ltd., 1997), 188-99; *Textual Criticism of the Hebrew Bible*, 313-49 (1st ed.) and 313-50 (2d ed.).

[29] See e.g. J. C. VanderKam and P. W. Flint, *The Meaning of the Dead Sea Scrolls: Their Significance for Understanding the Bible, Judaism, Jesus, and Christianity* (San Francisco: HarperCollins, 2002), 143, 146-47; P. W. Flint, "The Book of Leviticus in the Dead Sea Scrolls," in *The Book of Leviticus: Composition and Reception* (eds. R. Rendtorff and R. A. Kugler; VTSup 93; Leiden: Brill, 2003), 323-35, 332-35; cf. Lange, *Handbuch,* 15.

[30] Cf. I. Young, "The Stabilization of the Biblical Text in the Light of Qumran and Masada: A Challenge for Conventional Qumran Chronology?" *DSD* 9 (2002): 364–90; idem, "The Biblical Scrolls from Qumran and the Masoretic Text: A Statistical Approach," in *Feasts and Fasts: A Festschrift in Honour of Alan David Crown* (eds. M. Dacy, J. Dowling, and S. Faigan; Mandelbaum Studies in Judaica 11; Sydney: Mandelbaum, 2005), 81–140; Lange, *Handbuch,* 14-32.

[31] For the non-existence of group specific texts in the Second Temple period, see A. Lange, "From Literature to Scripture: The Unity and Plurality of the Hebrew Scriptures in Light of the Qumran Library," in *One Scripture or Many? Canon from Biblical, Theological, and Philosophical Perspectives* (eds. Chr. Helmer and Chr. Landmesser; Oxford: Oxford University Press, 2004), 51-107.

from the medieval MT as proto-Masoretic, while I will describe those who are close to the text of MT but deviate more than 2% as semi-Masoretic.

What remains debated in Tov's grid are his manuscript classifications, especially in the case of the books of the Pentateuch. The fragmentary character of the Qumran manuscripts often entails that those passages of the Pentateuch in which SP reads a significantly longer text are not preserved. In these cases a distinction between a pre-Samaritan and a semi-Masoretic manuscript is often not possible. Tov regards those manuscripts, which as a consequence of textual deterioration are equally close to MT and SP or to MT and LXX, as proto-Masoretic. While in my own classification of the biblical manuscripts among the Dead Sea Scrolls,[32] I did not find manuscripts which are equally close to MT and LXX for reasons of manuscript deterioration, I regard the group of manuscripts which are equally close to MT and SP for reasons of manuscript deterioration as significant. In order not to blur the statistical representation of the evidence, I regard it as important to list these manuscripts as a distinct statistical group. Furthermore, a large number of manuscripts from Qumran and elsewhere are so badly deteriorated that I find it problematic to classify them at all (any manuscript of which less than 100 words are preserved).[33] While Tov does not include all of these manuscripts in his statistics, he does include some. Furthermore, some of the so-called biblical manuscripts among the Dead Sea Scrolls are so deteriorated that the remaining text might as well represent a quotation of a biblical book in a non-biblical work.

Although based on Tov's research and in particular his classification grid, my own analysis of the textual character of various manuscripts of biblical books points hence into a somewhat different direction than the one of Tov. It is summarized in the following lists.[34]

47 non-aligned manuscripts: 4QRP^b (4Q364), 4QRP^c (4Q365 + 4Q365a), 4QRP^d (4Q366), 4QRP^e (4Q367), 4QGen^f (4Q6), 2QExod^a (2Q2), 4QExod^b (4Q13), 4QExod^c (4Q14), 4QExod–Lev^f (4Q17), 4QLev–Num^a (4Q23), 4QLev^b (4Q24), 11QpaleoLev^a (11Q1), 1QDeut^b (1Q5),

---

[32] Lange, *Handbuch*, passim.
[33] Exceptions to this rule of thumb are manuscripts which are badly deteriorated but attest without doubt to characteristic long- or short texts, such as 4QJer^b.
[34] For the arguments as to why I classify which manuscript how, the reader is referred to the discussions of the individual manuscripts in my *Handbuch*.

4QDeut^b (4Q29), 4QDeut^c (4Q30), 4QDeut^h (4Q35), 4QDeut^j (4Q37), 4QDeut^{k1} (4Q38), 4QDeut^{k2} (4Q38a), 4QDeut^n (4Q41), 4QpaleoDeut^r (4Q45), 4QJosh^a (4Q47), 1QJudges (1Q6), 4QSam^a (4Q51), 4QSam^c (4Q53), 6QpapKgs (6Q4), 1QIsa^a, 4QIsa^c (4Q57), 4QXII^a (4Q76), 4QXII^c (4Q78), 4QPs^a (4Q83), 4QPs^b (4Q84), 4QPs^d (4Q86), 4QPs^e (4Q87), 4QPs^f (4Q88), 4QPs^q (4Q98), 11QPs^a (11Q5), 11QPs^b (11Q6), 11QPs^c (11Q7), 4QJob^a (4Q99), 4QCant^a (4Q106), 4QCant^b (4Q107), 4QQoh^a (4Q109), 4QLam (4Q111), 4QDan^a (4Q112), 4QDan^b (4Q113), 4QDan^c (4Q114).

Two pre-Samaritan manuscripts: 4QpaleoExod^m (4Q22), 4QNum^b (4Q27).

Eleven manuscripts which are equally close to the text of MT and SP: 4QGen^c (4Q3), 4QGen^e (4Q5), 4QGen^g (4Q7), 4QGen^j (4Q9), 4QLev^c (4Q25), 4QLev^e (4Q26a), 4QDeut^d (4Q31), 4QDeut^f (4Q33), 4QDeut^i (4Q36), 4QDeut^o (4Q42), 5QDeut (5Q1).

Four manuscripsts which are close to the Hebrew Vorlage of the Septuagint:[35] 4QLev^d (4Q26), 4QDeut^q (4Q44), 4QSam^b (4Q52), 4QJer^b (4Q71).

20 semi-Masoretic manuscripts: 4QGen-Exod^a (4Q1), 4QpaleoGen–Exod^l (4Q11), 4QJosh^b (4Q48), 1QSam (1Q7), 4QKgs (4Q54), 4QIsa^a (4Q55), 4QIsa^b (4Q56), 4QIsa^d (4Q58), 4QIsa^e (4Q59), 4QIsa^f (4Q60), 2QJer (2Q13), 4QJer^c (4Q72), 4QEzek^b (4Q74), 11QEzek (11Q4), 4QXII^g (4Q82), 4QPs^c (4Q85), 4QProv^b (4Q103), 5QLam^a (5Q6), 1QDan^b (1Q72), 4QDan^d (4Q115).

Seven proto-Masoretic manuscripts: 4QDeut^e (4Q32), 4QDeut^g (4Q34), 1QIsa^b (1Q8), 4QJer^a (4Q70), 4QEzek^a (4Q73), 4QXII^e (4Q80), 2QRuth^a (2Q16).

83 manuscripts which cannot be classified text-typologically because of textual damage: 1QGen (1Q1), 2QGen (2Q1), 4QGen^d (4Q4), 4QGen^k (4Q10), 4QpaleoGen^m (4Q12), 4QpapGen^o (4Q483), 6QpaleoGen (6Q1), 8QGen (8Q1), 1QExod (1Q2), 2QExod^b (2Q3), 4QExod^d (4Q15), 4QExod^e (4Q16), 4QExod^g (4Q18), 4QExod^h (4Q19), 4QExod^j (4Q20), 1QpaleoLev–Num^a (1Q3 1–11, 12?, 15?), 2QpalooLev (2Q5), 4QLev^g

---

[35] The supralinear corrections of 5QDeut (5Q1) attest also to a text which is close the Hebrew *Vorlage* of the Deut-LXX (see below, 96).

(4Q26b), 11QLev^b (11Q2), 2QNum^a (2Q6), 2QNum^b (2Q7), 2QNum^c (2Q8), 2QNum^d? (2Q9), 1QDeut^a (1Q4), 2QDeut^b (2Q11), 2QDeut^c (2Q12), 4QDeut^a (4Q28), 4QDeut^l (4Q39), 4QDeut^m (4Q40), 4QDeut^p (4Q43), 4QDeut^t (4Q38c), 11QDeut (11Q3), 4QJudges^a (4Q49), 4QJudg-es^b (4Q50), 5QKgs (5Q2), 4QIsa^g (4Q61), 4QIsa^h (4Q62), 4QIsa^i (4Q62a), 4QIsa^j (4Q63), 4QIsa^k (4Q64), 4QIsa^l (4Q65), 4QIsa^m (4Q66), 4QIsa^o (4Q68), 4QJer^d (4Q72a), 1QEz (1Q9), 4QXII^b (4Q77), 4QXII^d (4Q79), 4QXII^f (4Q81), 4QpMi? (4Q168), 5QAmos (5Q4), MS Schøyen 4612/1, 1QPs^a (1Q10), 1QPs^b (1Q11), 2QPs (2Q14), 4QPs^g (4Q89), 4QPs^h (4Q90), 4QPs^j (4Q91), 4QPs^k (4Q92), 4QPs^l (4Q93), 4QPs^m (4Q94), 4QPs^o (4Q96), 4QPs^r (4Q98a), 4QPs^s (4Q98b), 5QPs (5Q5), 8QPs (8Q2), 11QPs^d (11Q8), 2QJob (2Q15), 4QJob^b (4Q100), 4Qpaleo-Job^c (4Q101), 4QProv^a (4Q102), 4QProv^c (4Q103a), 2QRuth^b (2Q17), 4QRuth^a (4Q104), 4QRuth^b (4Q105), 6QCant^d (6Q6), 4QQoh^b (4Q110), 3QLam (3Q3), 5QLam^b (5Q7), 1QDan^a (1Q71), 4QDan^e (4Q116), 6QpapDan (6Q7), 4QEzra (4Q117), 4QChron (4Q118).

35 manuscripts for which it is uncertain if they attest to a biblical book:
4QGen^{h1} (4Q8), 4QGen^{h2} (4Q8), 4QGen^{hpara} (4Q8), 4QGen^n (4Q576), 4QGen^p (4Q12a), 2QExod^c (2Q4), 4QExod^k (4Q21), 1QpaleoLev^b? (1Q3 16–19, 22–23, 12?, 15?,. 20?), 6QpaleoLev (6Q2), 2QDeut^a (2Q10), 4QDeut^{k3} (4Q38b), 4QpaleoDeut^s (4Q46), 6QpapDeut? (6Q3), 4QIsa^n (4Q67), 4QpapIsa^p (4Q69), 4QIsa^q (4Q69a), 4QIsa^r (4Q69b), 5QIsa (5Q3), 4QJer^e (4Q72b), 4QXII^c frag. 35, 3QEzek (3Q1), 4QEzek^c (4Q75), 1QPs^c (1Q12), 3QPs (3Q2), 4QPs^n (4Q95; is close to Ps-11QPs^a), 4QPs^p (4Q97), 4QPs^t (4Q98c), 4QPs^u (4Q98d), 4QPs^v (4Q98e), 4QPs^w (4Q98f), 4QPs^x (4Q98g), 6QpapPs? (6Q5), 11QPs^e? (11Q9), 6QpapProv? (6Q30), 4QCant^c (4Q108).

One manuscript wrongly identified as attesting to a biblical book:
4Qpap cryptA Lev^h? (4Q249j).[36]

My own statistics point hence to a different appreciation of the proto- and semi-Masoretic texts in the Second Temple period than the one of Tov and emphasize the textual plurality of the Hebrew Bible even more. The following table illustrates this.

---

[36] Against S. J. Pfann, "249j. 4Qpap cryptA Leviticus^h?" in S. Pfann et al., *Qumran Cave 4. XXVI: Cryptic Texts and Miscellanea Part 1* (DJD XXXVI; Oxford: Clarendon, 2000) 575-77, 575.

	Pentateuch according to Lange	Prophets and Ketubim according to Lange	Pentateuch according to Tov 2002	Prophets and Ketubim according to Tov 2002
Non-aligned	52.5%	51%	37.0%	53.0%
Pre-SP	5%		6.5%	
Vorlage of LXX	5%	4%	4.5%	3.0%
Equally close to MT and SP	27.5%			
semiMT	5%	35%	52.0%	44.0%
protoMT	5%	10%		

One last word of caution needs to be added with regard to the Septuagint. The above statistics are calculated based only on the Hebrew manuscripts from the Qumran library. But five Greek manuscripts were found in Qumran which attest either to the Old Greek text itself or a recension of it. Furthermore, three scrolls from Qumran attest to Aramaic translations of Leviticus and Job.

The above statistics show that especially in the case of the Pentateuch, with 10% of all manuscripts, proto- and semi-Masoretic texts played a significantly smaller role during the Second Temple period than Tov's statistics suggest. In the case of the other books belonging to the Prophets and Ketubim sections of the Hebrew Bible, 35% of their manuscripts are semi-Masoretic, while only 10% are proto-Masoretic. This means the proto-/semi-Masoretic text was for each biblical book only one text which was not even common in the second half of the Second Temple period. With about 50% of all manuscripts of biblical books from the Qumran library being non-aligned, the evidence suggests that these non-aligned manuscripts were not the exception but the rule of Second Temple textual reality and that proto-MT might not have been the dominant text of that time. The evidence poses two questions: how did the Masoretic standard text of the Hebrew Bible develop out of this textual plurality and how did the textual plurality of the books of the Hebrew Bible come to be. To answer the second question, I ask below for the various ways in which the textual witnesses to the books of the Hebrew Bible treated their respective *Vorlagen*. To engage with the first question exceeds the scope of this article. Instead of a full discussion of the question, I summarize results of research which I have published elsewhere.[37]

2 The proto-Masoretic Standard Text of the Hebrew Bible

From the perspective of my topic, the most important evidence for the development of the proto-Masoretic standard text the Hebrew Bible is provided by the biblical manuscripts which were found on the Masada as well as in Naḥal Ḥever, Wadi Murabba'at, Wadi Sdeir, Naḥal Ṣe'elim, and Naḥal Arugot. They can be classified text-typologically as follows.

Masada

Six proto-Masoretic manuscripts: MasLev[a] (Mas1a), MasLev[b] (Mas 1b), MasDeut (Mas1c), MasEzek (Mas1d), MasPs[a] (Mas1e; 1039-160), MasPs[b] (Mas1f; 1103-1742).

One manuscript which cannot be classified text-typologically because of textual damage: MasGen (Mas1).

Naḥal Ḥever, Wadi Murabba'at, Wadi Sdeir, Naḥal Ṣe'elim, and Naḥal Arugot

Nine proto-Masoretic manuscripts: MurGen–Exod.Num[a] (Mur1), SdeirGen (Sdeir1), 4QGen[b] (4Q2),[38] XLev[c] (MS Schøyen 4611), XḤev/SeNum[b] (XḤev/Se2), XJosh (MS Schøyen 2713), XJudges, MurXII (Mur88), 5/6ḤevPs (5/6Ḥev1b).

One manuscript attesting to the Kaige-Recension of the OG: 8ḤevXII gr (8Ḥev1; Rahlfs 943).

---

[37] "'They Confirmed the Reading' (*y. Ta'an.* 4:68a): The Textual Standardization of Jewish Scriptures in the Second Temple Period," in *From Qumran to Aleppo: A Discussion with Emanuel Tov about the Textual History of Jewish Scriptures in Honor of his 65th Birthday* (eds. A. Lange, M. Weigold, and J. Zsengellér; FRLANT 230; Göttingen: Vandenhoeck & Ruprecht, 2009), 29-80; Lange, *Handbuch*, 23-32.

[38] With regard to 4QGen[b] (4Q2), J. R. Davila, "2. 4QGen[b]," in E. Ulrich et al., *Qumran Cave 4.VII: Genesis to Numbers* (DJD XII; Oxford: Clarendon, 1994), 31-38, 31 argued: "The possibility, pointed out by F. M. Cross, must be raised that this manuscript may not have come from Qumran. Although the scribe is very skilled, the leather is coarse and poorly prepared, which is unusual for a Qumran manuscript. In addition, the script is either late Herodian or post-Herodian, and the text – reminiscent of the biblical scrolls from Muraba'at – is virtually identical with the Massoretic Text, exhibiting not a single textual variant from 𝔐 and only one orthographic divergence ... Moreover, no fragment from 4QGen[b] has been identified among the photographs of fragments recovered in controlled excavations from Cave 4. Thus, the question remain [sic] open that this manuscript possibly came from another cave and was inadvertently mixed with Cave 4 manuscripts by the Bedouin."

Seven manuscripts which cannot be classified text-typologically because of textual damage: Mur(?)Gen[b] (Mur[?]), ArugLev, 5/6HevNum[a] (5/6Hev1a), 34SeNum (34Se2), XHevSeDeut (XHevSe3), MurDeut (Mur2), MurIsa (Mur3).

The above lists show that all manuscripts from the sites in the Judean Desert that are connected with the first and second Jewish wars and that are preserved well enough for text-typological classification are proto-Masoretic in character. Does this mean that the proto-Masoretic standard text existed already during or before the first Jewish war? And if yes, how do the semi-Masoretic manuscripts from Qumran relate to this standard text? Are they later corruptions of on earlier proto-Masoretic text or is the proto-Masoretic text an artificial text, which was compiled out of semi-Masoretic manuscripts at the Jerusalem temple – as might be suggested by *y. Ta'an.* 4.68a?

A first answer to this question is provided by a correlation of the paleographic date with the textual character of the various biblical manuscripts from Qumran and the other sites around the Dead Sea. Table 1 and graph 1 illustrate a characteristic spread of the texts of the individual biblical books over the various Hebrew scripts used in Graeco-Roman times. The correlation between paleography and text-typology[39] shows that the non-aligned manuscripts are the largest group of textual witnesses until the middle of the first century C.E. In graph 1 they are grouped together with pre-Samaritan manuscripts and manuscripts which attest to the Hebrew *Vorlage* of the Old Greek as "other texts" because only very few manuscripts are preserved that attest to pre-SP and the Hebrew *Vorlage* of the LXX.[40] The proto-Masoretic manuscripts from the various sites of the Dead Sea are distributed differently over the paleographic epochs as compared to the nonaligned manuscripts. Although 4QJer[a] (4Q70) and 4QXII[e] (4Q80) go back to the years 225–175 and 75–50 B.C.E. respectively, proto-Masoretic manuscripts can be found in larger quantities only since the second half of the first century B.C.E. Semi-Masoretic manuscripts are attested as early as the first half of the second century B.C.E. (4QJer[c] [4Q72]) but occur more regularly only since the end of the second century B.C.E.

The largest quantities of non-aligned, semi- and proto-Masoretic manuscripts come from the second half of the first century B.C.E. This agrees

---

[39] For the paleographic dates and text-typological classifications of the biblical manuscripts from the Dead Sea, see their discussions in my *Handbuch*.
[40] Graph 1 does not recognize manuscripts for which it cannot be decided whether they attest to a semi-Masoretic or a pre-Samaritan text.

Table 1: Text-typological Chronology of the Hebrew Manuscripts of
Biblical Books from the Dead Sea

	Semi-MT	Proto-MT
Ca. 250 B.C.E.		
225–175 B.C.E.		4QJer^a (4Q70)
200–150 B.C.E.	4QJer^c (4Q72)	
175–150 B.C.E.		
Ca. 150 B.C.E.		
150–100 B.C.E.		
150–125 B.C.E.		
125–75 B.C.E.		
125–100 B.C.E.	4QGen–Exod^a (4Q1)	
100–25 B.C.E.	4QpaleoGen–Exod^l (4Q11), 1QDan^b (1Q72)	
100–50 B.C.E.	4QIsa^f (4Q60)	
100–75 B.C.E.		
Ca. 75 B.C.E.		
75–50 B.C.E.		4QXII^e (4Q80)
Ca. 50 B.C.E.	4QJosh^b (4Q48), 4QKgs (4Q54)	4QEzek^a (4Q73)
50–1 B.C.E.		MasPs^b (Mas1f; 1103–1742)
50–25 B.C.E.	4QIsa^a (4Q55), 4QIsa^b (4Q56)	4QDeut^c (4Q32), 1QIsa^b (1Q8)
30 B.C.E.–20 C.E.		
30–1 B.C.E.	1QSam (1Q7), 4QIsa^e (4Q59), 4QXII^g (4Q82), 4QDan^d (4Q115)	2QRuth^a (2Q16) MasLev^a (Mas1a), MasDeut (Mas1c), MasPs^a (Mas1e; 1039–160)
10 B.C.E.–30 C.E.	11QEzek (11Q4), 4QProv^b (4Q103)	MasLev^b (Mas1b)
1–50 C.E.		4QDeut^g (4Q34)
1–30 C.E.	2QJer (2Q13), 4QEzek^b (4Q74)	
25–50 C.E.		
20–68 C.E.		
Ca. 50 C.E.	5QLam^a (5Q6), 4QIsa^d (4Q58)	
50–135 C.E.		XJudg (X6)
50–100 C.E.		4QGen^b (4Q2; not from Qumran), XLev^c (MS Schøyen 4611), XJosh (MS Schøyen 2713) XḤev/SeNum^b (XḤev/Se2) SdeirGen (Sdeir1)
50–68 C.E.	4QPs^c (4Q85)	MasEzek (Mas1d) 5/6ḤevPs (5/6Ḥev1b)
100–135 C.E.		MurGen-Exod.Num^a (Mur1), MurXII (Mur88)

Semi-MT or pre-SP	Pre-SP	*Vorlage* of LXX	Non–aligned
		4QSam^b (4Q52)	4QExod–Lev^f (4Q17)
5QDeut (5Q1)		4QJer^b (4Q71)	
			4QQoh^a (4Q109)
			4QPs^a (4Q83)
			4QLev–Num^a (4Q23), 4QDeut^b (4Q29), 4QDeut^c (4Q30), 4QJosh^a (4Q47)
			1QIsa^a, 4QXII^a (4Q76)
4QDeut^d (4Q31)			
			6QpapKgs (6Q4), 4QDan^c (4Q114)
	4QpaleoExod^m (4Q22)		4QRP^e (4Q367), 4QpaleoDeut^r (4Q45)
4QDeut^i (4Q36)			4QJob^a (4Q99)
			4QSam^c (4Q53)
			4QXII^c (4Q78)
4QDeut^f (4Q33), 4QDeut^o (4Q42)			4QRP^b (4Q364), 4QRP^c (4Q365 + 4Q365a), 4QRP^d (4Q366)
4QGen^g (4Q7)			4QGen^f (4Q6), 4QLev^b (4Q24), 4QPs^d (4Q86), 4QPs^f (4Q88), 4QDan^a (4Q112)
			4QDeut^h (4Q35)
4QGen^e (4Q5), 4QGen^j (4Q9)			4QExod^c (4Q14), 4QSam^a (4Q51)
	4QNum^b (4Q27)	4QLev^d (4Q26)	4QExod^b (4Q13)
4QLev^e (4Q26a)			4QDeut^{k1} (4Q38), 4QDeut^{k2} (4Q38a), 4QDeut^n (4Q41), 1QJudg (1Q6), 4QCant^a (4Q106), 4QLam (4Q111)
			4QPs^q (4Q98)
		4QDeut^q (4Q44)	11QpaleoLev^a (11Q1), 11QPs^a (11Q5), 11QPs^c (11Q7)
			11QPs^b (11Q6)
			4QDan^b (4Q113)
4QGen^c (4Q3)			1QDeut^b (1Q5), 4QIsa^c (4Q57)
			4QDeut^j (4Q37), 4QPs^b (4Q84), 4QPs^e (4Q87)
4QLev^c (4Q25)			2QExod^a (2Q2)

well with the overall paleographic distribution of the Dead Sea Scrolls, which also peaks during the reign of Herod the Great (see graph 2). The largest amount of manuscripts found in the Qumran library were copied in scripts from the second half of the first century B.C.E.[41] The Masada manuscripts show that this paleographic peak of the Qumran library is not idiosyncratic but is part of an overall phenomenon. On the Masada, 15 manuscripts were found. Nine of these manuscripts were copied in the second half of the first century B.C.E.[42] (see graph 3). The paleographic evidence from Qumran and the Masada points thus to an increased manuscript production and an increased amount of scribal activity in the time after the Roman conquest of Judea (63 B.C.E.) and during the reign of Herod the Great. Even more interesting is that after the turn of the eras, the amount of non-aligned and semi-Masoretic manuscript decreases continuously while the number of proto-Masoretic manuscripts experiences another peak in the second half of the first century C.E. Even more so, after the year 68 C.E. only proto-Masoretic manuscripts can be found.

Graph 1: *Text-typological Chronology of the Hebrew Manuscripts of Biblical Books from the Dead Sea*

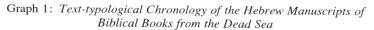

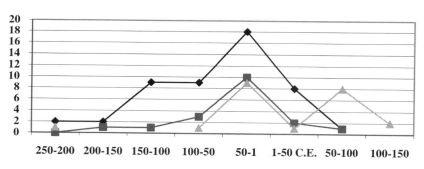

---

[41] Cf. B. Webster, "Chronological Index of the Texts from the Judaean Desert," in E. Tov, *The Texts from the Judaean Desert: Indices and Introduction to the Discoveries in the Judaean Desert Series* (DJD XXXIX; Oxford: Clarendon, 2002), 351–446, 373–74.

[42] For the paleographic dates of the non-biblical manuscripts from the Masada, see S. Talmon, "Hebrew Fragments from Masada," in idem and Y. Yadin, *Masada VI: Yigael Yadin Excavations 1963–1965: Final Reports* (Jerusalem: Israel Exploration Society, 1999), 1–149, 101, 106, 117–18, 120, 133–34, 136, 138–39, 157–58. For the paleographic dates of the Biblical manuscripts, see their discussions in my *Handbuch*.

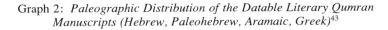

Graph 2: *Paleographic Distribution of the Datable Literary Qumran Manuscripts (Hebrew, Paleohebrew, Aramaic, Greek)*[43]

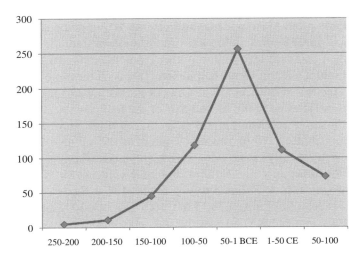

Graph 3: *Paleographic Distribution of the Datable Literary Masada Manuscripts*

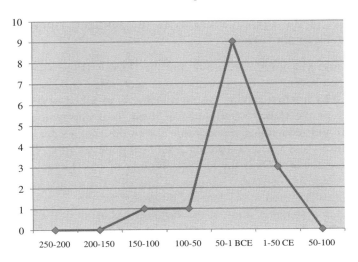

---

[43] Manuscripts written in cryptic alphabets are not included as the paleographic study of these scripts has not enough comparative material for precise dates. The paleographic dates are taken from the list of B. Webster ("Chronological Index to the Texts from the Judaean Desert," in *DJD* XXXIX: 351-446, 371-75).

The chronological distribution of the manuscripts of biblical books described above shows that the proto-Masoretic standard text was created in the second half of the first century B.C.E. as part of a scribal boom. Early proto-Masoretic manuscripts like 4QJerᵃ demonstrate that in the case of some biblical books existing manuscript traditions were chosen as their standard text while in other cases their standard text might be the result of a text-critical compilation. This is all the more likely since in Judea the first recensions of the Old Greek text towards a proto-Masoretic text are attested in the second half of the first cent. B.C.E.: 8HevXII gr and the *kaige* recension group as well as 4QLXXNum. Responsible for the first Judean efforts towards a standard text of Jewish scriptures were Jewish (priestly) elites who were highly educated both in the Jewish and the Graeco-Roman cultures. Rabbinic evidence (*b. Ketub.* 106a; *b. Mo'ed Qaṭ.* 18b; *y. Ta'an.* 4.68a; *y. Šeqal.* 4.3; *y. Sanh.* 2.6), remarks by Flavius Josephus (*Ant.* 3.38; 5.61; 10.57; 4.303–304) and the colophon of the Esther-LXX suggest that this standard text was created by priests in the Jerusalem temple. On the one hand the Jerusalem priests employed the principle of majority readings to create a standard text; on the other hand they selected for some books whole textual traditions and rejected other texts and/or textual versions outright.

3 Causes of the Textual Plurality of the Jewish Scriptures in the Second Temple Period

If the proto-Masoretic standard text of the Hebrew Bible was created in the second half of the first century B.C.E. and gained wide acceptance at the latest by the first century C.E., it remains to be asked how the textual plurality of the Hebrew Scriptures evolved. Is it due to a continuous editorial and redactional process that led to the coexistence of various text editions and redactions for each biblical book, as E. C. Ulrich suggests (see above)? Or is the textual plurality of the Hebrew Scriptures mainly the result of scribal changes of one *Urtext* for each book which was originally stored in the Jerusalem temple?[44]

Again, a systematic study of the various texts of biblical books in the Second Temple period would go beyond the constraints of this essay. Based on brief examples taken out of the Qumran library, I would therefore like to investigate in the following six different ways that scribes

---

[44] This seems to be the suggestions of an unpublished article by E. Tov ("Some Thoughts about Diffusion," passim).

changed the texts that they copied, i.e. scribal corruption, harmonistic editing, redaction and rewriting of texts, compilation of (poetic) texts, and recension. Based on my examples I then try to give an answer as to whether there is one or several causes for the textual plurality of the Second Temple period.

3.1 Scribal Corruption

A good example for scribal corruption of a text is 4QCant[b] (4Q107).[45] Of this scroll three fragments are extant that attest to 166 fully or partly preserved words from Cant 2:9–17; 3:1-2, 5, 9–11; 4:1–3, 8–11, 14–16; and 5:1.[46] The manuscript is written in an early Herodian book hand from the end of the first cent. B.C.E.[47] The manuscript is characterized by a large amount of scribal corruption. In total, 22 cases of unintentional scribal changes are extant in the 166 fully or partly preserved words of 4QCant[b]. Especially striking are thirteen Aramaisms. "Apocopated *mi-* is constantly replaced by *min* in 4QCant[b]":[48] מן לבנון (two times in Cant 4:8); מן ראשי (Cant 4:8); מן הררי (Cant 4:8); מן יין (Cant 4:10); מן כל (4:10); מן ג]דיו (Cant 4:16). Other Aramaisms include the use of הטללים and הררי in Cant 2:17, the two uses of את instead of אתי in Cant 4:8, as well as the plural forms אמונן in Cant 4:8 and בשמך in Cant 4:10. Both that the scribe can use Hebrew forms elsewhere in his manuscript (see e.g. the regular use of Hebrew plural forms) and that the Aramaisms occur in only three parts of 4QCant[b], i.e. frgs. 1 12-23; 2 ii 7-13; and 3 12, argue against a systematic Aramaizing revision of Canticles in 4QCant[b]. It seems more probable that the Aramaisms of 4QCant[b] are unconscious adjustments of the Hebrew text by the scribe of 4QCant[b]. Such unconscious adjustments could have easily happened when the scribe's attention slipped while copying a complicated Hebrew text like Canticles.

[45] For the canticles manuscripts at Qumran, see E. Tov, "Three Manuscripts (Abbreviated Texts?) of Canticles from Qumran Cave 4," *JJS* 46 (1995): 88–111; idem, "Canticles," in E. Ulrich et al., *Qumran Cave 4. XI: Psalms to Chronicles* (DJD XVI; Oxford: Clarendon, 2000), 195-219; P. Flint, "The Book of Canticles (Song of Songs) in the Dead Sea Scrolls," in *Perspectives on the Song of Songs – Perspektiven der Hohenliedauslegung* (ed. A. Hagedorn; BZAW 346; Berlin: Walter de Gruyter, 2005), 96–104.
[46] For the material reconstruction of 4QCant[b], see Tov, "Three Manuscripts," 90-91, 97-98; idem, "Canticles," 205–07.
[47] Thus Ada Yardeni according to Tov, "Three Manuscripts," 99, and "Canticles," 208.
[48] Tov, "Canticles," 209. For lists of the Aramaisms and scribal errors in 4QCant[b], see Tov, "Three Manuscripts," 99-100; and idem, "Canticles," 208-09.

Other scribal errors in 4QCant[b] include a haplography (שׁ[ועלים instead of שׁועלים שׁועלים [MT] in Cant 2:15),[49] a dittography (בלילות[לות בלי instead of בלילות [MT] in Cant 3:1), two cases of metathesis (התנאה instead of התאנה [MT] in Cant 2:13; בשׁקתי instead of בקשׁתי [MT] in Cant 3:1), an erroneous addition of עת in Cant 2:12 (crossed out by the scribe himself), another erroneous addition of a word in Cant 4:10 (deleted by way of *sigma* and *antisigma*?)[50], and the reading of אבאי instead תבואי (MT) in Cant 4:8. Furthermore, the scribe inserted אחותי into Cant 4:11 because of its similar occurrence in Cant 4:9, 10, 12; 5:1.[51] An added word might finally also be attested in a supralinear addition still visible on the photo PAM 40.604.

When all cases of scribal corruption are removed from the text of 4QCant[b], it becomes clear that its underlying *Vorlage* is rather close to the consonantal text of MT.[52] The 22 copyist errors extant in 166 fully or partly preserved words of 4QCant[b] demonstrate how scribal carelessness can be responsible for the unintended emergence of a new (non-aligned) Canticles text, which in terms of text-typology is rather far removed from its semi- or proto-Masoretic base text.

But scribal corruption is the not the only reason that different texts of one biblical book developed. While scribal corruption effects mostly textual changes that were not intended by any scribe, the Dead Sea Scrolls attest to intentional changes imposed by scribes on their *Vorlagen* as well. Such changes include redaction, harmonization, abbreviation, compilation, and recension.

3.2 Redaction and Rewriting

Rewriting – in the terminology of historical criticism also called redaction – is the most radical form of textual change that scribes could apply to their *Vorlagen*.[53] Such rewritings go back to the very beginnings of

---

[49] The identification of the haplography is based on the letter count of frg. 1 10, cf. Tov, "Three Manuscripts," 99 and "Canticles," 212.

[50] Cf. Tov, "Three Manuscripts," 106; "Canticles," 215; *Scribal Practices*, 202.

[51] Cf. Tov, "Three Manuscripts," 108; "Canticles," 216. This insertion reminds of the harmonizing editing discussed below.

[52] Cf. Lange, *Handbuch*, 478-79.

[53] For a broader perspective on rewriting, the so-called parabiblical literature and hypertextuality, see the collected volumes *Empirical Models for Biblical Criticism* (ed. J. H. Tigay; Philadelphia: University of Pennsylvania Press, 1985) and *In the Second Degree: Paratextual Literature in Ancient Near Eastern and Ancient Mediterranean Cultures and Its Reflections in Medieval Literature* (eds. P. S. Alexander, A. Lange, and R. Pillinger; Leiden: Brill), forthcoming.

ancient oral and written literature.[54] In Mesopotamia, the earliest Sumerian Gilgamesh narratives and poems reach back to the late third millennium, while the neo-Assyrian standard text of the *Gilgamesh Epic* developed in the first millennium in the time of the Neo-Assyrian Empire. The time-span between the first isolated Sumerian Gilgamesh texts and the final standard text marks a process of collecting and rewriting earlier Gilgamesh texts and the *Gilgamesh Epic*. Similarly, in ancient Egypt, the *Book of the Dead* evolved in several stages. Important milestones in the process of its redactional growth are marked by the Theban recension (1580 B.C.E.) and the Sais recension (650 B.C.E.). At the beginning of ancient Greek literature, the Homeric epics represent a radical rewriting of the mythical tradition later on collected in the *Mythic Cycle* – esp. the *Cypria*. Aside from the complicated textual history of the Homeric epics, which seems to point to extensive rewritings as well, even some of the classical Greek tragedies that take their themes and topics out of the Homeric epics stand in a kind of "parabiblical" or better paratextual relationship to them. Ancient Judaism is no exception to this rule. Even beyond the redactional histories of the books of the Hebrew Bible, which were reconstructed by historical-critical analysis, ancient Judaism produced a rich literature of rewritings of biblical books. Especially substantial is the so-called "parabiblical" or better paratextual tradition to the Pentateuch. Among its most prominent representatives are the *Book of Jubilees* and the *Temple Scroll*.

The most prominent example of such a reworking from within the canon is the proto-Masoretic redaction of the Book of Jeremiah. The question of how the Masoretic text of the book of Jeremiah and its Greek translation relate to each other is one of the most extensively debated issues in the study of Jeremiah and in the study of the textual history of the Hebrew Bible.[55] The differences between MT-Jeremiah and LXX-

---

[54] For the rewriting of authoritative literatures in Ancient Mesopotamia, Ancient Egypt, Ancient Greece, and Ancient Judaism, see J. H. Tigay, "The Evolution of the Pentateuchal Narratives in the Light of the Evolution of the *Gilgamesh Epic*," in Tigay, *Empirical Models,* 21-52, and the following contributions in the forthcoming volume *In the Second Degree*: A. Lange, "In the Second Degree: Ancient Jewish Paratextual Literature in the Context of Graeco-Roman and Ancient Near Eastern Literature;" G. J. Brooke, "Hypertextuality and the 'Parabiblical' Dead Sea Scrolls;" J. T. A. G. M. Van Ruiten, "The *Book of Jubilees* as Paratextual Literature;" A. Ambühl, "Trojan Palimpsests: The Relation of Greek Tragedy to the Homeric Epics;" G. Danek, "The Homeric Epics as Palimpsests;" B. Pongratz-Leiten, "From Ritual to Text to Intertext: A New Look on the Dreams in *Ludlul Bēl Nēmeqi*;" and S. H. Aufrère, "Priestly Texts, Recensions, Rewritings and Paratexts in the Late Egyptian Period."

[55] As this article does not allow even for a brief sketch of the history of research on the question, the reader is referred to the survey in my *Handbuch*, 304-14.

Jeremiah are so significant that one could almost speak of two different books of Jeremiah. The Masoretic text of Jeremiah is about 3097 or 14.7% shorter than the Greek one.[56] Both texts impose a significantly different structure on the book of Jeremiah as well. Based on the works of Emanuel Tov,[57] M. Bogaert,[58] and Y. Goldman,[59] I think that both versions go back to a common source. This is all the more likely since the badly preserved manuscript 4QJer[b] attests to the Hebrew *Vorlage* of Jeremiah-LXX.[60] Different from the proto-Masoretic text, the Hebrew *Vorlage* of the Jeremiah-LXX remained relatively close to this source although some extensions and abbreviations, etc., can be found in it as well. The proto-Masoretic text of Jeremiah (protoMT-Jer), on the other hand, restructured and reworked this common source extensively.[61] Textual observations in the additions of protoMT-Jer show that protoMT-Jer attests to a redaction of an earlier text of Jeremiah that is more faithfully represented by the Jer-LXX. ProtoMT-Jer has a tendency

---

[56] See Y.-J. Min, "The Minuses and Pluses of the LXX Translation of Jeremiah as Compared with the Massoretic Text: Their Classification and Possible Origins" (PhD diss., Hebrew University of Jerusalem, 1977), 1, 159, 181, 312, 315, 317.

[57] E. Tov, "L'incidence de la critique textuelle sur la critique littéraire dans le livre de Jérémie," *RB* 79 (1972): 189-99; idem, "Exegetical Notes on the Hebrew Vorlage of the LXX of Jeremiah 27," *ZAW* 91 (1979): 73-93; idem, "Some Aspects of the Textual and Literary History of the Book of Jeremiah," in *Le livre de Jérémie: Le prophète et son milieu, les oracles et leur transmission* (ed. P.-M. Bogaert; 2d ed.; BETL 54; Leuven: Peeters, 1997), 145-67, 430; idem, "The Literary History of the Book of Jeremiah in the Light of Its Textual History," in *Empirical Models for Biblical Criticism* (ed. J. H. Tigay; Philadelphia, Penn.:University of Pennsylvania Press, 1985), 211–37; idem, "The Characterization of the Additional Layer of the Masoretic Text of Jeremiah," *ErIsr* 26 (1999): 55-63, 229*; "The Book of Jeremiah: A Work in Progress," *BRev* 16 (2000): 32–38, 45.

[58] See e.g. P.-M. Bogaert, "De Baruch à Jérémie: Les deux rédactions conservées du livre de Jérémie," in *Le livre de Jérémie: Le prophète et son milieu, les oracles et leur transmission* (ed. P.-M. Bogaert; 2d ed.; BETL 54; Leuven: Peeters, 1997), 168-73, 430-32; idem, "Les mécanismes rédactionnels en Jér 10,1-16 (LXX et TM) et la signification des supplements," in Bogaert, *Le livre de Jérémie*, 222-38, 433-34; idem, "Urtext, texte court et relecture: Jérémie xxxiii 14-26 TM et ses préparations," in *Congress Volume: Leuven 1989* (ed. J.A. Emerton; VTSup 43; Leiden: Brill, 1991), 236-47; idem, "Le livre de Jérémie en perspective: Les deux rédactions antiques selon les travaux en cours," *RB* 101 (1994): 363–406. For further literature by P.-M. Bogaert on protoMT-Jer, see Lange, *Handbuch*, 320-21.

[59] Y. Goldman, *Prophétie et royauté au retour de l'exil: Les origins littéraires de la forme massorétique du livre des Jérémie* (OBO 118; Freiburg and Göttingen: Universitätsverlag and Vandenhoeck & Ruprecht, 1992).

[60] Thus first J. G. Janzen, *Studies in the Text of Jeremiah* (HSM 6; Cambridge, Mass.: Harvard University Press, 1973). For a survey of the history of research, see Lange, *Handbuch*, 304-14. Recently the closeness of 4QJer[b] to the Hebrew *Vorlage* of the Old Greek has been proven again by the reconstruction of R. J. Saley, "Reconstructing 4QJer[b] according to the Text of the Old Greek," *DSD* 17 (2010): 1-12.

[61] See my analysis of the evidence in *Handbuch*, 303-04, 314-19.

to complete names by way of adding patronyms as well as to add new details and explanations to the text flow and to extend formulas and idiomatic expressions. Mostly protoMT-Jer's longer additions are composed out of textual material taken from passages of the Book of Jeremiah or other Jewish scriptures. Furthermore, the longer additions of protoMT-Jer do not only employ other passages from the Book of Jeremiah but reference each other as well. Examples of such references include the parallel rhetoric between Jer 31:35-37 and Jer 33:20-26,[62] between Jer 29:10 and Jer 33:14,[63] as well as between Jer 29:14 and Jer 33:26. Therefore, against Stipp,[64] I see with Tov, Bogaert, and Goldman, no reason to perceive protoMT-Jer as consisting in itself of several redactional layers. This does, of course, not exclude the possibility of later scribal corruption of protoMT-Jer. This means that all extant versions of the Book of Jeremiah preserve only more or less extensive reworkings of the supposed common source of protoMT-Jer and Jer-LXX. The two main Jeremiah texts represent hence two different redactions of the Book of Jeremiah. Different from other books of the Hebrew Bible, the supposed *Urtext* of Jeremiah no longer exists. Taking the model of the redactional history of the Book Jeremiah that was developed among others by B. Duhm, S. Mowinckel, J. P. Hyatt, W. Rudolph, and W. Thiel[65] into consideration, the redactional history of the Book of Jeremiah can hence be graphically depicted as follows.

---

[62] Cf. Bogaert, "*Urtext*," 243-46; Goldman, *Prophétie*, 42-44.

[63] See e.g. W. Rudolph, *Jeremia* (3d ed.; HAT 1.12; Tübingen: Mohr [Siebeck], 1968), 185; G. Wanke, *Untersuchungen zur sogenannten Baruchschrift* (BZAW 122; Berlin: Walter de Gruyter, 1971), 45-46; idem, *Jeremia*, vol. 2: *Jeremia 25,15-52,34* (ZBK AT 20.2; Zürich: Theologischer Verlag Zürich, 2003), 315; W. L. Holladay, *Jeremiah 2: A Commentary on the Book of the Prophet Jeremiah Chapters 26-52.* (Hermeneia; Philadelphia, Pa.: Fortress, 1989), 228; Bogaert, "*Urtext*," 240-41; J. Lust, "Messianism and the Greek Version of Jeremiah," in *VII Congress of the International Organization for Septuagint and Cognate Studies Leuven 1989* (ed. C. E. Cox; SBLSCS 31; Atlanta, Ga.: Scholars Press, 1991), 87-122, 101-04; idem, "Diverse Text Forms of Jeremiah and History Writing with Jer 33 as a Test Case," *JNSL* 20.1 (1994) 31-48, 38; Goldman, *Prophétie*, 40-42; H.-J. Stipp, *Das alexandrinische und masoretische Sondergut des Jeremiabuches: Textgeschichtlicher Rang, Eigenarten, Triebkräfte* (OBO 136; Freiburg and Göttingen: Universitätsverlag and Vandenhoeck & Ruprecht, 1994), 134; W. McKane, *A Critical and Exegetical Commentary on Jeremiah. Vol. II.* (Edinburgh: T&T Clark, 1996), 861; K. Schmid, *Buchgestalten des Jeremiabuches: Untersuchungen zur Redaktions- und Rezeptionsgeschichte von Jer 30-33 im Kontext des Buches* (WMANT 72; Neukirchen-Vluyn: Neukirchener Verlag, 1996), 56-57, 61, 64.

[64] Stipp, *Sondergut*.

[65] See B. Duhm, *Das Buch Jeremia erklärt* (KHC 11; Tübingen: Mohr [Siebeck], 1901); S. Mowinckel, *Zur Komposition des Buches Jeremia* (Kristiana: Dybwad, 1914); J. P. Hyatt, "Jeremiah and Deuteronomy," *JNES* 1 (1942): 156-73; Rudolph, *Jeremia*; W. Thiel, *Die deuteronomistische Redaktion von Jeremia 1-25* (WMANT 52; Neu-

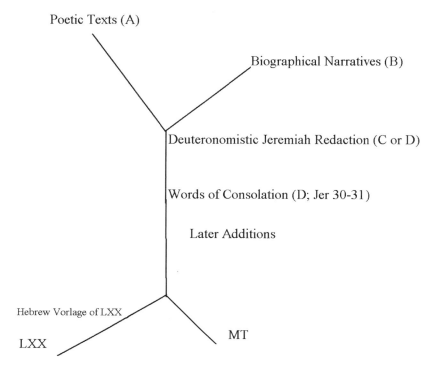

Poetic Texts (A)

Biographical Narratives (B)

Deuteronomistic Jeremiah Redaction (C or D)

Words of Consolation (D; Jer 30-31)

Later Additions

Hebrew Vorlage of LXX

LXX

MT

As an example[66] of how protoMT-Jer created the extensions of its *Vorlage*, Jer 29:1-23[67] is most instructive.[68]

kirchen-Vluyn: Neukirchener Verlag, 1973); idem, *Die deuteronomistische Redaktion von Jeremia 26-45* (WMANT 41; Neukirchen-Vluyn: Neukirchener Verlag, 1981). For a detailed history of research, see S. Herrmann, *Jeremia: Der Prophet und das Buch* (Erträge der Forschung 271; Darmstadt: Wissenschaftliche Buchgesellschaft, 1990); C. Maier, *Jeremia als Lehrer der Tora: Soziale Gebote des Deuteronomiums in Fortschreibungen des Jeremiabuches* (FRLANT 196; Göttingen: Vandenhoeck & Ruprecht, 2002), 14-41.

[66] Constraints of space do not allow for a full discussion of the scholarly literature on this passage. I will keep references to scholarly literature hence to a minimum and discuss Jer 29:1-23 elsewhere in more detail.

[67] For this chapter of Jeremiah, the priority of the LXX text has recently been established again by Raymond de Hoop. As the constraints of this article do not allow me to engage with the extensive debate about the relationship between MT-Jer and LXX-Jer in Jeremiah 29, the reader is referred to de Hoop's work instead: "Textual, Literary, and Delimination Criticism: The Case of Jeremiah 29 in 𝔐 and 𝔊," in *The Impact of Unit Delimination on Exegesis* (eds. R. de Hoop, M. Korpel, and S. Porter; Pericope 7; Leiden: Brill, 2009), 29-62.

[68] The below translation is guided by the NRSV. The long texts of protoMT-Jer are highlighted in italics. Parallels to other passages in Jeremiah are underlined and specified in parenthesis.

These are the words of the letter that the prophet Jeremiah sent from
Jerusalem to the *remaining* elders among the exiles, and to the priests,
the prophets, and all the people, *whom Nebuchadnezzar had taken
into exile from Jerusalem to Babylon.* ²This was after King Jeconiah,
and the queen mother, the court officials, the leaders of Judah and
Jerusalem⁶⁹, the artisans, and the smiths had departed from Jerusalem.
³The letter was sent by the hand of Elasah son of Shaphan and Gema-
riah son of Hilkiah, whom King Zedekiah of Judah sent to Babylon to
King *Nebuchadnezzar* of Babylon. It said: ⁴Thus says the LORD of
hosts, the God of Israel, to all the exiles whom I have sent into exile
from Jerusalem to Babylon: ⁵Build houses and live in them; plant
gardens and eat what they produce. ⁶Take wives and have sons and
daughters; take wives for your sons, and give your daughters in marriage, *that they may bear sons and daughters*; multiply there, and do
not decrease. ⁷But seek the welfare of the city⁷⁰ where I have sent you
into exile, and pray to the LORD on its behalf, for in its welfare you
will find your welfare. ⁸For thus says the LORD of hosts, the God of
Israel: Do not let the prophets and the diviners who are among you
deceive you, and do not listen to the dreams that they dream, ⁹for it is
a lie that they are prophesying to you in my name; I did not send
them, says the LORD.
10 For thus says the LORD: Only when Babylon's seventy years are
completed will I visit you, and I will fulfill to you my *good* words and
bring you back to this place. ¹¹*For surely I know the plans* I have for
you, *says the LORD*, plans for your welfare and not for harm, to give
you *future and hope.* ¹²*And when you call upon me and come* and pray
to me, I will hear you. ¹³When you search for me, you will find me;
if you seek me with all your heart, ¹⁴I will let you find me, *says the
LORD, and I will restore your fortunes and* <u>gather</u> *you from all the
nations and all the places where I have driven you, says the LORD, and
<u>I will bring you back</u>* (Jer 23:3; 30:3, 18) *to the place from which I
sent you into exile.*
15 Because you have said, 'The LORD has raised up prophets for us in
Babylon'— ¹⁶*thus says the LORD concerning the king who sits on the
throne of David, and concerning all the people who live in this city,
your kinsfolk who did not go out with you into exile:* ¹⁷*Thus says the
Lord of hosts, <u>I am going to let loose on them sword, famine, and
pestilence</u>* (cf. Jer 24:10), *and I will make them eat <u>rotten figs that are
so bad they cannot be eaten</u>* (cf. Jer 24:2). ¹⁸*I will pursue <u>them with
sword, with famine, and with pestilence</u>* (cf. Jer 24:10), <u>*and will make
them a horror to all the kingdoms of the earth, to be an object of curs-
ing, and horror, and hissing, and a derision among all the nations
where I have driven them*</u> (Jer 24:9), ¹⁹<u>*because they did not heed my*</u>

---

⁶⁹ LXX-Jer reads καὶ παντὸς ἐλευθέρου καὶ δεσμώτου ("and every free person and
prisoner").
⁷⁰ LXX-Jer reads τῆς γῆς ("the land").

> *words, says the Lord, when I persistently sent to you my servants the*
> *prophets, but they would not listen, says the Lord* (cf. Jer 25:4; 26:5;
> 35:15; 44:4). *²⁰But now, all you exiles whom I sent away from Jeru-*
> *salem to Babylon, hear the word of the* LORD: *²¹Thus* says the LORD of
> hosts, the God of Israel, concerning Ahab *son of Kolaiah* and Zedekiah
> *son of Maaseiah, who are prophesying a lie to you in my name*: I am
> going to deliver them into the hand of King *Nebuchadrezzar* of Bab-
> ylon, and he shall kill them before your eyes. ²²And on account of
> them this curse shall be used by all the exiles from Judah in Babylon:
> 'The LORD make you like Zedekiah and Ahab, whom the king of
> Babylon roasted in the fire', ²³because they have perpetrated outrage
> in Israel and have committed adultery with their neighbours' wives,
> and have spoken in my name *lying* words that I did not command
> them; I am the one who knows and bears witness, says the LORD.

Principally, protoMT-Jer rewrote its *Vorlage* in Jer 29:1-23 in two different ways. The smaller changes are more often than not harmonizations
(see below). These small changes can mostly be found in verses 1-9 and
21-23.

- In Jer 29:1, the added word יתר ("remnant") clarifies that not all
  elders but only those who were exiled to Babylon are addressed.
  At the end of v. 1, an addition of protoMT-Jer also specifies who
  had exiled the Jews and to which place they were brought ("whom
  Nebuchadnezzar had taken into exile from Jerusalem to Babylon").
- When in v. 2, LXX reads καὶ παντὸς ἐλευθέρου καὶ δεσμώτου
  ("and every free person and prisoner") the LXX reading creates the
  impression of an interruption of the list of exceptional people which
  were exiled beginning with the king and ending with artisans and
  smiths. The LXX, and thus in this case the Hebrew *Vorlage* of protoMT-Jer, puts a group of average free citizens in the middle of
  high-profile exiles. Proto-MT-Jer rectifies the situation by changing
  the reading to "the leaders of Judah and Jerusalem."
- In v. 3, protoMT-Jer clarifies which Babylonian king is meant by
  adding the name Nebukadnezzar (cf. v. 21).
- In v. 4, protoMT-Jer inserts two specifications. כל clarifies that all
  exiles are addressed in this letter and בבלה specifies that vv. 4-7
  speak to the exiles in Babylon and not the whole diaspora, as do vv.
  10-14 (see below).
- In v. 6, protoMT-Jer specifies the purposes of the marriages which
  parents were supposed to arrange for their children, i.e. "that they
  may bear sons and daughters."

- In v. 7, protoMT-Jer changes τῆς γῆς ("the land"; probably originally הארץ in the LXX-*Vorlage*) into העיר ("the city") because it emphasized in v. 1 that the Jews were exiled to the city of Babylon.
- In v. 9, protoMT-Jer construes בשקר with the preposition ב (בשקר) as opposed to שקר in the *Vorlage* of LXX. Because in the Book of Jeremiah the verb נבא is construed with בשקר otherwise only in Jer 5:31; 20:6, it seems as if with this subtle change protoMT-Jer wants to refer back to Pashur in Jer 20:6 of whom Jeremiah predicts a death in the Babylonian exile because of prophesying lies.
- In v. 21 protoMT-Jer adds the patronyms "son of Kolaiah" and "son of Maaseiah" to the names of the two false prophets in the Babylonian exile respectively. It furthermore specifies which Babylonian king is meant in v. 21 by adding the name Nebudadnezzar (cf. v. 6). By adding the phrase "who are prophesying a lie to you in my name" protoMT-Jer also clarifies why God gave the two prophets into the hand of this king
- In v. 23, protoMT-Jer adds the word שקר to show that Ahab and Zedekiah spoke not just some words but words of rebellious lies.

Next to these smaller changes, protoMT-Jer rewrote Jer 29:10-20 drastically. While not changing the basic structure of Jeremiah's letter significantly, protoMT-Jer adds a long excursus to the letter in 29:16-20 about those remaining in Jerusalem and extends verses 10-14 significantly.

> Jer 29:1-3 Prescript
> Jer 29:4-7 Word about the length and life in Mesopotamia
> Jer 29:8-9 Word about false prophets
> Jer 29:10-14 Word about the return to Jerusalem
> Jer 29:15-23 Word about two false prophets
> Jer 29:16-19 Excursus: Word about those remaining in Jerusalem

In protoMT-Jer's *Vorlage*, Jeremiah's letter gives only a little comfort for the exiles in Mesopotamia.[71] Only after 70 years will they return home (Jer 29:10). They should ensconce themselves in Mesopotamia, search the good of that country, and live their lives there. The Jewish existence in the Mesopotamian diaspora is endangered by false prophets. Following their false words of hope of return leads into catastrophe, as evidenced by the terrible punishment visited on Ahab and Zedekiah.

---

[71] For an interpretation of Jeremiah's letter, see A. Lange, *Vom prophetischen Wort zur prophetischen Tradition: Studien zur Traditions- und Redaktionsgeschichte innerprophetischer Konflikte in der Hebräischen Bibel* (FAT 34; Tübingen: Mohr Siebeck, 2002), 244-56.

Instead, Jeremiah assures the exiles that God will be available to them not only in Jerusalem but in Mesopotamia as well.

ProtoMT-Jer's redactional measures change this letter dramatically into a text concerned with both the future of exiles and the future of those still living in Judah. ProtoMT-Jer's long text at the end of verse 14 creates an inclusion with verse 10.[72]

V. 10   להשיב   אל המקום הזה
V. 14 והשבתי אתכם אל מקום אשר הגליתי אתכם משם

In protoMT-Jer's *Vorlage*, Jer 29:10-14 was a word of consolation. The exiles need to stay in Mesopotamia for 70 years before it will be possible for them to return. But even in Mesopotamia God plans Shalom for the exiles. If they pray to him he will hear them in Mesopotamia just like he used to hear them in Israel. In protoMT-Jer, the emphasis of this text changes to the theme of return to Jerusalem by way of the inclusion between v. 10 and v. 14. While in the *Vorlage* God's plans of Shalom for the exiles concerned their life's during their seventy year stay in Mesopotamia, the insertion of the phrase "future and hope" re-characterizes God's plans of Shalom as the return of the exiles to Jerusalem (v. 11). Consequently, protoMT-Jer qualifies the words of God mentioned in v. 10 as "my good word" by inserting הטוב. The disastrous news of return only after seventy years in the *Vorlage* becomes "my good word" for protoMT-Jer. An almost verbal parallel can be found in Jer 33:14, which is part of another proto-Masoretic addition (Jer 33:14-26).[73] The proto-Masoretic addition in Jer 33:14-26 thus promises the reinstitution of Davidic kingship and levitical priesthood as a specification of what will happen after 70 years. In Jer 29:11 and 14 God's good word is further qualified as a prophecy through the two additions of the formula נאם יהוה by protoMT-Jer.

Furthermore, protoMT-Jer reorients through subtle changes the assurance of protoMT-Jer's *Vorlage* that God will hear the prayers of the exiles and will be accessible for them even in Mesopotamia. ProtoMT-Jer precedes the והתפללתם אלי ושמעתי אליכם ("and pray to me, I will hear you") with וקראתם אתי והלכתם ("and when you call upon me and come"). Although קרא does not always denote a cultic communication,[74] the

---

[72] Italics mark the additional text in protoMT-Jer.

[73] See e.g. Rudolph, *Jeremia*, 185; Wanke, *Untersuchungen*, 45-46; idem, *Jeremia*, 315, Holladay, *Jeremiah 2*, 228; Bogaert, "*Urtext*," 240-41; Lust, "Messianism," 101-04; idem, "Diverse Text Forms," 38; Goldman, *Prophétie*, 40-42; Stipp, *Sondergut*, 134; McKane, *Jeremiah*, 861; Schmid, *Buchgestalten*, 56-57, 61, 64.

[74] For the cultic and non-cultic connotations of קרא, see G. Schauerte, קרא, *ThWAT* VII: 117-47 (esp. 128-29).

combination with the following הלך points in the context of prayer to the Jerusalem Temple as the place to which someone goes to pray to the God of Israel. That protoMT-Jer re-orients Jer 29:10-14 towards a return to Jerusalem means it promises the exiles not only their return to Jerusalem, but also that they will be able to communicate in the context of the Jerusalem temple cult again with their God. What was opening the possibility of a universal prayer in the *Vorlage* of protoMT-Jer is restricted by protoMT-Jer itself to the promise of future participation in the Jerusalem temple cult.

Another radical change of the message of the letter of Jeremiah in protoMT-Jer's *Vorlage* can be found in v. 14: "and I will restore your fortunes and gather you from all the nations and all the places where I have driven you." In verses 1-3, Jeremiah's letter was addressed only to the Babylonian exiles. In verse 14 the addressees of the letter's Shalom-prophecies are widened radically though. Now it is not only the Babylonian exiles to whom the letter promises return. On the contrary, God will gather exiled Jews from all the nations (מכל־הגוים) and from all the places (מכל־המקומות) and return them to Jerusalem. Not only the Babylonian Jews, but the whole diaspora is addressed now.[75] As elsewhere, ProtoMT-Jer uses rhetoric from other parts of the Book of Jeremiah to phrase this promise. In Jer 29:14 it employs the promises of Jer 23:3; 30:3, 18.[76] How much protoMT-Jer is interested in a universalization of Jeremiah's promises of return to all the diaspora can be seen in Jer 23:3, too. LXX-Jer reads here "Then I myself will gather the remnant of my flock out of all the land (τῆς γῆς) where I have driven them." The singular refers clearly to Mesopotamia. ProtoMT-Jer changes the singular of "the land" (τῆς γῆς – in Hebrew הארץ) in the plural "the lands" (הארצות): "Then I myself will gather the remnant of my flock out of all the lands where I have driven them."[77] Now Jer 23:3 concerns not only Mesopotamian Jewry, but the whole diaspora.

My interpretation of Jer 29:1-14 contradicts recent claims[78] that LXX-Jer and MT-Jer share a common perspective on the exile. Both texts

---

[75] Cf. Wanke, *Jeremia*, 267-68.

[76] Cf. Goldman, *Prophétie,* 70-73 and L. C. Allen, *Jeremiah: A Commentary* (OTL; Louisville, Ky.: Westminster John Knox Press, 2008), 326.

[77] Translation according to NRSV.

[78] Against Raymond de Hoop, "Perspective after the Exile: The King, עבדי, 'My Servant' in Jeremiah—Some Reflections on MT and LXX," in *Exile and Suffering: A Selection of Papers Read at the 50th Anniversary Meeting of the Old Testament Society of South Africa OTWSA/OTSSA, Pretoria August 2007* (eds. B. Becking and D. Human; OTS 50; Leiden: Brill, 2009), 105-21.

view the exiles and their fate very differently. For the text of LXX-Jer
and the Hebrew *Vorlage* of protoMT-Jer, the exile is a punishment. The
exiles need to settle down in Mesopotamia for the rest of their lives.
Only after seventy years is a return possible. The only consolation Jeremiah can give the Babylonian exiles is that their God will be accessible
to them in Mesopotamia as well. The text of protoMT-Jer turns the letter
into a prophecy of salvation. The exiles of all the world will return to
Jerusalem where they will rebuild country and temple and begin the temple cult anew. Far from bringing grave news, Jewish exiles all over the
world are depicted in protoMT-Jer as the hope of Judaism. This radical
rewriting of the letter of Jeremiah poses questions of where and when
protoMT-Jer was written.

Before I can address these questions, the last and most extensive addition of protoMT-Jer to Jeremiah 29 needs to be discussed, i.e. verses
16-20. The above translation already illustrates that to phrase this addition protoMT-Jer employed the language of Jeremiah 24. This chapter
compares the remaining population of Judah under King Zedekiah with
rotten figs that cannot be eaten and to which people respond with horror.
Like bad figs, God will destroy them. Those whom God will not kill,
he will exile to the nations where the current exiles are. With the phrase
אשר הדחתים שם in Jer 29:19, protoMT-Jer links the fate of Judeans
about to be exiled with the exiles to whom Jer 29:14 promises return
from all nations and places where God exiled them (אשר הדחתי אתכם שם;
Jer 29:14). These (first) exiles among the nations are the good figs of
Jeremiah 24 which will return to Judah and reestablish God's people.
Jer 29:16-20 incorporates only the description of the bad figs from
Jeremiah 24 because the positive future of the exiles is already described
in verses 10-14.

What remains to be asked for protoMT-Jer after Jer 29:10-14 is if the
whole diaspora will return to Judah and Jerusalem and what happens
with those Jews that remained in Judah and Jerusalem. The answer is
horrible and straightforward. The people of Judah and Jerusalem did not
listen to the often repeated message of God's prophets (Jer 29:19). The
sub-clause "because they did not heed my words, says the Lord, when I
persistently sent to you my servants the prophets, but they would not
listen" occurs similarly in Jer 7:25, 25:4; 26:5; 35:15; 44:4. In Jer
25:4; 35:15; 44:4 it denotes the veneration of other gods by Israel and
in the context of Jer 7:25 it compares Israel's sacrificial cult with the
veneration of other gods. It seems therefore likely that protoMT-Jer
accuses the remaining population of Judah in Jer 29:19 also of the

veneration of other gods. God will thus destroy the king of Jerusalem and his people.

ProtoMT-Jer rewrites Jeremiah's letter to the Mesopotamian exiles thus in two ways. 1) It inserts a salvation prophecy for the whole diaspora. All Jews will return from all over the world to Judah and Jerusalem and venerate God in his temple. 2) It inserts a doom prophecy for the Jews still in Judea. The citizens of Judah and Jerusalem, foremost their ruler, will be destroyed and sent into exile where they will be an object of disgust for their host countries. This dichotomy between the Jews of the diaspora and the Jews of Judah raises the question when protoMT-Jer was written and by whom.

Excursus: The Date of the Proto-Masoretic Jeremiah Redaction

Recently either protoMT-Jer as a whole[79] or parts of it – especially Jer 33:14-26[80] – have been dated to early Hasmonean times. This idea is not new. Already B. Duhm suggested a Hasmonean date for Jer 33:14-26.[81] In opposition to such a late setting, other exegetes argue for a date of Jer 33:14-26 in particular and protoMT-Jer in general in the late six century B.C.E.[82] or in the middle of the fifth century B.C.E.[83] Against a Hasmonean setting it needs to be emphasized that for protoMT-Jer, the *terminus ante quem* is established by the paleographic date of the proto-Masoretic manuscript 4QJer[a] (4Q70) in the years 225-175 B.C.E.[84] Because scribal errors show that 4QJer[a] (4Q70) is not an autograph, protoMT-Jer was written

[79] E.g. A. Schenker, "La rédaction longue du livre de Jérémie doit-elle être datée au temps des premiers Hasmonéens?" *ETL* 70 (1994): 281-93.

[80] Cf. C. Levin, *Die Verheißung des neuen Bundes in ihrem theologiegeschichtlichen Zusammenhang ausgelegt* (FRLANT 137; Göttingen: Vandenhoeck & Ruprecht, 1985), 194-96; P. Piovanelli, "JerB 33,14-26, ou la continuité des institutions à l'époque maccabéenne," in *The Book of Jeremiah and its Reception/Le livre de Jérémie et sa reception* (eds. A. H. W. Curtis and T. Römer; BETL 128; Leuven: Peeters, 1997), 255-76.

[81] Cf. B. Duhm, *Das Buch Jeremia erklärt* (KHC 11; Tübingen: Mohr [Siebeck], 1901), 274, 276; cf. *op. cit.*, xx.

[82] A. Laato, *Josiah and David Redivivus: The Historical Josiah and the Messianic Expectations of Exilic and Postexilic Times* (CBOTS 33; Stockholm: Almqvist & Wiksell, 1992), 117; Goldman, *Prophétie*, 225-35.

[83] M. Pietsch, *"Dieser ist der Sproß Davids ...:" Studien zur Rezeptionsgeschichte der Nathanverheißung im alttestamentlichen, zwischentestamentlichen und neutestamentlichen Schrifttum* (WMANT 100, Neukirchen-Vluyn: Neukirchener Verlag, 2003), 78-79, 85-86.

[84] For the paleographic date of 4QJer[a], see the oral communication by F. M. Cross in D. N. Freedman and K. A. Mathews, *The Paleo-Hebrew Leviticus Scroll (11QpaleoLev)* (Philadelphia, Penn.: American Schools of Oriental Research, 1985), 55.

at the latest in the third century B.C.E. As for a *terminus post quem*, Bogaert was able to establish it in the late fourth or early third century B.C.E.[85] Bogaert argues that Jer 47:1 ("before Pharaoh attacked Gaza") points to the sack of Gaza by Ptolemy I Soter in 312 B.C.E., while protoMT-Jer's mention of Caphtor in Jer 47:4 relates to Soter's conquest of Cyprus in 294 B.C.E. Bogaert's observations argue against earlier settings of protoMT-Jer.

The proto-Masoretic version of Jeremiah's letter to the Babylonian exiles is particularly important when it comes to the question of where protoMT-Jer was produced. The harsh predication of the total annihilation of the citizens of Judah and Jerusalem make it highly unlikely that protoMT-Jer was written in Judah. Because protoMT-Jer universalizes the salvation prophecy of Jer 29:10-14 to pertain not only to the Babylonian exiles but to the whole diaspora, it seems also unlikely that protoMT-Jer was written by Mesopotamian Jews. As evidenced by several sources, since the late fourth and early third cent. B.C.E., a large Jewish diaspora developed in Egypt. The *Letter of Aristeas* (12-27) attests to a deportation of large numbers of Jews from Judah to Ptolemaic Egypt during the reign of Ptolemy I Soter. This report is supplemented by a quotation from Hecateus in Josephus' apology *Against Apion* (1.186-87), which speaks about a voluntary immigration of a leading priest by the name of Hezekiah to Ptolemaic Egypt at the same time.[86]

> Ptolemy got possession of the places in Syria after that battle at Gaza; and many, when they heard of Ptolemy's moderation and humanity, went along with him to Egypt, and were willing to assist him in his affairs; one of whom (Hecateus says) was Hezekiah, an archpriest[87] of

[85] Bogaert, "Baruch," 431-32; idem, "Relecture et déplacement de l'oracle contre les Philistine: Pour une datation de la rédaction longue du livre de Jérémie," in *La Vie de la Parole: De l'Ancien au Nouveau Testament: Études offertes à Pierre Grelot* (Paris: Desclée, 1987), 139-50, 145–50; idem, "*Urtext*," 237; idem, "La datation per souscription dans les rédactions courte (LXX) et longue du livre de Jérémie," in *L'apport de la Septante aux etudes sur l'antiquité: acts du colloque de Strasbourg, 8-9 novembre 2002* (eds. J. Joosten and P. Le Moigne; LD 203; Paris: Cerf, 2005) 137-59.
[86] Translation according to W. Whiston, *The Life and Works of Flavius Josephus the Learned and Authentic Jewish Historian and Celebrated Warrior ... to Which Are Added Seven Dissertations concerning Jesus Christ, John the Baptist, James the Just, God's command to Abraham, etc.* (New York: Holt, Rinehart and Winston, 1957), 870.
[87] Whiston translates "the high priest of the Jews." But the Greek does not have a definite article. The appropriate translation would thus be "a high priest of the Jews." J.-D. Gauger, "Zitate in der jüdischen Apologetik und die Authentizität der Hekataios-Passagen bei Flavius Josephus und im Ps. Aristeas-Brief," *JSJ* 13 (1982): 6-46, 45 (cf. e.g. J. C. Vanderkam, *From Joshua to Caiaphas: High Priests after the Exile* [Minneapolis: Fortress Press, 2004], 117) has shown that Hecateus employs the term

the Jews; a man of sixty-six years of age, and in great dignity among his own people. He was a very sensible man and could speak very movingly, and was very skilful in the management of affairs, if any other man ever were so.

In the late fourth and early third century B.C.E., i.e. at the time when Bogaert dates the proto-Masoretic text of Jeremiah, the only other sizeable population of Jews outside of Judah next to the Mesopotamian diaspora was the Egyptian diaspora which began in large number under the reign of Ptolemy I. That protoMT-Jer predicts the destruction of Judean Jewry in favor of the whole diaspora and that protoMT-Jer reorients Jer 29:10-14 away from the Mesopotamian exiles to the whole diaspora points in my opinion to Egyptian Judaism as the setting of the proto-Masoretic Jeremiah redaction. Whether protoMT-Jer comes out of the group around the archpriest Hezekiah mentioned by Hecateus is a question that cannot be answered in the constraints of this article but will be discussed elsewhere.

Two corroborations exist for my proposed Egyptian setting of protoMT-Jer. 1) Boegaert's observations concerning protoMT-Jer's subtle allusions to the sack of Gaza by Ptolemy I Soter and to his conquest of Cyprus in Jer 47:1, 4 corroborate an Egyptian setting. While the military achievements of Ptolemy I Soter were surely well known in Egypt and other parts of the Ptolemaic realm it seems unlikely that knowledge of these events were widespread enough among Mesopotamian Jews that they could have understood the slight changes which protoMT-Jer inserted into the text of Jer 47:1, 4 to refer to military successes of Ptolemy I Soter. 2) That Jews from early Ptolemaic Egypt rewrote the Book of Jeremiah to express their rejection of Judean Jewry and to articulate their own hopes of return to Judah in order to replace the Judean Jews should not come as a surprise. In Jeremiah 43-44, the Book of Jeremiah points itself to a fictional Egyptian setting by describing how Jeremiah ended his life in Egypt. Furthermore, the book of Jeremiah was received in the literature of Egyptian Judaism. In the third cent. B.C.E., Demetrius the Chronographer refers to Jeremiah 52 (Demetrius 6.1 = Clement of Alexandria, *Strom.* 1.141.1) and in the middle of the second cent. B.C.E., the third Sibyline Oracle alludes to Jer 25:11 (3Sib 3:280).

If protoMT-Jer was produced by Jews from Ptolemaic Egypt, its date becomes more precise as well. Because Egyptian Jews preferred to write

---

ἀρχιερεύς here in the Greek sense of a leader of a temple community and not as pointing to a Jewish high priest. This should not surprise as Hecateus was a non-Jewish author writing for a non-Jewish audience.

in Greek already early in the third cent. B.C.E., it stands to reason that protoMT-Jer must have been written by first generation immigrants in the early third cent. B.C.E. at the latest – probably soon after the mass migration of Jews to Egypt during the reign Ptolemy I.

End of excursus

Given the narrow time window in which protoMT-Jer must have reworked the Book of Jeremiah, it seems quite likely that it argued against the intensified Hellenization of Judean Jewry after Judah became Ptolemaic. Such Hellenizing tendencies are well documented by the book of Ecclesiastes[88] and by what is known about the Tobiad family.[89] This is especially well illustrated by the polytheistic prescript of a letter which Toubias sent on May 12th 257 to Apollonios, the *dioiketes* of the Ptolemaic Empire (Pap.Cair.Zen. I 59076; CPJ 1.4):

> "Toubias to Apollonios greeting. If you and all your affairs are flour-ishing, and everything else is as you wish it, many thanks to the gods!"[90]

It is because of tendencies like these that protoMT-Jer compares the future of the Ptolemaic province of Yehud to the one of Jerusalem under the rule of Zedekiah. Like the Jews of the late pre-exilic period were punished with the destruction of state, city, and temple, Judah will suffer the same fate again during the war of the diadochi because of its Hel-lenizing. As before – in the perception of Jewish history by protoMT-Jer –, the returning diaspora will reestablish the chosen people and their cult in Judah and Jerusalem. That such harsh predictions were not unusual in the third century B.C.E. is attested by the Enochic *Book of Watchers* (*1 Enoch* 1-36). In polemizing against the Hellenizing tendencies of Judean Jewry under Ptolemaic rule it compared the situation of the third cent. B.C.E. with the mixed marriages of the fallen heavenly watchers and their teaching of knowledge to their human wives. In its description of the Watchers and their Promethean function as negative cultural heroes,

---

[88] For Greek influence on Ecclesiastes, see e.g. R. Braun, *Koheleth und die frühhelle-nistische Popularphilosophie* (BZAW 130; Berlin: Walter de Gruyter, 1973); L. Schwienhorst-Schönberger, *Nicht im Menschen gründet das Glück (Koh 2,24): Kohelet im Spannungsfeld jüdischer Weisheit und hellenistischer Philosophie* (Herders Biblische Studien 2; Freiburg i.B.: Herder, 1994).

[89] For the Tobiad family and its Hellenizing preferences, see P. Schäfer, *The History of the Jews in the Greco-Roman World* (rev. ed.; London: Routledge, 2003), 18-20, 32-34.

the *Book of Watchers* combines Greek with Jewish myth to slander Hellenistic culture as something that was taught already by the Watchers to their exogamous wives. As a consequence the deluge came. The implication for a time of increased Greek cultural influence is evident. Greek acculturation is comparable with the teachings of the fallen heavenly watchers. Its consequences will be as bad as the deluge was.[91]

With its reworking of Jeremiah's letter to the Babylonian exiles, the proto-Masoretic Jeremiah redaction creates a typology which is coined by a particular idea of Jewish history. Because the Jews of Judah venerated other gods, Judah, Jerusalem, and the temple were destroyed in 587 B.C.E. by the Babylonians. In another addition (Jer 39:4-13), protoMT-Jer even goes through a significant narrative effort to ensure that Jerusalem was destroyed and empty after the 587 B.C.E. conquest. Those who were not killed or exiled fled shortly afterwards to Egypt (see Jer 40:7-43:7). Judah was empty and desolated – thus the historical fiction of the Book of Jeremiah. After these events, Judaism was represented by the exiles which remained true to the covenant. They were to come back and rebuild Judah and the Temple cult. The universalization of Jeremiah's promise of return to the whole diaspora shows that protoMT-Jer applies this earlier experience in fictional Jewish history to the situation of the early third cent. B.C.E. As in the past, the Jews of Jerusalem and Judah in the early third cent. B.C.E. venerate other gods and will be destroyed – one could speculate whether protoMT-Jer imagines this destruction in the context of the wars of the diadochi. True Judaism is represented by the diaspora of the third cent. B.C.E. The diaspora will repopulate Judah, rebuild it and begin the Temple cult anew. That with this typology protoMT-Jer reflects a broader interpretative tradition of Jeremiah's promise of a return after seventy years (Jer 25:12-12; 29:10) becomes evident in the *Letter of Jeremiah*. Written in the Babylonian diaspora during the reign of Antiochus III,[92] the *Letter of Jeremiah* promises a return to Judah for the exiles after seven generations.

---

[90] Translation according to L. H. Schiffman, *Texts and Traditions: A Source Reader for the Study of Second Temple and Rabbinic Judaism* (Hoboken, N.J.: Ktav Publishing House, 1998), 139.

[91] For this interpretation of final stage of the *Book of Watchers*, see my "The Significance of the Pre-Maccabean Literature from the Qumran Library for the Understanding of the Hebrew Bible: Intermarriage in Ezra/Nehemiah – Satan in 1 Chr. 21:1 – the Date of Psalm 119," in *Congress Volume Ljubljana 2007* (ed. A. Lemaire; VTSup 133; Leiden: Brill, 2010), 171-218, 187-91, and the literature quoted there.

[92] Cf. R. G. Kratz "Der Brief des Jeremia: Übersetzt und erklärt," in O. H. Steck, R. G. Kratz, and I. Kottsieper, *Das Buch Baruch, Der Brief des Jeremia, Zusätze zu Ester und Daniel* (ATD Apokryphen 5; Göttingen: Vandenhoeck & Ruprecht, 1998), 71-108, 81-84.

> When, therefore, you come into Babylon, you will be there for rather
> many years, even for a long time, as long as seven generations. But
> after this, I will bring you from there with peace.[93]

To summarize: ProtoMT-Jer rewrites an earlier version of the Book of
Jeremiah drastically to create a new text of the book. The reworking is
not restricted to small changes. While protoMT-Jer is also harmonizing
its base text it goes far further. The example of Jeremiah 29 shows that
this redaction creates a different text with a different message. In the
case of Jeremiah, the *Vorlage* of protoMT-Jer was not only reworked by
protoMT-Jer but also by the Hebrew *Vorlage* of Jer-LXX. As both texts
continued to exist, the example of protoMT-Jer shows that reworkings
are one cause of textual plurality. ProtoMT-Jer proves thus that in some
cases the textual witnesses of a biblical book attest to different redactions
of it while their shared *Vorlage* most probably looked again different
from each of them. It seems difficult to me to still dub this postulated
shared source of protoMT-Jer and the Hebrew *Vorlage* of LXX-Jer the
Urtext of the Book Jeremiah. The Book(s) of Jeremiah point the student
of ancient literature instead to the fact that for some ancient (biblical)
books the one *Urtext* never existed.[94]

3.3 Harmonistic Editing – The Example of 4QDeut^n (4Q41)

ProtoMT-Jer is the most radical example of rewriting known from the
textual traditions of the ancient Jewish scriptures. While similar but less
radical rewritings can be encountered in the case of other biblical books
as well – e.g. the Book of Ezekiel – most textual witnesses to biblical
books fall into a different category of textual variation. In a comparison
between the rewritings of Jewish scriptures and the Samaritan Pentateuch, Tov describes the differences between biblical manuscripts and
what he calls rewritten Bible as follows.[95]

> We think … that the two groups are distinct, since the SP group must
> have been considered an authoritative Bible text limiting its some-
> times major reworking …, to the addition of sentences or periscopes
> from elsewhere in the Bible. The SP group, it should be stressed, did
> not add new sections, nor did it change the Bible text freely. The

---

[93] Translation according to *A New English Translation of the Septuagint* (eds. A. Pietersma
and B. G. Wright; New York: Oxford University Press, 2007), 944.
[94] The contribtion of F. Garcia Martinez to this volume ("The Dead Sea Scrolls and the
Book of Joshua") argues a similar case for the Book of Joshua.
[95] E. Tov, "Rewritten Bible Compositions and Biblical Manuscripts, with Special Attention to the Samaritan Pentateuch," *DSD* 5 (1998): 334-54, 354.

rewritten Bible compositions, on the other hand, freely added new details, and probably were not considered authoritative.

While it might be questioned in how far categories like Bible can be applied to a time before the closure of the Hebrew canon,[96] Tov's observation regarding the differences in terms of character and extent between texts like pre-SP on the one hand and a rewriting on the other hand are still valid. The editorial reworking of the pre-Samaritan Pentateuch is not of the same magnitude as the rewriting which the proto-Masoretic Jeremiah redaction applied to its *Vorlage*, although the latter employed the harmonizing editing so prominent in pre-SP as well.

Already in my analysis of Jeremiah 29, I have presented the type of variant readings that correct their base text and harmonize individual passages with the rest of the Book of Jeremiah. This so-called harmonization is well known from several Qumran scrolls.[97] As one of the best preserved manuscripts from the Qumran library, 4QDeut[n] (4Q41) is a good example.[98] Of its six columns, only col. V is slightly damaged and col. VI more significantly. With its small height[99] of 7.1cm (5.5cm column height equaling twelve lines), even in its original total length, 4QDeut[n] was too small to have contained the whole Book of Deuteronomy. It is hence classified since its discovery as an excerpted text,[100]

---

[96]   Cf. the contribtion of F. Garcia Martinez to this volume ("The Dead Sea Scrolls and the Book of Joshua").

[97]   For harmonizing texts among the Dead Sea Scrolls, see E. Tov, "The Nature and Background of Harmonization in Biblical Manuscripts," *JSOT* 3 (1985): 3-29; idem, "Textual Harmonizations in the Ancient Texts of Deuteronomy," in idem, *Hebrew Bible, Greek Bible, and Qumran: Collected Essays* (TSAJ 121; Tübingen: Mohr Siebeck, 2008), 217-82; E. Eshel, "4QDeut[n] – A Text That Has Undergone Harmonistic Editing," *HUCA* 62 (1991): 120-21, 147-52; S. White Crawford, *Rewriting Scripture in Second Temple Times* (Studies in the Dead Sea Scrolls and Related Literature; Grand Rapids, Mich.: Eerdmans, 2008), 19-37.

[98]   For 4QDeut[n], see S. A. White, "The All Souls Deuteronomy and the Decalogue," *JBL* 109 (1990): 193-206; S. White Crawford, "41. 4QDeut[n]," in E. Ulrich et al., *Qumran Cave 4. IX: Deuteronomy, Joshua, Judges, Kings* (DJD XIV; Oxford: Clarendon, 1995), 117-28; Eshel, "4QDeut[n]," passim.

[99]   For the measures of 4QDeut[n] and its material reconstruction, see White Crawford, "41. 4QDeut[n]," 117-18.

[100] Thus first H. Stegemann, "Weitere Stücke von 4 Q p Psalm 37, von 4 Q Patriarchal Blessings und Hinsweis auf eine unedierte Handschrift aus Höhle 4 Q mit Exzerpten aus dem Deuteronomium," *RevQ* 6 (1967-69): 191-217, 217-27; cf. S. A. White, "4QDt[n]: Biblical Manuscript or Excerpted Text?" in *Of Scribes and Scrolls: Studies on the Hebrew Bible, Intertestamental Judaism, and Christian Origins* (Lanham, Md.: University Press of America, 1990), 13-20; Eshel, "4QDeut[n]," 117-54; J. A. Duncan, "Considerations of 4QDt[j] in Light of the 'All Souls Deuteronomy' and Cave 4 Phylactery Texts," in *The Madrid Qumran Congress: Proceedings of the International Congress on the Dead Sea Scrolls, Madrid 18-21 March 1991* (eds. J. Trebolle Barrera and L. Vegas Montaner; 2 vols.; STDJ 11; Leiden: Brill, 1992), 1:199-215. For

which probably did not contain significantly more text than what is still extant of it, i.e. Deut 8:5–10; 5:1– 29, 31–33; 6:1. Being copied in an early Herodian book hand,[101] 4QDeut^n employs a fuller orthography than MT but uses mostly the short morphological forms known from MT.

Since F. M. Cross's first published remarks[102] about 4QDeut^n, the scroll has been regarded as a collection of Deuteronomy references compiled for liturgical purposes because of its small size. Recently, it was proposed by Finsterbusch that excerpted (liturgical) texts like 4QDeut^n should be regarded separately in the text-critical study of the Book of Deuteronomy in particular or of the Hebrew Bible in general as they display special textual characteristics due to their excerpted nature.[103] Similarly, Duncan speculates whether the textual variants of excerpted texts go back to copying from memory in a way comparable to the Phylacteries and *Mezuzot* from Qumran.[104] Against such considerations it should be noted that although some excerpted manuscripts might attest to variant readings that were introduced into their biblical texts only for purposes of abbreviation (see below on abbreviation), it is at least as likely that the textual variation attested by the excerpted manuscripts goes back to the scribal *Vorlagen* from which they were excerpted. The example of the Phylacteries from Qumran demonstrates furthermore that while they display similarities with excerpted manuscripts in their harmonizing approach, the phylacteries attest at the same time to more and less systematic textual change than excerpted texts like 4QDeut^n do. Concerning the text-critical value of excerpted texts, Tov's 1995 statement still brings it to the point:

> the excerpted manuscripts from the Qumran library, see also E. Tov, "Excerpted and Abbreviated Biblical Texts from Qumran," *RevQ* 16 (1994-95): 581-600; idem, "The Biblical Texts from the Judaean Desert," 149-50; J. A. Duncan, "Excerpted Texts of *Deuteronomy* at Qumran," *RevQ* 18 (1997-98): 43-62; B. A. Strawn, "Excerpted Manuscripts at Qumran: Their Siginificance for the Textual History of the Hebrew Bible and the Socio-Religious History of the Qumran Community and Its Literature," in *The Bible and the Dead Sea Scrolls: The Princeton Symposium on the Dead Sea Scrolls* (ed. J. H. Charlesworth; 3 vols.; Waco, Tex.: Baylor University Press, 2006), 2:107-67.

[101] See F. M. Cross, *Scrolls from the Wilderness of the Dead Sea* (London: British Museum, 1965), 31; cf. White Crawford, "4QDeut^n," 117-18.

[102] F. M. Cross, *Wilderness*, 31; see especially M. Weinfeld, "Prayer and Liturgical Practice in the Qumran Sect," in *The Dead Sea Scrolls: Forty Years of Research* (eds. D. Dimant and U. Rappaport; STDJ 10; Leiden: Brill, 1992), 241-58, 251-55; idem, "Grace after Meals in Qumran," *JBL* 111 (1992): 427-40, 427-29.

[103] Thus recently K. Finsterbusch, "Identität in der Differenz: Anmerkungen zur Textüberlieferung der Deuteronomium-Handschriften vom Toten Meer," in *Juda und Jerusalem in der Seleukidenzeit: Herrschaft- Widerstand – Identität: Festschrift für Heinz-Josef Fabry* (eds. U. Dahmen and J. Schnocks; BBB 159; Göttingen: V & R Unipress, 2010), 339-62, 339 note 2.

[104] Duncan, "Excerpted Texts," 60-61.

> For the textual analysis of the Bible the excerpted or abbreviated texts
> provide the same type of evidence as running biblical texts, with the
> exception that the lack of pericopes should be ascribed to excerpting
> or shortening, and not to the special textual character of the scroll.[105]

Among the 51 variants of 4QDeutⁿ towards MT, SP, and LXX a significant number of harmonizing readings can be found. E. Eshel speaks
about seventeen such harmonizing readings in 4QDeutⁿ. Some but not all
of these readings are also found in SP, the LXX, the Nash Papyrus, and
other Qumran witnesses as well. 4QDeutⁿ though is an ideal sample case
to illuminate how scribes harmonized the texts of their *Vorlagen* with
other passages from Deuteronomy, from the overall Pentateuch, or even
from other Jewish scriptures. In 4QDeutⁿ, these harmonizing readings
are especially common in Deut 5:6-21. They align the Deuteronomy
Decalogue with the one in Exod 20:2-17. In light of similar harmonizations in the Nash Papyrus as another text which was excerpted for
liturgical purposes, it is quite possible that the harmonizing alignment of
the two versions of the Decalogue in 4QDeutⁿ was undertaken to allow
for its daily recitation as prescribed in *m. Tamid 5:1*. 4QDeutⁿ would in
this case illustrate how the liturgical use of a text influences its textual
history.[106] The following table summarizes the smaller harmonizations
between the two versions of the Pentateuch in 4QDeutⁿ.

Table 2: Harmonizations with Exod 20:2-17 in n 4QDeutⁿ

	MT	SP	4QDeutⁿ	Exod 20:2-17 MT
Deut 5:8	כל	וכל	וכול	וכל
Deut 5:9	ועל שלשים	על שלשים	על שלשים	על שלשים
Deut 5:14	וכל בהמתך	וכל בהמתך	ובהמתך	ובהמתך
Deut 5:18	ולא	לא	לוא	לא
Deut 5:19	ולא	לא	לוא	לא
Deut 5:20	ולא	לא	לוא	לא
Deut 5:21	ולא תחמוד	לא תחמוד	לוא תחמוד	לא תחמוד
Deut 5:21[107]	ולא תתאוה בית רעך	לא תחמוד בית רעך	לוא תחמוד בית רעיך	לא תחמד בית רעך

---

[105] Tov, "Excerpted and Abbreviated Biblical Texts," 599.

[106] For the influence which the liturgical use of a text had on its textual history, see
A. Lange and M. Weigold, "The Text of the Shema Yisrael in Qumran Literature and
Elsewhere" (forthcoming in a Festschrift).

[107] In SP and Exod 20:17MT לא תחמוד בית רעך is the first stichos of the tenth commandment while in Deut 5:21 MT and 4QDeutⁿ it is the second.

The eight smaller harmonizations with the Exodus version of the Decalogue show that the scribe of 4QDeut[n] or his *Vorlage* harmonized the
Decalogue in Deuteronomy with its Exodus version. Most of these harmonizations involve small details like the deletion or addition of a *waw
copulativum*. Only in one case was a word deleted (כל in Deut 5:14) and
only in one other case a word was changed (תחמוד instead of תתאוה).
Larger changes in the text are mostly avoided. The only exception to this
rule is a long addition to the Sabbath command at the end of Deut 5:15
which is taken from Exod 20:11a.[108]

Deut 5:15 according to 4QDeut[n][109]	Deut 5:15 according to MT	Exod 20:11
You shall remember that you were a servant in the land of Egypt, and the Lord your God brought you out from there with a mighty hand and an outstretched arm. Therefore the Lord your God commanded you to *keep* the sabbath day *to hallow it. For in six days the Lord made heaven and earth, the sea, and all that is in them and rested the seventh day; so the Lord blessed the Sabbath day to hallow it.*	You shall remember that you were a servant in the land of Egypt, and the Lord your God brought you out from there with a mighty hand and an outstretched arm. Therefore the Lord your God commanded you to *perform* the sabbath.	For in six days the Lord made heaven and earth, the sea, and all that is in them and rested the seventh day; so the Lord blessed the Sabbath day and hallowed it.

Because the two versions of the Decalogue give different reasons for the
Sabbath command the scribe of 4QDeut[n] has combined them by inserting
a part of the Exodus text into the Deuteronomy one. This particular
aspect of harmonizing witnesses, i.e. the large scale conflation of various

---

[108] Cf. e.g. J. H. Tigay, "Conflation as a Redactional Technique," in *Empirical Models for Biblical Criticism* (ed. J. H. Tigay; Philadelphia: University of Pennsylvania Press, 1985), 53-95, 55-57; White, "All Souls," 200-01; S. White Crawford, "Reading Deuteronomy in the Second Temple Period," in *Reading the Present in the Qumran Library: The Conception of the Contemporary by Means of Scriptural Interpretations* (SBLSymp 30; Atlanta: SBL, 2005), 127-40, 129-30; eadem, *Rewriting Scripture*, 31-32; Eshel, "4QDeut[n]," 145-46; Duncan, "Excerpted Texts," 55-56.

[109] Translation according to M. Abegg, P. Flint, and E. C. Ulrich, *The Dead Sea Scrolls Bible: Translated and with Commentary* (Edinburgh: T & T Clark, 1999), 154. Difference between MT and 4QDeut[n] are marked in italics.

parallel yet different passages to one new text, is close to the phenomenon of redaction and rewriting because it corresponds to the merging of
sources in earlier redactional layers of e.g. the Pentateuch.[110]

But harmonization with Exod 20:2-17 is not the only aim of 4QDeut[n].
Both inside and outside the Decalogue 4QDeut[n] harmonizes its Deuteronomy text with other Deuteronomy- or Exodus-passages as well.[111]

- The addition of אלוהיכם to יהוה in Deut 5:5 was added under the
  influence of 42 parallel expressions in Deuteronomy alone which
  speak of "the Lord, your God."[112]
- Deut 5:14 is harmonized with Exod 35:2 by an addition of בו; and
  with Exod 16:26 et al. by the reading וביום.
- Deut 5:15bβ is harmonized with Deut 5:12a.
- Deut 8:6 is harmonized with "texts in Deuteronomy dealing with
  the general command 'to love God' (such as 11:22; 19:9, et al[113])."
- Deut 8:7 is harmonized with Exod 3:8.
- Deut 5:22 is harmonized with Deut 4:11.

That the harmonizations of 4QDeut[n] agree sometimes but not always
with SP while further agreements with the LXX and the Nash Papyrus
as well as nonaligned readings occur warns against simply grouping
4QDeut[n] with SP in one textual family of harmonizing texts. 4QDeut[n]
attests to its own harmonizing text which in several readings agrees with
SP and pre-SP texts but is non-aligned in character.[114] It can be compared with SP and pre-SP texts in its harmonizing reworking though.
Like other harmonizing texts, 4QDeut[n] systematically improves its Deu-
teronomy-base-text. E.g., when a given part of the Deuteronomy Decalogue disagrees with its counterpart in Exodus, 4QDeut[n] adjusts the text
of the Deuteronomy Decalogue to the one in Exodus thus harmonizing
the disagreement.

This points on the one hand to a consciousness of the scribe of 4QDeut[n]
or of its *Vorlage* for the possibility of textual corruption of the text of the
Pentateuch. On the other hand, this systematic effort to streamline the

---

[110] Cf. Tigay, "Conflation," passim.
[111] This list is compiled from Eshel's study ("4QDeut[n]"). For a complete discussion of
these harmonizations, see Eshel, "4QDeut[n]," 142-47.
[112] Eshel, "4QDeut[n]," 144.
[113] Eshel, "4QDeut[n]," 144.
[114] See Tov, "The Biblical Texts from the Judaean Desert," 156; E. Owen, "4QDeut[n]: A
Pre-Samaritan Text?" *DSD* 4 (1997):162-78; S. White Crawford, "A Response to
Elisabeth Owen's '4QDeut[n]: A Pre-Samaritan Text?'," *DSD* 5 (1998): 92-94; Lange,
Handbuch, 97-98.

text of Deuteronomy illustrates also how new texts of the book of Deuteronomy developed. Because 4QDeut[n] attest to an excerpt of Deuteronomy, which collects passages of Deuteronomy occuring otherwise in Phylacteries, *Mezuzot*, and the Nash Papyrus, it is quite likely that it was originally used for liturgical purposes (see above, 85). But whether in the case of 4QDeut[n] its harmonized text of Deuteronomy was developed for liturgical purposes or not is of little interest for my question of how textual plurality came to be. It just shows that in the case of 4QDeut[n] its harmonizations were motivated by liturgical reasons. Whether liturgically motivated or not, in the end, the harmonizations of 4QDeut[n] created yet another text of the Book of Deuteronomy or – to be more precise – of parts of it. This is all the more true as it is widely recognized that the same type of harmonizations occur in the Samaritan Pentateuch, in the Hebrew *Vorlagen* of the Old Greek translations of the Pentateuch, as well as in the pre-Samaritan manuscripts 4QpaleoExod[m] (4Q22) and 4QNum[b] (4Q27),[115] although these textual witnesses were not written for liturgical purposes. What was illustrated here by the paradigm of 4QDeut[n] occurs hence elsewhere following the same motivations and employing the same mechanisms without liturgical reasons.

3.4 Abbreviation – the Example of 4QCant[a] (4Q106)

That 4QDeut[n] presents the reader with an excerpted text from Deuteronomy makes it similar to but different from the next category of textual change. An excerpted text like the one attested by 4QDeut[n] collects various passages from one or several biblical books. An abbreviated text cuts various passages out of the book it attests to.[116] Abbreviated manuscripts are not common among the biblical manuscripts of the Qumran library, but they do occur. One of the most radical examples is 4QCant[a] (4Q106).[117] Of this manuscript only six fragments are extant which attest to 108 partly or fully preserved words out of Cant 3:4-5, 7; 6:11; 7:7. The original scroll was only 9.3 cm high. The scribe wrote the manuscript in a very tiny early Herodian book hand. At 4QCant[a] 2 ii, the text of Cant 4:8 and 6:10 is missing without any doubt. Because the missing text amounts to about 30% of the whole book of Canticles, it is unlikely

[115] E.g. Eshel, "4QDeut[n]," 117; White Crawford, "Reading Deuteronomy," 131-32; eadem, *Rewriting Scripture*, 22-35; Tov, "Textual Harmonizations," passim.
[116] Cf. Tov, "Excerpted and Abbreviated Biblical Texts," 597-99.
[117] For this manuscript, its edition, description, paleography, and orthography see Tov, "Three Manuscripts," 91-97, and "Canticles," 199-204.

that it was deleted accidentally by way of *homoioteleuton*.[118] If scribal accident can be excluded as a cause for the short text of 4QCant[a] 2 ii three possible explanations remain.

- 4QCant[a] 2 ii could attest to an earlier shorter text of Canticles. In this case, Cant 4:8-6:10 would be a latter addition to the book of Canticles.[119]
- 4QCant[a] 2 ii could attest to a later abbreviation of the book of Canticles. In this case, Cant 4:8-6:10 would have been cut out of the Canticles text by the scribe of 4QCant[a] or some earlier copyist in the copying chain of this text.[120]
- 4QCant[a] could have attested to the text of Cant 4:8-6:10 elsewhere in the not preserved parts of the manuscript. In this case 4QCant[a] would be a manuscript with a different textual sequence than proto-MT Canticles.

Similarities between Cant 4:1-7 and Cant 6:11-7:5 warrant for a smooth transition of the Canticles text between Cant 4:7 and 6:11. These similarities allowed for an abbreviation of Cant 4:8-6:10. Both Cant 4:4 and 7:5 compare a neck with a tower. Both Cant 4:5 and 7:3 liken a woman's breasts to a gazelle. Both Cant 4:3 and 6:11 mention pomegranates. Both Cant 4:1 and 7:5 refer to eyes. The wording of Cant 4:5a and 7:4 is almost identical. Only Cant 4:4 and 7:5 use the word מגדל ("tower") in the book of Canticles.[121] Tov adds to these arguments observations that show that Cant 4:8-6:10 was perceived as one or more textual units in antiquity.

> ... at the point where 4QCant[a] col. III 1-2 leaves out a large section, Cant 4:8-6:10, a partially empty and a completely empty line were probably found in the reconstructed text. Furthermore, the last verse

---

[118] Cf. G. W. Nebe, "Qumranica I. Zu unveröffentlichten Handschriften aus Höhle 4 von Qumran," *ZAW* 106 (1994): 307-22, 310; Tov, "Three Manuscripts," 96-97; idem, "Canticles," 203. Nebe[118] thinks that the reading of 4QCant[a] 2 ii goes back to an associative correlation of the word לבונה ("frankincense" Cant 4:6) with the word לבנה ("moon"; Cant 6:10) as well as of the two uses of word the יפה ("beautiful") in Cant 4:7 and 6:10.

[119] Thus E. C. Ulrich, "Our Sharper Focus on the Bible and Theology Thanks to the Dead Sea Scrolls," *CBQ* 66 (2004): 1-24, 8; idem, "The Text of the Hebrew Scriptures at the Time of Hillel and Jesus," in *Congress Volume Basel 2001* (ed. A. Lemaire; VTSup 92; Leiden: Brill, 2002), 85-108, 104-05.

[120] Thus Tov, "Three Manuscripts," 89-91; idem, "Canticles," 195-96; idem, "Excerpted and Abbreviated Biblical Texts," 591-92; S. White Crawford, "Five Scrolls," *Encyclopedia of the Dead Sea Scrolls* (eds. L. H. Schiffman and J. C. VanderKam; 2 vols.; Oxford: Oxford University Press, 2000), 1:295-97, 295.

[121] Cf. Tov, "Three Manuscripts," 89, 97; idem, "The Biblical Texts from the Judaean Desert," 591-92; idem, "Canticles," 195-96.

of the omitted section 4:4-7, in 4QCant[a] and the next verse in the
scroll, Cant 6:11, starts off another unit, indicated in M with a closed
paragraph after 6:10.[122]

It is most likely that the scribe of 4QCant[a] was concerned not to have
enough space on his small scroll for the whole book of Canticles. This
concern is evident in the exceptionally tiny handwriting of the manuscript. When the parallels between Cant 4:1-7 and 6:11-7:5 allowed in
his opinion for abbreviation he decided to exclude Cant 4:8-6:10 from
his manuscript. The abbreviation of Cant 4:8-6:10 in 4QCant[a] created a
substantially different text for the book of Canticles. The next scribe who
would have copied 4QCant[a] would have transmitted and multiplied this
altered text in the textual tradition of Canticles. By way of its abbreviation 4QCant[a] would have thus contributed to the textual plurality of the
book of Canticles in the Second Temple period.

That 4QCant[a] is no exception but only the most radical example preserved of an ancient Jewish scribal practice is shown by 4QCant[b] (4Q107),
which in addition to its scribal corruptions (see above), seems to be an
abbreviating manuscript, too. Tov[123] argues with regard to the missing text
of Cant 4:4-7 in 4QCant[b] 2 ii 6-7, that "the omission of Cant 4:4-7 is
indicated by an open paragraph at the end of line 6, after v 3, and a large
indentation at the beginning of the next line before the text of v 8." Similarly, he regards the omission of Cant 3:6-8 in 4QCant[b] 2 i 7 as intentional.

Whatever the reasons for the omissions in 4QCant[a] and 4QCant[b], neither manuscript compiles collected passages for liturgical use as was the
case with 4QDeut[n] (see above). But as a consequence of the scribal
abbreviation in both manuscripts a new, shorter texts of Canticles came
to be, which would have added to the textual plurality of the Second
Temple Judaism in case they were copied. But the ommisions of
4QCant[a,b] are not attested by any other textual witness to Canticles. It
must hence remain unclear whether these particular abbreviating manuscripts had a larger impact on the textual history of Canticles or not.

3.5 Compilation of Poetic Texts – Psalms versus Hodayot

Different textual witnesses of one biblical book can attest to divergent
text sequences in this book. Such re-sequencing of a given book can be
part of a reworking by a redactor. Prominent examples for a redactional

---

[122] Tov, "Canticles," 196.
[123] Tov, "Canticles," 196, cf. ibid., 216.

resequencing of a biblical book are the proto-Masoretic Jeremiah redaction (see above) and the divergent sequence of Ezekiel 36; 38-39; 37 in Papyrus 967.[124] In comparison to these at least in part narrative texts, the compilation and collection of poetic texts seems to have followed its own rules in ancient Judaism.[125] A comparison between the different Psalms-manuscripts from the Qumran library[126] shows that the text of the individual psalms in these manuscripts is – with few exceptions – more stable than the text of many other biblical books.[127] The main difference between the individual Psalms manuscripts from Qumran lies in which psalms they include and in which sequence these psalms follow each other. Based on which songs a given Psalms manuscript from Qumran contains in which sequence the following canonical and non-canonical Psalms-collections can be identified in Qumran and at the other sites from the Dead Sea:

1. Ps-MT (4QPs^c?; vgl. 4QMidrEschat$^{a.b}$; cf. MasPs$^{a.b}$; 5/6ḤevPs)
2. Ps-11QPs^a (11QPs$^{a.b}$; vgl. 4QPs^e)
3. 4QPs$^{a.q}$
4. 4QPs^b
5. 4QPs^d
6. 4QPs^f
7. 4QPs^k
8. 4QNon-Canonical Psalms A
9. 4QNon-Canonical Psalms B
10. 4QWorks of God + 4QCommunal Confession[128]

The below list illustrates which psalms the individual manuscripts of each psalms collection contained in which sequence.[129]

---

[124] Ezekiel 36 misses in Papyrus 967 verses 23b-38. For a detailed study of Ezekiel 36-39 in Papyrus 967, see A. S. Crane, *Israel's Restoration: A Textual-Comparative Exploration of Ezekiel 36-39* (VTSup 122; Leiden: Brill, 2008).

[125] For a more detailed study of this phenomenon, see A. Lange, "Collecting Psalms in Light of the Dead Sea Scrolls" (the article will be published in a yet unfinished Festschrift).

[126] For the textual history of the Psalms in light of the Dead Sea Scrolls, see P. W. Flint, *The Dead Sea Scrolls and the Book of Psalms* (STDJ 17; Leiden: Brill, 1997); Lange, *Handbuch*, 373-450, and the literature quoted there.

[127] Cf. A. Lange, "Die Endgestalt des protomasoretischen Psalters und die Toraweisheit: Zur Bedeutung der nichtessenischen Weisheitstexte aus Qumran für die Auslegung des protomasoretischen Psalters," in *Der Psalter in Judentum und Christentum* (ed. E. Zenger, Herders Biblische Studien 18; Freiburg i.B.: Herder, 1998), 101-36, 109-11.

[128] For 4QWorks of God + 4QCommunal Confession as parts of one manuscript attesting to a psalms-collection, see D. Falk, "Works of God and Communal Confession," in E. Chazon et al., in consultation with J. VanderKam and M. Brady, *Qumran Cave 4.XX: Poetical and Liturgical Texts, Part 2* (DJD XXIX; Oxford: Clarendon, 1999), 23-61, 23-24.

[129] Below, → marks if two psalms follow each other on one fragment. Only those Qumran manuscripts are listed whose text sequence still allows for an allocation to a particular psalms collection.

1. Ps-MT (for Ps-MT the reader is referred to its critical editions)
2. 11QPs[a] (... Ps 101–103→...→109→...→118→104→147→105→146
   →148→...→121–132→119→135→136 + 118:1, 15, 16, 8, 9, X, 29?
   →145→154→Plea for Deliverance→Ps 139→137–138→Sir 51:13–30
   →Apostrophe to Zion→Ps 93→141→133→144→155→142–143→149–
   150→Hymn to the Creator→2 Sam 23,[1–]7→David's Compositions→
   Ps 140→134→151A→151 B ...); 11QPs[b] (Ps 77→78; 119; 118;1,
   15–16; Plea for Deliverance; Apostrophe to Zion; Ps 141→133→144);
   4QPs[e] (Ps 76→77,1; 78; 81; 86; 88; 89; 103→109; 114; 115→116;
   118→104; 105→146; 120; 125→126; 129→130)
3. 4QPs[a] (Ps 5→6; 25; 31→33; 34→35→36; 38→71; 47; 53→54; 56;
   62→63; 66→67; 69); 4QPs[q] (Ps 31→33[→34→]35)
4. 4QPs[b] (Ps 91[→]92[→]93[→]94; 96; 98; 99[→]100; 102→103[→]112;
   113; 115; 116; [117→]118)[130]
5. 4QPs[d] (Ps 106→147→104)
6. 4QPs[f] (Ps 22; 107; 109→Apostrophe to Zion; Eschatological Hymn[→]
   Apostrophe to Judah)
7. 4QPs[k] (Ps 135[→]99)[131]

The lists illustrate that not one but several Psalms collections existed in the Second Temple period. These psalms collections combined the various existing psalms differently. The proto-Masoretic Psalter was thus just one among many existing psalms collections. While in some cases several manuscripts attest to one psalms collection in other cases only one manuscript is known.

The same phenomenon of different combinations of a certain category of poetic texts in various manuscripts is also known from the Qumran *Hodayot*. Again various manuscripts which contain the same type of poetic texts differ significantly from each other in both which songs they contain and in which sequence they combine them. Eileen Schuller summarizes the evidence as follows in her *editio princeps*.[132]

> The full collection of psalms that is found in 1QH[a] is preserved in one other copy, 4QH[b] ...
> 4QH[a] ... has a different order of psalms. All the material in 4QH[a] that overlaps with material in 1QH[a] is from psalms of the 'Hymns of the Community' type. The proposed length of the scroll as it has been reconstructed (*c.* 3.7 m) indicates that this was a much smaller collection than that found in 1QH[a] ... According to the identification of the fragments that belong to 4QH[e] and the reconstruction of the scroll that

---

[130] For the material reconstruction of 4QPs[b], see P. W. Skehan, E. C. Ulrich, and P. W. Flint, "Psalms," in *DJD* XVI: 1-170, 21-48. The material reconstruction of this manuscript allows for the identification of some psalm-sequences although they are not preserved. They are marked above with [→].

[131] For Ps 99 following Ps 135 in 4QPs[k], see Skehan, Ulrich, and Flint, "Psalms," 123-25.

[132] Schuller, "Hodayot," *DJD* XXIX: 69-254, 74-75.

is proposed, only one psalm from the beginning of the manuscript has been preserved. If it is correct to consider the *Hodayot* manuscript, the order of the psalms is clearly different in this copy than the order in 1QH^a. The material evidence of 4QH^c, with its very short columns of only twelve lines, suggests that this manuscript contains a much smaller collection of psalms ... All the preserved material is from the 'Hymns of the Teacher' collection, and this manuscript may have contained only psalms of that type with perhaps an introductory psalm ... In the preserved section of 4QpapH^f, there are fragments of the 'Creation Hymn' (corresponding to 1QH^a IX 1-X 5 ...) and of the 'Hymns of the Teacher' section (1QH^a X 6-XVII 36 ...) ... According to the proposed reconstruction of the scroll, the preserved fragments were the beginning of the scroll ... It is impossible to determine if there were further layers containing more columns which have not survived.

The comparison between the *Hodayot* and Psalms manuscripts from Qumran shows that poetic texts followed their own text-critical rules in antiquity. Each psalm or *hodayah* was regarded as an independent text which could be combined more or less randomly in the various psalms and *hodayot* collections. This more or less random combination of the individual psalms and *hodayot* led in the end to the existence of several psalms and *hodayot* collections next to each other, i.e. to textual plurality of collections of poetic texts.

3.6 Recension – the Examples of Papyrus Fouad Inv. 266b and 266c, 4QLXXNum und 8HevXII gr

In the case of Greek manuscripts of biblical books several revisions of the Old Greek text towards a (proto-Masoretic) Hebrew text were found in Egypt (Papyrus Fouad Inv. 266b and 266c),[133] Qumran (4QLXX-Num),[134] and Nahal Hever (8HevXII gr).[135] At least in the case of

---

[133] See R. Hanhart for Papyrus Fouad Inv. 266b, "Die Söhne Israels, die Söhne Gottes und die Engel in der Masora, in Qumran und in der Septuaginta: Ein letztes Kapitel aus Israel in hellenistischer Zeit," in *Vergegenwärtigung des Alten Testaments: Beiträge zur biblischen Hermeneutik: FS R. Smend* (eds. C. Bultmann, W. Dietrich, and C. Levin; Göttingen: Vandenhoeck & Ruprecht, 2002), 170–78, 171; idem, review of F. Dunand, *Papyrus grecs bibliques (Papyrus F. Inv. 266.)*, *OLZ* 73 (1978): 39–45, 42–45; L. Koenen, "Introduction," in Z. Aly, *Three Rolls of the Early Septuagint: Genesis and Deuteronomy: A Photographic Edition Prepared with the International Photographic Archive of the Association Internationale de Papyrologues* (Papyrologische Texte und Abhandlungen 27; Bonn: Habelt, 1980), 1–23, 1–2, 9. For Papyrus Fouad Inv. 266c, see ibid., 9, 18–20.

[134] P. W. Skehan, "4QLXXNum: A Pre-Christian Reworking of the Septuagint," *HTR* 70 (1977): 39–50, 39 (cf. pp. 39–40); cf. also J. W. Wevers, "An Early Revision of the Septuagint of Numbers," *ErIsr* 16 (1982): 235*–39*; U. Quast, "Der rezensionelle

4QLXXNum (4Q121)[136] and 8ḤevXII gr (8Ḥev 1)[137] these recensions belong to larger recension groups which continued to exist through late antiquity.[138] Although the early recensions of the Old Greek text were mostly intended to bring it closer to the proto-Masoretic text and in this way standardized the Hebrew and Greek texts of the Hebrew Bible with each other,[139] in the end such recensional efforts added to the textual plurality of the biblical books in the Second Temple period on the one hand and to the textual plurality of the Greek Old Testament on the other hand. Examples for such recensional reworkings include the following readings.

Num 3:40
OG: ἐπιίσκεψαι ("examine")
4QLXXNum: αριθμησο[ν ("coun[t")
MT: פקד ("count")

Num 4:6, 8, 11
OG: ἀναφορεῖς ("[carrying]-poles")
4QLXXNum: αρτηρας ("carrying-poles")
MT: בדים ("carrying-poles")

Num 4:12
OG: καὶ ἐμβαλοῦσιν ("and they shall lay")
4QLXXNum: και θησουσιν ("and they shall put")
MT: ונתנו ("and they shall put")

Charakter einiger Wortvarianten im Buche Numeri," in *Studien zur Septuaginta: FS R. Hanhart* (eds. D. Fraenkel, U. Quast, and J. W. Wevers; MSU 20; Göttingen: Vandenhoeck & Ruprecht, 1990), 230–52, 248–50.
[135] Cf. e.g. D. Barthélemy, *Les devanciers d'Aquila: Première publication intégrale du texte des fragments du Dodécaprophéton trouvés dans le désert de Juda, précédée d'une étude sur les traductions et recensions grecques de la Bible réalisées au premier siècle de notre ère sous l'influence du rabbinat palestinien* (VTSup 10; Leiden: Brill, 1963), 179–272; Tov, *Greek Minor Prophets Scroll*, 145–58; K. H. Jobes and M. Silva, *Invitation to the Septuagint* (Grand Rapids, Mich.: Baker Academic, 2000), 171–73.
[136] Cf. Quast, "Der rezensionelle Charakter," 231–50.
[137] See Barthélemy, *devanciers*, 203–65; See e.g. G. Howard, "The Quinta of the Minor Prophets," *Bib* 55 (1974): 15–22; A. van der Kooij, *Die alten Textzeugen des Jesajabuches: Ein Beitrag zur Textgeschichte des Alten Testaments* (OBO 35; Freiburg, Schweiz: Universitätsverlag, 1981), 127–50; Jobes and Silva, *Invitation*, 171–73, 284–87; N. Fernández Marcos, *The Septuagint in Context: Introduction to the Greek Version of the Bible* (Leiden: Brill, 2001), 142–54.
[138] Cf. e.g. Quast, "Der rezensionelle Charakter," 248–50; Barthélemy, *Les devanciers d'Aquila*, 179–272; Tov, *Greek Minor Prophets Scroll*, 145–58; Jobes and Silva, *Invitation*, 171–73.
[139] Cf. Lange, "They Confirmed the Reading," 56–61.

Deut 22:9

OG: μετὰ τοῦ γενήματος τοῦ ἀμπελῶνός σου ("with the yield of your vineyard")

Pap. Fouad.   καὶ το γενη[μα του αμπελωνος σου ("and the yield of
Inv. 266b: your vineyard")

MT: ותבואת הכרם ("and the yield of your vineyard")

Deut 33:19

OG: ἔθνη ἐξολεθρεύσουσιν καὶ ἐπικαλέσεσθε ("They shall utterly destroy nations, and you shall call")

Papyrus Fouad \εθν[η επι]/κ[αλ]εσο[νται̣α εις το ορος ("they] sh]all
Inv. 266c:[140]]ca[ll peopl[es to the mountain")

MT: עמים הר יקראו ("they shall call peoples to the mountain")

Jonah 3:3

OG: καθυὼς ἐλάλησε κύριος ("as the Lord spoke")

8HevXII gr: κατ]α το ρημα h[why ("according to the word of the Lord")

MT: כדבר יהוה ("according to the word of the Lord")

That such recensional reworkings are not restricted to the Greek textual traditions of biblical books might be suggested by 5QDeut. 5QDeut was copied in the first half of the second century B.C.E.[141] In Deut 7:15; 8:2, 19; 9:2, supralinear corrections were added to 5QDeut in an early Herodian bookhand (30–1 B.C.E.). As far as the manuscript is preserved, the main text of 5QDeut reads against the Old Greek in every variant. But the four supralinear additions correct the main text of 5QDeut every time towards the Hebrew *Vorlage* of the Old Greek.[142] Therefore, the supralinear corrections of 5QDeut can be viewed as a recension of a Hebrew text towards the Hebrew *Vorlage* of the Old Greek.

---

[140] For the reconstruction of Pap. Fouad 266 inv. at this place, see Koenen, "Introduction," 16, 18.

[141] See J. T. Milik, "Deutéronome," in M. Baillet, J. T. Milik and R. de Vaux, *Les 'petites grottes' de Qumrân* (DJD III; 2 vols.; Oxford: Clarendon, 1962); 1:169–71, 169.

[142] See Milik, "Deutéronome," 170–71. For a critical view on Milik's understanding of the supralinear corrections in 5QDeut, see E. Tov, "The Textual Base of the Corrections in the Biblical Texts Found at Qumran," in *The Dead Sea Scrolls: Forty Years of Research* (eds. D. Dimant and U. Rappaport; STDJ 10; Leiden: Brill, 1992), 299–314, 307–08.

4. Conclusion

The work of Emanuel Tov has pointed to the plurality of the textual histories of the books of the Hebrew Bible. Each book had its own individual pre-canonical textual history that was in most cases characterized by a plurality of various textual witnesses. Without having addressed the issues systematically, Tov implies in his publications (see above) that the various texts of each biblical book all derive from one mastercopy which was deposited in the Jerusalem temple. Textual plurality would thus, on the one hand, be a result of scribal changes of this *Urtext*. On the other hand, Tov recognizes in some cases – like the Book of Jeremiah – the existence of parallel editions. Ulrich (see above) links the textual plurality of the Second Temple period exclusively with the redactional and editorial history of the biblical books and claims that the different texts of each biblical book attest to coexisting variant literary editions. This study has shown that the various texts and text forms of each biblical book developed for different reasons. Scribal corruption, redactions and editions, harmonistic editing, compilations, abbreviations, and recensions are responsible for the development of the variant texts of each biblical book and thus for the textual plurality of the Second Temple period. Only towards the end of the Second Temple period when Judaism began to develop a closed canon of Hebrew scriptures did the proto-Masoretic text as it is known today become the Jewish standard text of this canon. Tov argued in considering the mechanisms of textual transmission and manuscript collection in antiquity that this compilation of the proto-Masoretic text of the Hebrew Bible as a whole brings together texts of different textual character for each book.[143] The research of this article corroborates Tov's interpretation as it shows how the proto-Masoretic text of Jeremiah represents a radical expansion of its *Vorlage* while the proto-Masoretic text of Canticles seems to be relatively original as opposed to 4QCant[a] and 4QCant[b].

---

[143] "The Coincidental Textual Nature of the Collections of Ancient Scriptures," in *Congress Volume Ljubljana 2007* (ed. A. Lemaire; VTSup 133; Leiden: Brill, 2010), 153-69.

THE DEAD SEA SCROLLS AND
THE BOOK OF JOSHUA

Florentino GARCÍA MARTÍNEZ, K.U.Leuven

It is a privilege and a great honor for me to participate in this meeting on "The Dead Sea Scrolls and the Books of the Bible" and to pay tribute to Professor Emanuel Tov, a colleague who has so greatly increased our knowledge of both the Greek and Hebrew Bibles, and particularly of the Dead Sea Scrolls. During the last twenty years, as Editor-in-Chief of the *Discoveries in the Judaean Desert* Series, he has been the engine behind the project, and has invested an incalculable amount of time and energy in order to complete the edition of the Dead Sea Scrolls. He has been the midwife who has facilitated the births of 31 of the 38 volumes which comprise the series.[1] In the Preface to volume 23 of the DSD series, I expressed my thanks to Professor Tov with the following words: "His personal involvement in all phases of the production of the manuscript secured uninterrupted progress and encouraged us to lay aside other obligations in order to complete this work."[2] It was out of this sentiment of gratitude and admiration for the work that Emanuel has done (as well as for his unfailing personal support) that I could not refuse the invitation of our colleague Armin Lange to speak here in his honor, even though I realized that the topic Professor Lange had assigned to me, as one who has worked mostly with the non-biblical texts of the collection, would have been better in the hands of other more qualified colleagues.

In the e-mail with his invitation, Professor Lange wrote: "your talk should address the question [of] how the Dead Sea Scrolls help to better understand the books of the Hebrew Bible. I will address in my *laudatio* of Emanuel a lot of his work on the textual history." Therefore the part of Tov's work that I know better, because I have been teaching it for

---

[1] These statistics were accurate as of October 2008. The current count is 33 out of 40, since volume 37 by É. Puech and volume 40, by Stegemann – Schuller, have been published.

[2] F. García Martínez, E. J. C. Tigchelaar, and A. S. van der Woude, *Qumran Cave 11.II: 11Q2-18, 11Q20-31* (DJD XXIII; Oxford: Clarendon, 1998), xv.

many years to my students in Groningen and in Leuven,[3] will not be the topic of my talk, but will be dealt with in the *Laudatio* of Prof. Lange. Nor will the topic of my talk be the area of his work with which I am most proud to be associated (as editor of the Series in which it has been published)[4]: Tov's *Scribal Practices and Approaches Reflected in the Texts Found in the Judean Desert*, a summa of scribal features culled from his unique familiarity with the manuscripts, and so important for understanding the scribes, the compositions they copied, and the transmission of texts in Antiquity. What I am briefly presenting here, as requested, is simply "the question of how the Dead Sea Scrolls help us to understand the books of the Hebrew Bible."

We are thus going to talk about the "books" and not about "the Hebrew Bible," since in the context of the collection of manuscripts we call Dead Sea Scrolls, "the Hebrew Bible" is clearly an anachronism.[5] There is no such a thing as "the Hebrew Bible" at Qumran. Since it is impossible to talk of the contribution of the Scrolls to our understanding of all twenty-two books that later on will form "the Hebrew Bible," in the short time that I have at my disposal and without burdening you excessively, I needed to make a selection. The most obvious and appropriate way to do this was to look at the manuscripts that have been published personally by Professor Tov and use these manuscripts as the basis of my lecture, but he has published too much! A look at the Indexes in DJD XXXIX[6] reveals that (in addition to his contributions to this volume and a small contribution to Volume 36 of Miscellanea[7]) Professor Tov has published the Greek Minor Prophets Scroll from Naḥal Ḥever as the sole author of volume 8,[8] and that he has contributed to volumes 12, 14, 15, 16, which contain so-called "Biblical Texts" from

---

[3] The textbook for this course was none other than E. Tov, *Textual Criticism of the Hebrew Bible* (2d rev. ed.; Minneapolis and Assen: Fortress and Van Gorcum, 2001).

[4] E. Tov, *Scribal Practices and Approaches Reflected in the Texts Found in the Judean Desert* (STDJ 54; Leiden: Brill, 2004).

[5] See F. García Martínez, "Rethinking the Bible: Sixty Years of Research on the Dead Sea Scrolls and Beyond," in *Authoritative Scriptures in Ancient Judaism*. (ed. M. Popovic; Supplements to the Journal for the Study of Judaism 141; Leiden: Brill, 2010), 19-36.

[6] E. Tov, *The Texts from the Judaean Desert: Indices and Introduction to the Discoveries in the Judaean Desert Series* (DJD XXXIX; Oxford: Clarendon, 2002).

[7] E. Tov, "4Q338, 4QGenealogical List?," in S. Pfann et al., *Qumran Cave 4. XXVI: Cryptic Texts and Miscellanea Part 1* (DJD XXXVI; Oxford: Clarendon, 2000), 290, pl. XIX.

[8] E. Tov, *The Greek Minor Prophets Scroll from Naḥal Ḥever (8ḤevXIIgr)* (DJD VIII; Oxford: Clarendon, 1990).

Cave 4, and to volume 13 of "para-biblical texts" also from Cave 4. In volume 12, he published four manuscripts of the book of Leviticus;[9] in volume 14 one of the manuscripts of the book of Joshua;[10] in volume 15 five manuscripts of the book of Jeremiah;[11] and in volume 16 three manuscripts of the book of Canticles.[12] In his work on volume 13, Tov has published, with Sidnie White, the four manuscripts of the so-called 4QReworked Pentateuch,[13] and with Torleif Elgvin a "Paraphrase of Genesis and Exodus."[14]

It is obvious then that it is not possible to deal here with all of these books of the Hebrew Bible. We could form clusters of books to reduce their number. A first cluster could be the Pentateuch, in which we could deal with Leviticus, but also with the Reworked Pentateuch and the Paraphrase of Genesis and Exodus, since I understand that Emanuel now considers 4QReworked Pentateuch to be a "biblical" manuscript. But since we have a well-known disagreement regarding the interpretation of some of the evidence (concerning the character of 4Q365a), it would not be elegant to discuss the matter here. Another cluster could be formed by the Prophets, where we could deal with Jeremiah and with the Greek Minor Prophets. However, I am quite certain that Emanuel's work, both on Jeremiah and on the Minor Prophets, will be dealt with by Professor Lange in his discussion of Tov's research on textual history. What remains, therefore, are the book of Canticles (one of the Five Scrolls) and the book of Joshua.

Two of the manuscripts of Canticles published by Tov (4Q106 and 4Q107) are particularly interesting since they "lack substantial segments of text found in the other textual witnesses." In the words of Tov:

> The two texts thus undoubtedly present manuscripts of Canticles, rather than commentaries or paraphrases, but they constitute biblical

---

[9] E. Tov, "4Q25, 26, 26a, 26b, 4QLev^{c,d,e,g}," in E. Ulrich et al., *Qumran Cave 4.VII: Genesis to Numbers* (DJD XII; Oxford: Clarendon, 1994), 189-204, pl. XXXV-XXXVII.

[10] E. Tov, "4Q48, 4QJosh^b," in E. Ulrich et al., *Qumran Cave 4. IX: Deuteronomy, Joshua, Judges, Kings* (DJD XIV; Oxford: Clarendon, 1995), 153-60, pl. XXXV.

[11] E. Tov, "4Q70, 71, 72, 72a, 72b, 4QJer^{a,b,c,d,e}," in E. Ulrich et al., *Qumran Cave 4. X: The Prophets* (DJD XV; Oxford: Clarendon, 1997), 145-206, pl. XXIV-XXXVII.

[12] E.Tov, "4Q106-108, 4QCant^{a,b,c}," in E. Ulrich et al., *Qumran Cave 4. XI: Psalms to Chronicles* (DJD XVI; Oxford: Clarendon, 2000), 195-219, pl. XXIV-XXV.

[13] E. Tov and S. White, "4Q364-367, 4QReworked Pentateuch^{b,c,d,e}," in H. Attridge et al., *Qumran Cave 4. VIII Parabiblical Texts, Part 1* (DJD XIII; Oxford: Clarendon, 1994), 187-351, pl. XIII-XXXVI.

[14] T. Elgvin and E. Tov, "4Q422, 4QParaphrase of Genesis and Exodus," in *DJD* XIII: 417-441, pl. XLII-XLIII.

manuscripts of a special kind. With some hesitation they are described
here as abbreviated texts, although there are no exact parallels for this
assumption among the Qumran texts.[15]

Professor Tov develops this further:

> The biblical book of Canticles contains a conglomeration of love
> songs, and not one coherent composition, so that segments could be
> removed from it without harming the context. This is the case with the
> two Qumran scrolls, each of which has been shortened in a different
> way, and following the sequence of the text as extant in other textual
> witnesses. Underlying this description is thus the understanding that
> the Qumran scrolls shortened an earlier existing text, while the
> assumption that they represent early literary crystallizations of the
> book differing from the one represented by the other textual witnesses,
> though not impossible, is discarded.[16]

I think little more can be said about these manuscripts than what Tov has
so concisely and elegantly written. Therefore I will focus my remarks
here how the Dead Sea Scrolls help us to better understand the book of
Joshua.

The Dead Sea Scrolls and the Book of Joshua

Presenting the contribution of the Dead Sea Scrolls towards our understanding of the book of Joshua is greatly facilitated by an integrative
article on the topic written by Emanuel Tov himself for the *Encyclopedia
of the Dead Sea Scrolls*, in which he discusses the "biblical" manuscripts of Joshua, and also refers to other manuscripts related to the book
of Joshua but not considered copies of the biblical book. Professor Tov
opens his article on the Book of Joshua with these words: "If the number
of copies of a manuscript found at Qumran is an indication of their popularity within the Qumran community, Joshua was not a popular book,
represented merely by two copies in Cave 4."[17] In light of the popularity
of the Book of Deuteronomy, for example, with its many copies, this
aspect is certainly relevant. But before we start making inferences from
this fact for hotly debated issues (particularly in German Biblical scholarship) such as the formation of the Pentateuch, or of the Hexateuch, or
of the Enneateuch, or of the understanding of the Deuteronomistic work,
etc., we need to consider the evidence preserved, both the "biblical" and
the "non-biblical" manuscripts of Joshua.

---

[15] Tov, *DJD* XVI: 195-96.
[16] Tov, *DJD* XVI: 196.
[17] E. Tov, "Joshua, Book of," in *Encyclopedia of the Dead Sea Scrolls* (eds. L. H. Schiffman
and J. C. VanderKam; 2 vols.; New York: OUP, 2000) 1: 431.

(a) The evidence of the "biblical" manuscripts of Joshua can be briefly summarized. Before the Qumran discoveries, the book of Joshua was known in two forms: one represented by the Masoretic Text and the other by the Septuagint. These two forms were so different that it was generally accepted that: (1) they represent two different editions of the book, each one reflecting a different stage in its development; and (2) the textual form represented by the Greek translation was the oldest one of the two, its Hebrew *Vorlage* representing a more original form of the text that the one transmitted in Hebrew. At Qumran, only two manuscripts of the biblical book have been found, both in Cave 4: 4Q47 (4QJosh[a]), a formal Hasmonaean manuscript, published by Ulrich, and 4Q48 (4QJosh[b]), a late Hasmonaean (or early Herodian) manuscript, published by Tov, both in DJD XIV. The manuscript published by Tov agrees in general with the text represented by the Masoretic Text (with a small number of readings which agree with the Septuagint, although in one interesting case, in Josh 3:15, the text has been corrected interlinearly, and the correction agrees with the Septuagint against MT). The manuscript published by Ulrich, however, has not only proven true the two previous assumptions of critical scholarship (existence of different editions, and priority of the Septuagint) but has considerably changed our understanding of the process of formation of the biblical book. This manuscript, 4QJosh[a],[18] represents yet a third edition or recension of the book, different from both the Masoretic Text and the Septuagint, and this edition is without a doubt the oldest, the shortest and the most original of the three that we now possess.

The key element is the building and placement of first altar immediately after crossing the Jordan at Gilgal and the entry into the land described in chapter 4, and not, as is the case in the Masoretic Text and the Septuagint, after several battles in chapters 8 and 9 respectively. As Ulrich notes, the location of the building of the altar in MT and LXX is puzzling: the altar's construction is delayed, there is an perplexing military expedition to build the altar in unprotected territory in order to abandon it immediately afterwards, and Mount Ebal is never again linked with this altar, but exclusively with the place of the curse. In contrast, the narrative of 4QJosh[a] is simple and directly fulfills the command of Deuteronomy 27:2-3.[19]

[18] E. Ulrich, "4Q47, 4QJosh[a]," in *DJD* XIV: 143-52, pl. XXXIIX-XXXIV.
[19] Ulrich, DJD XIV: 145-46. See also the preliminary publication of the fragment by E. Ulrich, "4QJosh[a] and Joshua's First Altar in the Promised Land," in, *New Qumran Texts and Studies* (eds. G. J. Brooke and F. García Martínez; STDJ 15; Leiden: Brill, 1994), 89-104.

As Emanuel Tov says:

> When comparing the different attestations of the pericope of the build-
> ing of the altar and the reading of the Torah, one clearly recognizes
> their secondary nature. This section was meant to stress Joshua's
> faithfulness to the commandments of the Torah: As soon as the Isra-
> elites crossed the Jordan, they implemented the command of Deuter-
> onomy 27, which ordered to build an altar on Mount Ebal (or Mount
> Garizim, according to the Old Latin and the Samaritan Pentateuch).
> This pericope was inserted secondarily in some manuscripts of Joshua
> in the course of the development of the book, and, as often happens,
> it was inserted in three different places in the different textual wit-
> nesses. But, while in the tradition behind the Masoretic Text and Sep-
> tuagint, this pericope is secondary, its position in Joshua[a] seems to be
> original. The version of Joshua[a] is therefore hailed by Ulrich and Rofé
> as presenting an earlier and more logical version of Joshua than the
> Masoretic Text and Septuagint, since it presents the Israelites as build-
> ing an altar as soon as they had safely traversed the Jordan. The sec-
> ondary nature of 8.30-35 in its present context in the Masoretic Text
> is evident, as this section is very loosely connected with the context.
> This pertains also to the Septuagint in which it occurs at a slightly
> different place. (9.2)[20]

In my opinion, these two Qumran manuscripts of the book of Joshua, so
different from each other, bring to the fore an important aspect towards
our understanding of the book's formation and of its gradually acquired
authoritative status. Concerning the formation of the book of Joshua, we
know now that the process was longer than we had previously suspected:
the three editions must have coexisted for over three centuries, since the
oldest edition of the book, the one represented by Joshua[a], is still known
to Flavius Josephus. According to the Jewish historian (*Ant.* 5.16-20),
Joshua built an altar upon crossing the Jordan and sacrificed upon it (as
in Joshua[a]), although later in the narrative he also recounts the building
of the altar at Sechem after having installed the tabernacle at Siloh (*Ant.*
5.68-69). With respect to the gradually acquired authoritative status of
the book of Joshua, we can note the friendly coexistence in the same
collection of two of the editions, represented by the two manuscripts
(Joshua[b] can be considered a representative of the edition we know from
the Masoretic Text). Further, as we will see in a moment, the "non-
biblical" manuscripts of Joshua attest to numerous readings characteristic of the edition now known in the Greek translation, showing that all
three editions were known and used within the same collection. This

---

[20] Tov, "Joshua, Book of," 432.

proves, I think, that the approach to the authoritative character of a composition is independent of its textual form (as Ulrich has repeatedly
emphasized[21]). What was considered authoritative was the book itself,
and not its concrete textual form, since all of these forms and editions
were harmoniously kept together in the same collection, and they were
used indiscriminately in the formation of new compositions. These new
compositions that developed and expanded different elements from the
book of Joshua, to which now we turn our attention, have been labelled
"non-biblical," "para-biblical," "apocryphal" and the like, but they also
contribute greatly to our understanding of the "biblical" book of Joshua.

(b) The presentation of the evidence of the "non-biblical" manuscripts related to the book of Joshua is less straightforward than that of
the "biblical" manuscripts. Their presentation is complicated by their
fragmentary character, the uncertainty of their assignment to the same
composition, their different provenance, and the different ways that they
have been interpreted. Fortunately, in this case as well, I can refer to a
detailed article written by the honoree, entitled: "The Rewritten Book of
Joshua as Found at Qumran and Masada," which brings order to the
materials and puts them in perspective.[22]

Tov considers six different manuscripts, published under different
names, as representing, with different degrees of certainty, a single apocryphal composition based upon the book of Joshua and which, according
to him, can be considered as a "paraphrase of Joshua." These manuscripts
include: two copies of 4QApocryphon of Joshua, published by Newsom
(4Q378 and 4Q379),[23] 4Q522, published by Puech as 4QProphecy of
Joshua,[24] 5Q9 published by Milik as "Composition with Toponyms,"[25]
and two very fragmentary and uncertain compositions, 4QpaleoParaJosh

[21] See the articles collected in E. Ulrich, *The Dead Sea Scrolls and the Origins of the Bible* (SDSSRL; Grand Rapids: Eerdmans, 1999).

[22] E. Tov, "The Rewritten Book of Joshua as Found at Qumran and Masada," in *Biblical Perspectives: Early Use and Interpretation of the Bible in Light of the Dead Sea Scrolls* (eds. M.E. Stone and E. Chazon; STDJ 28; Leiden: Brill, 1998), 233-56.

[23] C. Newsom, "4Q378-379, 4QApocryphon of Joshua[a-b]," in G. Brooke et al., *Qumran Cave 4.XVII: Parabiblical Texts, Part 3* (DJD XXII; Oxford: Clarendon, 1996), 237-88, pl. XVII-XXIV.

[24] É. Puech, "4Q522, 4QProphétie de Josué (4QapocrJosué[c] ?)," in É. Puech, *Qumrân grotte 4. XVIII: Textes hébreux (4Q521-4Q528, 4Q576-4Q579)* (DJD XXV; Oxford: Clarendon, 1998), 39-74, pl. IV-V.

[25] J. T. Milik, "5Q9, 5QOuvrage avec toponimes," in M. Baillet, J. T. Milik, and R. De Vaux, *Les 'Petites grottes' de Qumrân* (DJD III; Oxford: Clarendon, 1962), 179-80, pl. XXXVIII.

published by Ulrich,[26] and MasParaJosh published by Talmon.[27] We shall leave the Masada and the PalaeoHebrew manuscripts out of consideration here, because the preserved evidence is so minute that no concrete conclusions can be extracted from them. Instead, we shall concentrate on the other four manuscripts.

4Q378 and 4Q379 have been described by their editor, Carol Newsom, in this way:

> The text may represent an example of the literary activity known as the 'rewritten Bible'. It can be postulated that it covered roughly the same narrative scope as the canonical book of Joshua. If so, the material near the beginning of the work is preserved in 4Q378. That manuscript, however, suggest that the Apocryphon of Joshua had a different beginning than does the canonical book, since 4Q378 14 includes a description of the Israelites' mourning for Moses after his death. This description was apparently followed by an account of Joshua's accession to leadership (4Q378 3-4, paralleling Joshua 1) and a long speech by Joshua to the people, modeled after Moses' speech in Deuteronomy, especially chaps. 1-3 and 28-31. The other manuscript, 4Q379, contains material from a slightly later part of the composition, since it preserves references to crossing the Jordan (parallel to Joshua 3) and the curse on the rebuilder of Jericho from Josh 6:26. The number of fragments that contain admonitory speeches, prayers, and curses suggests that the author of the composition may have been more interested in these rhetorical forms of speech than in the narration of event *per se*.[28]

5Q522 has been described by its editor, Émile Puech, as a midrash on the historical books (Joshua, Judges, 1 and 2 Samuel, 1 Kings and 1 Chronicles): "pouvant être parallèle ou faire suite au midrash de *l'Apocryphon de Josué*."[29] The composition apparently deals with the conquest of the land by the different tribes of Israel, among which Simeon, Dan, Issachar and Asher are named, but also with Jerusalem (called "the rock of Zion") and the construction of the Temple. The first column of the best preserved fragment (frg. 9) contains a list of the cities conquered (or not conquered) by the tribes, extending from Syria and Lebanon to the Negev, and from the Sea to Galilee. The list is similar to

[26] E. Ulrich, "4Q123, 4QpaleoParaJoshua," in P. Skehan, E. Ulrich, J. E. Sanderson, *Qumran Cave 4.IV: Paleo-Hebrew and Greek Biblical Manuscripts* (DJD IX; Oxford: Clarendon, 1992) 201-03, pl. XLVI.
[27] Sh. Talmon, "1039-211, Joshua Apocryphon (MasapocrJosh)," in *Masada VI.: Yigael Yadin Excavations 1963-1965: Final Reports* (Jerusalem: Israel Exploration Society, 1999), 105-16.
[28] Newson, *DJD* XXII: 237-38.
[29] Puech, *DJD* XXV: 71.

the one contained in 5Q9, but it is impossible to establish where many of the places named are located. The second column of this fragment refers to the future arrival of David, his conquest of the "Rock of Zion," the expulsion of the Amorites, and to David's intention to build the temple. Four other small fragments contain the text of Psalm 122, which has been reconstructed in its entirety.

Although there is no overlap among these four manuscripts, it seems reasonably certain to assume that 4Q378 and 379 are copies of a single composition and that 4Q522 and 5Q9 are also copies of a single composition. It is indeed possible that these two compositions originally belonged to the same work and corresponded to different parts of the composition, as Tov has proposed and Puech reluctantly seems to accept; but for my purpose here, this is not really important, and my argument will be even stronger if they represent two different compositions. What is important is that all four manuscripts, and therefore the composition or compositions they represent, rewrite and reinterpret the book of Joshua in one way or another (the respective editors duly signal when one or another of the editions of Joshua are reflected in the readings of the manuscripts) and in this way they contribute towards establishing the authority of the biblical book, making it move (as George Brooke say) "from being authoritative in a limited way to belonging firmly to a canonical list."[30]

In the ancient world so different from ours, the primary, and perhaps the most obvious way, for a writing to establish its own authority was by referring to other, already accepted, authoritative literature. At the same time, the writings that attracted secondary developments, that were modified, interpreted or adapted, by the same token had their authority enhanced and more firmly established. We can say that the intertext was used to authorize the new text, and that the new composition reinforced the authority of the existing text. We see this process of "authorization" already in use in the compositions which would later become the "Bible." If we consider the Hebrew canon, we see that several books, such as Deuteronomy or Chronicles, which are rewritings of other authoritative writings, have ended as canonical books – for example Deuteronomy rewrites legal materials from Exodus, Leviticus and Numbers, and Chronicles rewrites materials from Samuel-Kings. The same process is

---

[30] G. J. Brooke, "Between Authority and Canon: The Significance of Reworking the Bible for Understanding the Canonical Process," in *Reworking the Bible: Apocryphal and Related Texts at Qumran* (eds. E. G. Chazon, D. Dimant, and R. A. Clements; STDJ 58; Leiden: Brill, 2005), 104.

at work here in the case of the book of Joshua and the "rewritten" Joshua book or books which these four manuscripts represent.

Rewritten compositions obviously take their authority from the text that they rework, and in this way attest to their authoritative status. They, in turn, contribute towards establishing even further the authority of the book which they rewrite. The phenomenon of rewriting as an authority conferring strategy therefore works in both directions: the new composition attests to the authority of the source composition, and reinforces it; at the same time the new composition claims for itself a share in the authority attributed to the source. And in our case, we have proof that the reworking of the book of Joshua attained authoritative status among the group that collected and preserved the manuscripts. This proof is contained in the well known *4QTestimonia*.[31] This manuscript is a single sheet of leather, written by the same copyist who penned 1QS and 4QSamuel^c,[32] and uses the same convention as other scrolls of replacing the tetragrammaton with four dots. It contains a collection of four quotations without further commentary or explanation, though each quotation is clearly delimited, by both three blank spaces and marginal marks after each quote. The first quotation (lines 1–8) is taken from Exodus 20:18b according to the Samaritan tradition, a text which brings together Deuteronomy 5:28–29 and Deuteronomy 18:18–19 of the Masoretic Bible. It announces the coming of a prophet like Moses, which the Samaritans used to foster the expectation of the coming of the Taheb, and which is used here to express the belief in the coming of the eschatological Prophet. The second quote (lines 9–13) is taken from Numbers 24:15–17 in a textual form similar to the one preserved in the Masoretic text, but with several differences – not only orthographical, but some also of substance – as compared to both the Masoretic and Samaritan traditions. This second quotation interprets the oracle of Balaam on the Scepter and the Star as referring to the coming of a future messianic figure. The third

---

[31] Edited by J. M. Allegro, "4Q175, 4QTestimonia," in J. M. Allegro, *Qumrân Cave 4.I:4Q158-4Q186* (DJD V; Oxford: Clarendon, 1968), 57-60, pl. XXI. The manuscript has been studied very intensively. For a select bibliography, see A. Steudel, "Testimonia," in Schiffman and VanderKam, *Encyclopedia of the Dead Sea Scrolls*, 2:936–38, to which should be added the new edition by F. M. Cross in *Hebrew, Aramaic, and Greek Texts with English Translations. Volume 6B* (The Princeton Theological Seminary Dead Sea Scrolls Project 6B; Tübingen and Louisville: Mohr and Westminster John Knox, 2002), 308–27.

[32] On this scribe, see E. Tigchelaar, "In Search of the Scribe of 1QS," in *Emanuel: Studies in Hebrew Bible, Septuagint, and Dead Sea Scrolls in Honor of Emanuel Tov* (eds. S. M. Paul, R. A. Kraft, L. H. Schiffman and W.W. Fields; SVT 94; Leiden: Brill, 2003), 439–52.

quote (lines 14–20) is taken from Deuteronomy 33:8–11, also with some variants from the Masoretic text, applying the blessing of Levi to the expected priestly messiah. The fourth quotation (lines 21–30) is taken from the *4QApocryphon of Joshua*, as it is preserved in 4Q379.

We can logically conclude that these quotations, which are all set at the same level and are introduced with similar introductory formulae, were considered to provide proof from authoritative writings for the collector's ideas and can thus tell us something about the shape of the authoritative writings at that time. These authoritative sources are an expanded and harmonised version of Exodus, attested at Qumran in several scrolls, which later came to be the "Bible" for the Samaritans, and is considered by Tov as closely related to the "rewritten Bible compositions"; two slightly modified versions of Numbers and Deuteronomy, two books which later become the "Bible" for Jews and Christians; and our *Apocryphon of Joshua,* a reworking of the book of Joshua, very similar to other compositions found at Qumran and which are usually classified as "rewritten Scripture," but which is considered here as authoritative as the other three writings. What is particularly interesting in this case is that it is not the "canonical book of Joshua" which is quoted as authoritative Scripture in *4QTestimonia,* but the Apocryphal one, the reworked form of the canonical book.

A second important contribution of the apocryphal composition based on the book of Joshua, as represented by 4Q522, is the light it sheds upon our understanding of the book of Psalms, since fragments 22-25 of that manuscript preserve Psalm 122 in its entirety in a textual form that is close to the MT.[33] Although no less than 22 copies of the book of Psalms have been found on Cave 4, Psalm 122 has not been preserved there, and its only other attestation at Qumran (in a textual form different from the MT) is in column 3 of 11Q5, where it appears in between Psalms 121 and 123.[34] Due to the fragmentary nature of the evidence of 4Q522, we are deprived of the context of the quote of the Psalm, and we will never know how it was attached to the rest of the narrative of which it now forms a part or what its precise function in the narrative was. But its presence is significant, by virtue of the fact that, apparently, the whole Psalm was included in the quote. It is probably for this reason that these small fragments have been published twice in DJD: as part of 4Q522, the composition to which they belong, but also in DJD XVI, the volume

---

[33] Puech, *DJD* XXV: 68-70
[34] J. A. Sanders, *The Psalms Scroll of Qumrân Cave 11 (11QPsᵃ* (DJD IV; Oxford: Clarendon, 1965), 24, pl. IV.

which contains the biblical manuscripts of the book of Psalms from Cave 4.[35]

Quotations of this sort are truly exceptional in the Scrolls. The only parallels I can recall are the quotation of Psalm 91 in column six of 11Q11 (11QApocryphal Psalms),[36] where this Psalm against the demons is completely integrated with the other psalms of exorcism which form the composition, and the acrostic poem on wisdom attested both as part of the book of Ben Sira (51:13-30) and as an independent poem in 11Q5 xxi 11-xxii7 1.[37] Perhaps it is not accidental that all the examples that we have of this sort of quotation (of a complete block of text) are complete poems, which were apparently more prone to travel from one text to another. However, these quotations are clearly different from other quotations of biblical (or other) books which we find in the Scrolls. We can compare it, for example, with the quote in the *Hymn to the Creator* in 11Q5 column XXVI, of the "floating" passage that we know from its double appearance in Jeremiah 10:12-13 and 51:15-16, and from its presence in Psalm 135:6-7, and which is reused with very little variation in the Qumran poem,[38] and the differences are immediately apparent.

But it is time to close. Are we allowed to extract a general conclusion for our understanding of the Hebrew Bible in the light of the Scrolls from these Joshua manuscripts and from the two small details in the composition or compositions that rework the book of Joshua? I think we are, and this conclusion is that our category "Bible" is completely inadequate in the historical context that the Scrolls represent, and that we should get used to considering the collection as a whole, without our artificial divisions between "biblical" and "non-biblical" manuscripts.

We have seen the harmonious coexistence of three editions of the book of Joshua, and one or two rewritings of this book in different copies, all in the same collection. Our discussion of the reworked forms of Joshua proved two points: first, that a rewritten composition, inspired by the book of Joshua, can attain the same (or higher) authoritative status than the original book on which it was based; and second, that even such an authoritative book like the book of Psalms can be considered as a conglomerate of raw materials that can be plundered for new literary constructions, in this case the rewriting of the book of Joshua. All of this

---

[35] Ulrich et al., *DJD* XVI: 169-170.
[36] García Martínez, Tigchelaar, and van der Woude, *DJD* XXIII: 181-205, pl. XXII-XXV.
[37] Sanders, *DJD* V: 42-43 and 79-85, pl. XIV.
[38] Sanders, *DJD* V: 47 and 89-91, pl. XVI.

proves, in my opinion, that for the people who formed and preserved the collection of manuscripts found in and around Qumran, all of these writings were exactly that, religious writings which, without distinction, informed their lives.

Professor Emanuel Tov has taught us all that in the light of the Qumran finds we can no longer speak of a "biblical text," but rather "biblical texts" (in the plural). For the majority of the compositions represented in the collection, the only context we know is the collection as such. I therefore propose that we dispense with the usual labels and consider the collection as a whole, in which more or less authoritative writings are preserved.[39]

---

[39] F. García Martínez, "¿Sectario, no-sectario o qué? Problemas de una taxonomía correcta de los textos qumránicos," RevQ 23/91 (2008): 383-394.

DIE REZEPTION BIBLISCHER TEXTE IN FRÜHJÜDISCHER ZEIT IM LICHT DER QUMRANTEXTE

Gastvorlesung aus Anlass der Ehrenpromotion von Prof. Dr. Emanuel TOV an der Universität Wien

Prof. Dr. Heinz-Josef FABRY, Universität Bonn

Emanuel Tov war der erste Qumrangelehrte, der der Weltöffentlichkeit einen vollständigen Katalog aller Qumrantexte vorlegte. Seine Indices "The Texts from the Judaean Desert" in DJD 39, 2002, bilden zwar den formalen Abschluss dieser gewaltigen Publikationsreihe, sind aber die lückenlose Zusammenfassung aller vorangegangener Teil-Kataloge, deren Erscheinen von den Qumranologen jeweils mit großer Spannung erwartet wurde, fand man doch hier von kompetenter Hand gefertigt jeweils die neueste Übersicht dessen, was war, was ist und was sein würde.

Seiner Übersicht ist auch zu verdanken, dass wir schon sehr früh wussten, dass ca. 200 der mehr als 800 Handschriften Bibeltexte[1] enthalten. Da diese Bibeltexte in textgeschichtlicher Hinsicht die ältesten Bibeltexte sind, die wir haben, d.h. die hebräischen Bibeltexte sind z.T. mehr als 1000 Jahre älter als unsere älteste hebräische Bibel, die griechischen Handschriften sind z.T. mehr als 500 Jahre älter als unsere ältesten griechischen Bibeln, haben diese Bibeltexte von Beginn der Qumranforschung an höchstes Interesse bei den Bibelwissenschaftlern gefunden.

Ist dieser hohe Prozentsatz biblischer Handschriften für eine jüdische Gruppierung chasidisch-priesterlicher Prägung, wie sie zweifelsohne in Qumran gegeben ist, nicht weiter verwunderlich, so ist doch der Umgang mit diesen Texten, die Art ihrer Auslegung und vor allem der Blick auf den Qumran-Kanon für uns höchst interessant. Gerade in solchen Fragen fühlen sich Exegeten katholischer und evangelischer Herkunft nicht

---

[1] Die Bezeichnung "Bibeltexte" oder "biblische Texte" ist im Blick auf die Handschriften von Qumran nicht unproblematisch, da zur Zeit Qumrans die Kanonisierungsprozesse noch längst nicht abgeschlossen waren. Mit diesen Bezeichnungen sind hier Bücher und Texte gemeint, die später einmal entweder in den jüdischen/und/oder christlichen Kanon biblischer Schriften aufgenommen worden sind.

unwesentlich fremdbestimmt, ist uns doch von unserer Kirche vorgege-
ben, was zum christlichen Kanon biblischer Texte gehört und was nicht,
ja es ist uns auch die Methodik vorgeschrieben, wie wir die Texte zu
interpretieren haben. Da kann ein Blick in die Zustände, wie sie denn
damals waren, eine gewisse befreiende Wirkung haben.

Nun, als Exeget fühle ich mich nicht unfrei. Mein Interesse besteht
nicht darin, mich gegen kirchliche Setzungen aufzulehnen, vielmehr
treibt mich die Frage nach der historischen Entwicklung um. Es ist interessant, das Gewordene zu beobachten, interessanter ist es jedoch, das
Werden des Gewordenen nachzuvollziehen. Jede historische Grenzzie-
hung ist interessant im Blick auf das Eingegrenzte. Um das Eingegrenzte
aber richtig verstehen zu können, ist der Blick auf das Ausgegrenzte
wesentlich: das ist das Wesen des Kanons; in dieser Frage hat Qumran
ein entscheidendes Mitspracherecht. Dieses Interesse bildet nun auch den
Ausgangspunkt für unsere heutige Fragestellung. Dabei soll es uns
primär um die unterschiedlichen Arten des Umganges der Qumrangemeinde mit den biblischen und auch außerbiblischen Texten gehen.

1. Der Pesher als die für Qumran typische Kommentarform

Wiederholt ist wohl zu Recht vermutet worden, dass in Qumran zum
ersten Mal in der Weltliteratur der Unterschied zwischen dem Text eines
Autors und einem Kommentar gemacht wurde. Bis dahin und vielfach
auch später noch wurden Kommentare als Marginalie an den Textrand
geschrieben. Diese Marginalie wurde von einem späteren Abschreiber in
den Text hineingenommen und wurde damit Bestandteil des Textes
selbst. Dies gab es in Qumran auch, aber daneben entstand eine Form der
Kommentierung, die den Text aufnahm und in der Regel Vers für Vers
mit einem Kommentar (hebr. *pešer*)[2] durchschoss. Damit wurde ein

---

[2] Zur Klärung dieses Begriffes vgl. H.-J. Fabry und U. Dahmen, פשר *pešær*, *ThWAT* VI:
810-16; zur Pesher-Literatur insgesamt vgl. P. Horgan, *Pesharim: Qumran Interpretations of Biblical Books* (CBQMS 8; Washington: Catholic Biblical Association of America, 1979) und G. J. Brooke, "Qumran Pesher: Towards the Redefinition of a Genre,"
RevQ 10 (1979/81): 483-503; B. Ejrnaes, "Pesher-litteraturen fra Qumran," in *Døde-
havsteksterne og Bibelen* [Contributions to an International Conference on Qumran at
Gentofte, Denmark, June 19-22, 1995] (eds. N. Hyldahl and Th. L. Thompson; Forum
for Bibelsk Eksegese 8; Kobenhavn: Museum Tusculanums Forlag, 1996), 27-39;
M. Kister, "A Common Heritage: Biblical Interpretation at Qumran and its Implications," in *Biblical Perspectives: Early Use and Interpretation of the Bible in Light of
the Dead Sea Scrolls. Proceedings of the First International Symposium of the Orion
Center for the Study of the Dead Sea Scrolls and Associated Literature, 12-14 May,
1996* (eds. M. E. Stone and E. G. Chazon; STDJ 28; Leiden: Brill, 1998), 101-11;

eigenständiger Text geschaffen, der zwar in enger Beziehung zum kommentierten Text stand, sich aber als eigenständige Schrift von ihm absetzte. Beachtlich ist, dass solche *pešarîm* primär zu prophetischen Büchern angefertigt wurden, wenn auch nicht ausschließlich.

1.1. Mehr als **30 *pešarîm***, Kommentare zu biblischen Büchern, primär zu Jes und zu Texten aus dem Dodekapropheton (bes. Hab), dann auch zu Ps 37 sind erhalten. Tora-Texte wurden offensichtlich nicht ausgelegt, obwohl in 4Q239, 4Q240 und 4Q252 *pešarîm* zum Genesis-Buch vorliegen, mit Gen 6 und 49 aber nur erzählende, nicht jedoch gesetzliche Texte auslegen. Die *pešarîm* haben die spezifische Eigenart, die prophetische Botschaft in die Jetztzeit des Kommentators zu holen. Der Kommentator ist überzeugt, dass sich die Botschaft aus der Zeit des jeweiligen Propheten nicht auf jene zurückliegende Zeit, sondern auf die Endzeit bezieht und dass diese Endzeit jetzt angebrochen ist. Zum theologischen Profil dieser *pešarîm* gehören ein ausgeprägter Dualismus, die Betonung von Erwählung und Determinismus und die Aufnahme apokalyptischer Motive. Damit erweisen sich diese Schriften als für Qumran besonders typisch. Nach 1QpHab ii 7-10; vii 4-5 hat der "Lehrer der Gerechtigkeit" selbst diese machtvolle und autoritative Propheteninterpretation in Qumran eingeführt. Er wusste sich im Besitz einer Sonderoffenbarung, die ihn dazu legitimierte, die Propheten verbindlich auszulegen.

Verweilen wir kurz bei einer Betrachtung der drei auf sechs Handschriften verteilten Jesaja-Kommentare[3], um uns ein wenig mit den *pešarîm* vertraut zu machen.

1.1.1. Zu einem ersten Kommentar gehören **4Q163(4QpJes^c)** und **4Q165(4QpJes^e)**; er wurde um 100 v. Chr. komponiert und artikulierte den qumranischen Anspruch, das einzig wahre Israel zu sein. Er umfasst eine Kommentierung von Jes 8-14; 19; 29-31 sowie – wenn tatsächlich 4QpJes^e dazugehört – Jes 21; 32 und 40. Interessanterweise werden einige

---

H. G. Snyder and H. Gregory, "Naughts and Crosses: Pesher Manuscripts and Their Significance for Reading Practices at Qumran," *DSD* 7/1 (2000): 26-48; S. L. Berrin, "Qumran Pesharim," in *Biblical Interpretation at Qumran* (ed. M. Henze; Studies in the Dead Sea Scrolls and Related Literature; Grand Rapids, Mich.: Eerdmans, 2005) 110-33.

[3] G. J. Brooke, "Isaiah in the Pesharim and Other Qumran Texts," in *Writing and Reading the Scroll of Isaiah: Studies of an Interpretive Tradition, Formation and Interpretation of Old Testament Literature* (eds. C. C. Broyles and C. A. Evans; 2 vols.; VTSup 70.2; Leiden: Brill, 1997), 2:609-32; idem., "The Qumran Pesharim and the Text of Isaiah in the Cave 4 Manuscripts," in *Biblical Hebrew, Biblical Texts: Essays in Memory of Michael P. Weitzman* (eds. A. Rapoport and A. and G. Greenberg; JSOTSup 333; Sheffield: Sheffield Academic Press, 2001), 304-20.

Hos-, Jer- und Sach-Zitate eingefügt und kommentiert; deshalb weiß sich dieser Pesher nicht nur dem Propheten Jesaja, sondern letztlich dem gesamten *corpus propheticum* verpflichtet. Obwohl dieser Kommentar äußerst fragmentarisch ist, zeigt er doch, dass er die Botschaft des Propheten auslegen und applizieren will auf die gegenwärtige Gemeinschaft von Qumran, die er als die Gemeinde der Endzeit versteht, für die einzig und allein der Prophet Jesaja seine Botschaft verkündet hat.

1.1.2. Zu einem zweiten Kommentar gehören **4Q161(4QpJes^a)** und **4Q164(4QpJes^d)**. Er wurde um 70 v. Chr. formuliert und weist eine mehr entwickelte Eschatologie und Messianologie auf. Das als unmittelbar bevorstehend gedachte Weltende mit dem Kampf der Gerechten gegen die Ungerechten gibt diesem Kommentar eine sehr eindringliche Note. Entsprechend nahe steht er der qumranischen Kriegsrolle. Die im Pesher kommentierten Abschnitte beschreiben Gottes Fürsorge für sein Volk Juda angesichts der andrängenden Assyrer und enthalten eine messianische Prophezeiung des "Sprosses" aus der Wurzel Jesse. Die Pesher-Interpretation appliziert diese Prophezeiungen auf die Gegenwart des Verfassers, also auf zeitgenössische militärische Aktionen in Palästina/Juda, deren Entschlüsselung für die Qumranologen von höchstem Interesse ist. Die messianischen Prophezeiungen bezieht der Pesher auf die eschatologischen Erwartungen der Qumrangemeinde und liefert damit einen wichtigen Baustein für die qumranische Messianologie.[4]

1.1.3. Ein dritter Kommentar liegt möglicherweise in **4Q162(4QpJes^b)** aus der Mitte des 1. Jh. v. Chr. vor. Exemplarisch soll ein gut erhaltener Text zitiert werden: Auf ein Zitat von Jes 5:10 (?) folgt der Pesher: "Die *Deutung* (*pišrô*) des Wortes bezieht sich auf das Ende der Tage, wenn das Land wüst daliegt vor dem Schwert/vor der Dürre und vor Hunger. Dann wird es geschehen am Ende der Heimsuchung des Landes". Es folgt das Zitat von Jes 5:11: "Wehe, Zecher des Rauschtrankes am frühen Morgen, die ihr auf Wein aus seid bis zum Einbruch der Dämmerung!" Die folgende Auslegung bietet die Identifikation: "Das sind die Männer des Spottes, die in Jerusalem sind. Sie sind es, die die Tora JHWHs verwerfen und das Wort des Heiligen Israels verschmähen". Es kann kaum Zweifel daran bestehen, dass der Pesher das Drohwort des Propheten auf die Sadduzäer ("Männer des Spottes") in Jerusalem ummünzt, die in CD 1,14 als Feinde des "Lehrers der Gerechtigkeit" auftreten (vgl. auch 1QpHab 10,9).

---

[4] Dazu vgl. H.-J. Fabry und K. Scholtissek, *Der Messias* (Neue Echter-Bibel – Themen 5; Würzburg: Echter Verlag, 2002).

1.2. Neben die gebräuchliche Form des fortlaufenden – den Bibeltext entlanggehenden Pescher (*pesher continu*; z.B. 1QpHab) tritt der thematische Pescher (*pesher thématique*, J. Carmignac)[5], der dann aber bereits den Übergang zum Midrasch signalisiert. Aus der Art des Schriftbezuges und der Verwendung der Zitationsformel lässt sich eine formal simplifizierende Entwicklung erkennen, die ein allmähliches Auslaufen dieser Auslegung in der Mitte des 1. Jh. v. Chr. anzeigt.

1.3. Zwischenfazit: Die *pešarîm* zum Jesajabuch legen Heilsorakel und Unheilsweissagungen des Propheten aus, übergehen aber die geschichtlichen Abschnitte in Jes 36-39. Einige *pešarîm* gehen kontinuierlich dem Text entlang, andere springen und exzerpieren, wiederum andere ziehen auch weitere Prophetenzitate bei und interpretieren somit Jesaja in der Perspektive des gesamten Prophetenkorpus. Aus den Auseinandersetzungen Israels mit den Assyrern des 8. Jh. v. Chr. lesen sie jetzt die Auseinandersetzung zwischen Guten und Bösen, zwischen Gerechten und Ungerechten in der unmittelbaren Gegenwart heraus. Es ist leicht einzusehen, dass gerade in der Messiasfrage das Jesajabuch gute Vorlagen bot. Wie die apokalyptischen Texte nehmen nun auch die *pešarîm* eindeutige Identifizierungen vor und gebrauchen dazu Bezeichnungen, die damals durchaus von jedem verstanden werden konnten, für uns heute aber z.T. nur mit Mühe zu entschlüsseln sind.

Wollen die älteren Jes-*pešarîm* noch für die Gemeinschaft von Qumran als das neue Gottesvolk werben, haben die jüngeren Kommentare damit fertig zu werden, dass sich große Teile Israels dieser Gemeinde noch nicht angeschlossen haben. Sie intensivieren die unmittelbare Naherwartung des Endgerichtes, entsprechend betonen sie die Vorzüge qumranischer Ekklesiologie und Messiashoffnung (vgl. auch 1/4QpPs), haben dann aber auch das Ausbleiben der eschatologische Wende zum berechneten Zeitpunkt (70 v. Chr.) zu verarbeiten. Man suchte bei den Propheten nach Angaben für die Zeit danach und der jüngste Pesher 1QpHab räsoniert darüber, "dass sich die letzte Zeit in die Länge zieht" (vii 7f. im Anschluss an Hab 2:3).

Die im Pesher vorliegende Rezeption einer biblischen Schrift geschieht mit Vollmacht. Wir wissen, dass die meisten biblischen Bücher erst in den letzten Jahrhunderten v. Chr. ihre "endgültige" Gestalt erhalten haben. Bis hierher wurden diese Bücher fortgeschrieben und wir haben in Qumran viele Beispiele für solche Fortschreibungen. Im Pesher

---

[5] G. J. Brooke, "Thematic Commentaries on Prophetic Scriptures," in Henze, *Biblical Interpretation at Qumran*, 134-57.

geschieht aber etwas anderes als Fortschreibung. Der fortschreibende Redaktor impliziert in seinen redaktionellen Einfügungen die gegenwärtige Situation, belässt dabei aber dem biblischen Text die Primäraussage und die inspirierende Vorgabe. Jetzt weiß sich der Kommentator selbst inspiriert und befähigt, den ihm vorliegenden Text in seinem Selbststand zu belassen, seinen für die aktuelle Gegenwart geltenden Sinn jedoch in verbindlicher Weise in einem eigenständigen Buch darzustellen. Jetzt ist die Aktualisierung nicht mehr durch die Inspiration des aktualisierten Textes getragen, sondern sie wird durch die Inspiration des Kommentators ermöglicht. Hinter jedem Pesher steht jemand, "dessen Wort Macht hat".

2. Vom Pesher zum Midrasch

2.1. Vom Pesher als Offenbarung in der Form eines Kommentars ist der **Midrasch** als Schriftforschung zu unterscheiden, kann aber in Qumran über die haggadische und halakhische Exegese zur Gesetzes-Bestimmung mit Offenbarungsqualität tendieren (Maier, Steudel). Kennzeichnend für den qumranischen Midrasch in Abhebung vom Midrasch der Rabbinen ist das Ziel, eine Sonderoffenbarung für Qumran zu erläutern, die allen übrigen Menschen verborgen bleibt. Die dazu notwendige Offenbarergestalt "wie Moses" ist der Gemeinde im *doreš hattôrah* gegeben.

2.2. Nach seiner Rekonstruktion aus 4Q174 und 4Q177 (zusätzlich noch 4Q182 und 4Q178?) kann der **"Midrasch zur Eschatologie"** (**4QMidrEschat**[a.b]) als der wichtigste thematische Midrasch[6] in Qumran gelten. Es handelt sich um eine strukturell dem Tanakh (Tora, Propheten, Schriften) nachgestaltete eschatologische Schrift, nach der die von Belial beherrschte Zeit der Läuterung ("das Ende der Tage") bereits angebrochen ist, die bald durch die Ankunft des Messias beendet werden wird. Die Forschung diskutiert gegenwärtig den im Midrasch genannten Ausdruck "Heiligtum aus/von Menschen" (*miqdaš 'adam*)[7], der die *jahad*-Gemeinschaft als spiritualisierende Metapher für den Tempel versteht, in dem Werke des Dankes als Opfer dargebracht werden. Die Auseinander-

---

[6] Wird von G. J. Brooke zu den thematischen *pešarîm* gerechnet.
[7] Vgl. dazu G. J. Brooke, "Miqdash Adam, Eden and the Qumran Community," in *Gemeinde ohne Tempel/Community without Temple: Zur Substituierung und Transformation des Jerusalemer Tempels und seines Kults im Alten Testament, antiken Judentum und frühen Christentum* (eds. B. Ego, A. Lange and P. Pilhofer in cooperation with K. Ehlers; WUNT I.118; Tübingen: Mohr Siebeck, 1999), 285-301.

setzung des Midrasch mit den Pharisäern ("Männer, die Glattes suchen") lässt eine Datierung zur Zeit der Alexandra Salome geraten erscheinen.

2.3. Der **Melchisedek-Midrasch** (**11Q13**)(dazu 4Q180/181)[8] ist ein thematischer Midrasch aus der Mitte des 1. Jh. v. Chr. Er geht aus von einer eschatologischen Ausdeutung des atl. Erlassjahres (Lev 25) als Endzeit, in der Melchisedek, der Altpriester des jebusitischen Jerusalem (Gen 14), hohepriesterliche (vgl. Hebr 7), königlich-richterliche (Ps 82:1) und messianische (Jes 61:1-3) Funktionen hat. Als Anführer der Engel kämpft er gegen Belial, übt das Strafgericht über alles Böse in der Welt aus und führt den Anbruch der Heilszeit herbei.[9]

2.4. Der **Midrasch zur Genesis (4Q252)**[10] wurde in der bisherigen Forschung wegen der in Kol. III-VI enthaltenen Segenssprüche des Patriarchen Jakob (Gen 49) 4QPatriarchal Blessings genannt. Diese qumranische Schrift aus dem 1. Jh. v. Chr. selektiert die Patriarchengeschichte so, dass in ihr die Wurzeln der gegenwärtigen Gemeinde als das wahre Israel heraus präpariert werden. Sie will den Anspruch auf das Land legitimieren und paränetisch zum Tora-Gehorsam führen, damit dieser Erbanspruch eingelöst werden kann.

2.5. Der **Midrasch Sefer Mosche (4Q249)** ist in kryptischer Schrift geschrieben und ist nach St. Pfann[11] eine der wenigen Rollen, die von einem qumranischen Bibliothekar mit einer Titulatur auf der Rückseite versehen worden ist, aus der paläographisch eine Datierung aus der Frühzeit Qumrans (um 150 v. Chr.) zu erschließen ist. Der Text steht offensichtlich in Beziehung zu Lev (14:40-45 im Zusammenhang der Reinheitsgesetze, die beim Befall eines Hauses durch Schimmel/Aussatz anzuwenden sind. Die befallenen Steine sind zu ersetzen, notfalls muss das ganze Haus abgerissen und der Bauschutt außerhalb der Stadt abgelagert werden. Unklar ist, warum eine Notiz von den krepierenden Fischen der ersten ägyptischen Plage (Ex 7:18) in diesen Text eingefügt ist; möglicherweise soll kontextuell verdeutlicht werden, dass auch der

---

[8] J. J. M. Roberts, Melchizedek, in *The Dead Sea Scrolls: Hebrew, Aramaic, and Greek Texts with English Translations*. Vol. 6b: *Pesharim, Other Commentaries, and Related Documents* (eds. J. H. Charlesworth and H. W. M. Rietz; The Princeton Theological Seminary Dead Sea Scrolls Project; Tübingen: Mohr Siebeck, 2002), 264-73.

[9] P. J. Kobelski, *Melchizedek and Melchiresa* (CBQMS 10; Washington D.C.: The Catholic Biblical Association of America, 1981).

[10] J. L. Trafton, "Commentary on Genesis A," in Charlesworth and Rietz, *The Dead Sea Scrolls*, 203-19.

[11] S. Pfann, "4Q249 Midrash Sefer Moshe," in *Legal Texts & Legal Issues: Proceedings of the Second Meeting of the International Organization of Qumran Studies, Published in Honour of Joseph M. Baumgarten* (eds. M. Bernstein, F. García Martínez and J. Kampen; STDJ 23; Leiden: Brill, 1997), 11-18.

Befall eines Hauses nicht von allein kommt, sondern letztlich eine von
Gott geschickte Plage ist. Oder im Blick auf die rabbinische Auslegung:
Wenn der Fisch stirbt, stirbt der ganze Nil. Wenn ein Stein befallen ist,
ist das ganze Haus befallen (*Leqach Tov*), ein typisch rabbinischer *Qal-
Wachomer*-Schluss.

2.6. Zwischenfazit: Midrasch und Pesher sind in ihren Grundzügen
ähnlich, aber in formaler Hinsicht deutlich voneinander zu unterscheiden.
Wie der Pesher sich primär auf prophetische Texte bezieht, so bezieht
sich der Midrasch primär auf Gesetzestexte und bildet auf diese Weise die
Vorstufe zur jüdischen Halakha. Aber bereits in Qumran war der Midrasch nicht darauf beschränkt: Der Begriff steht bald schon für eine „Exegese", die nicht einem Text entlang geht, sondern bestimmte sprachliche
Begriffe und Wendungen auslegt. Im Midrasch können jetzt viele unterschiedliche Auslegungen zusammengetragen werden, während der Pesher
nur eine einzige Auslegung vorlegt. Beide Formen der Rezeption biblischer Texte spiegeln die verantwortliche Deutung von Geschichte und
Gegenwart durch die Gemeinde von Qumran und ihre Vorläufergemein-
den, ihre Suche nach Identität und sozialer Integration, ihre Besonderheit,
aber auch ihre Zugehörigkeit zum Volk Israel. "Rather, it was a form of
intensive religious expression and experience in itself, veritably a form of
worship, a locus for experiencing the divine presence in their midst. Soci-
ally, such study strengthened the bonds of religious community"[12].

3. Abschreiben und Kopieren als Akt der Interpretation

Im Blick auf die Rezeption biblischer Texte wird eine reine Abschrift
eines Textes in der Regel nicht weiter beachtet, setzt man hier doch eine
unbedingte Texttreue voraus. Abweichungen werden meist ohne Auf-
wand in den Bereich der textkritisch relevanten Abschreibefehler ver-
bannt. Entsprechend hat die Große Jesajarolle (1QJesᵃ) lange Zeit als
primär lediglich textkritisch interessante Quelle gegolten, wozu sie nach
den Vorarbeiten von M. Burrows[13], H. M. Orlinsky[14] und W. H. Brown-

[12] S. D. Fraade, "Midrashim," in *Encyclopedia of the Dead Sea Scrolls* (eds. L. H. Schiffman and J. C. VanderKam; 2 vols; Oxford: Oxford University Press, 2000) 1:549-52,
bes. 551.
[13] M. Burrows, ed., *The Dead Sea Scrolls of St. Mark's Monastery. Volume I: The Isaiah
Manuscript and the Habakkuk Commentary* (New Haven: American Schools of Oriental Research, 1950).
[14] H. M. Orlinsky: "Studies in the St. Mark's Isaiah Scroll," *JBL* 69 (1950): 149–66;
JNES 11 (1952): 153–6; *JJS* 2 (1950–1951): 151–4; *JQR* 43 (1952–1953): 329–40;
IEJ 4 (1954): 5–8; *HUCA* 25 (1954): 85-92.

lee[15] bestens ausgestattet war. Mit S. Talmon[16], A. Rubinstein[17] und nahezu zeitgleich J. V. Chamberlain[18] wurde diese textkritische Phase überwunden. Man fragte nun zumindest ansatzweise nach den exegetischen Valenzen der Varianten. Für jede weitere Arbeit an der Jesajarolle wurde das inzwischen erschienene monumentale Werk von E. Y. Kutscher[19] zur unverzichtbaren Grundlage. Mit J. Høgenhaven[20] und A. van der Kooij[21] setzte dann endlich die von S. Talmon angestoßene Frage nach den exegetischen Valenzen der Varianten neu ein, die zuletzt in der umfassenden Monographie von P. Pulikottil[22] noch einmal erweitert werden konnte zugunsten einer tieferen Einsicht in die editorischen Tätigkeiten der damaligen Kopisten. Pulikottil machte darauf aufmerksam, dass die interpretierenden und aktualisierenden Varianten nur dann richtig erfasst werden können, wenn man sie konsequent mit parallelen Angaben in den *pešarîm* und den sonstigen qumran-eigenen Handschriften konfrontiert. Damit ist ein Forschungsbedarf angezeigt, der im Folgenden präzisiert werden soll:

Grundsätzlich hat man 1QJes[a] für eine Kopie des biblischen Jesajabuches mit vielen textkritisch relevanten Varianten gehalten. Dabei fällt aber auf, dass die Verfasser der sechs Jesaja- *pešarîm*[23] nicht diese Jesajarolle, sondern den protomasoretischen Jesajatext als Grundlage für ihre *pešarîm* gewählt haben. Sie haben offensichtlich darum gewusst, dass 1QJes[a] nicht nur eine Kopie des Bibeltextes ist. Worin aber besteht das Plus dieses Textes? Testet man die Varianten mit den Mitteln der Literar-

[15] W. H. Brownlee, *The Meaning of the Qumrân Scrolls for the Bible, with Special Attention to the Book of Isaiah* (New York: Oxford University Press, 1964).
[16] S. Talmon, "DSIa as a Witness to Ancient Exegesis of the Book of Isaiah," *ASTI* 1 (1962): 62–72 = idem, *The World of Qumran from Within* (Jerusalem: Magnes, 1989), 131–41; idem, "Observations on the Variant Readings in the Isaiah Scroll (1QIsaᵃ)," in idem, *The World of Qumran From Within: Collected Studies* (Leiden: Brill, 1990), 117–130.
[17] A. Rubinstein, "Theological Aspects of Some Variant Readings in the Isaiah Scroll," *JJS* 6 (1955): 187–200.
[18] J. V. Chamberlain, "The Functions of God as Messianic Titles in the Complete Qumran Isaiah Scroll," *VT* 5 (1955): 366-372.
[19] E. Y. Kutscher, *The Language and Linguistic Background of the Isaiah Scroll (1QIsᵃ)* (STDJ 6; Leiden: Brill, 1974).
[20] J. Høgenhaven, "The First Isaiah Scroll from Qumran (1QIsᵃ) and the Massoretic Text. Some Reflections with Special Regard to Isaiah 1–12," *JSOT* 28 (1984): 17–35.
[21] A. van der Kooij, *Die alten Textzeugen des Jesajabuches. Ein Beitrag zur Textgeschichte des Alten Testaments* (OBO 35; Freiburg und Göttingen: Universitätsverlag und Vandenhoeck & Ruprecht, 1981).
[22] P. Pulikottil, *Transmission of Biblical Texts in Qumran—The Case of the Large Isaiah Scroll 1QIsaᵃ* (JSOTSup 34; Sheffield: Sheffield Academic Press, 2001).
[23] 4Q161 (4QpJesᵃ) bis 4Q165 (4QpJesᵉ) und 3Q4 (3QpJes).

kritik ab, fragt man also, ob diese Varianten Ergebnis einer bestimmten editorischen Intention sein können, dann hat man zumindest heuristisch den Übergang von der Textkopie zum Pesher in Betracht gezogen. Der tatsächliche Fortschreibungscharakter von 1QJes[a] soll im Folgenden an einigen Beispielen gezeigt werden.

3.1. Die Rolle enthält den Text des gesamten Jesajabuches auf 54 Kolumnen. Die Handschrift ist paläographisch in die Zeit der Hasmonäer (ca. 125-100 v. Chr.)[24] einzuordnen, ist wenig sorgfältig geschrieben[25] mit sehr vielen Schreibfehlern, die vom Schreiber selbst oder von späteren Korrektoren aus der hasmonäischen (ca. 100–75 v.Chr.), spät-hasmonäischen (50–25 v. Chr.) und herodianischen Zeit (30–1 v.Chr.) korrigiert wurden.

3.2. Wie E. Y. Kutscher eindrucksvoll gezeigt hat, sind in 1QJes[a] alle Arten von Varianten vorhanden, die üblicherweise zu textkritischen Operationen führen: Verlesungen, Auslassungen und Zufügungen, Metathesen, falsche Wort-Trennungen, Ungenauigkeiten; daneben Versuche der Textverbesserung oder -erleichterung. Andere Varianten lassen auf mehrere Vorlagen des Schreibers schließen (Jes 22:14; Jes 37:25; Jes 38:19f.). Zur textkritischen Valenz dieser Varianten sind drei Bereiche zu benennen: meistens bestätigt 1QJes[a] den MT gegen LXX. An 21 Stellen stimmt 1QJes[a] mit LXX gegen MT überein. Es gibt schließlich Belege, in denen 1QJes[a] gegen MT und LXX steht. Solche Varianten sind textkritisch interessant und bestätigen die Ansicht von E. Tov[26] und H.-J. Fabry[27], dass in Qumran mehrere Textlinien nebeneinander existierten.

3.3. Schon J. V. Chamberlain[28] sah hinter einigen Varianten messianische Tendenzen; A. Rubinstein[29] glaubte in manchen Varianten theologische Tendenzen erkennen zu können, die etwas von der Sonderstellung

[24] E. Tov, "The Text of Isaiah at Qumran," in *Writing & Reading the Scroll of Isaiah: Studies of an Interpretive Tradition* (eds. C. C. Broyles and C. A. Evans; VTSup 70, 1–2; Leiden: Brill, 1997) 2:491–511. 494 datiert mit *F. M. Cross* die Rolle auf 150-125 v. Chr.
[25] Vgl. E. Tov, "The Textual Base of the Corrections in the Biblical Texts Found at Qumran," in *The Dead Sea Scrolls. Fourty Years of Research* (eds. D. Dimant and U. Rappaport; STDJ 10; Leiden and Jerusalem: Brill and Magnes Press, 1992), 299-314.
[26] E. Tov, *Der Text der hebräischen Bibel. Handbuch der Textkritik* (Stuttgart: Kohlhammer, 1997), 83–97.
[27] H.-J. Fabry, "Der Text und seine Geschichte," in *Einleitung in das Alte Testament* (eds. E. Zenger et al.; 7th ed.; Stuttgart: Kohlhammer, 2008), 34–59, bes. 41–47.
[28] Chamberlain, "The Functions of God," 366–72.
[29] Rubinstein, "Theological Aspect," 187-200.

der Qumrangemeinde anzeigten. P. Pulikottil kommt zu einem ersten
Ergebnis: „It has been observed that the scribe has mainly two exegetical concerns: historical and theological".[30] Das nun möchte ich im Folgenden an einigen Beispielen präzisieren:

3.3.1.   Jes 8:11

MT: כִּי כֹה אָמַר יְהוָה אֵלַי כְּחֶזְקַת הַיָּד וְיִסְּרֵנִי מִלֶּכֶת בְּדֶרֶךְ הָעָם־הַזֶּה לֵאמֹר:

Denn so spricht JHWH zu mir, als *die Hand* (*mich*) packte und er
mich abwandte davon, auf dem Weg dieses Volkes zu gehen.

1QJes[a]: כי כה אמר יהוה אלי כחזקת יד יסרנו מלכת בדרך העם־הזה לאמר:

Denn so spricht JHWH zu mir, als *eine Hand* (*uns*) packte und er *uns*
abwandte davon, auf dem Weg dieses Volkes zu gehen.

Die Variation des Textes ist geringfügig, aber wirkungsvoll. Der Schreiber bezieht den Text durch den Plural "uns" auf das Selbstverständnis
der Qumrangemeinde, die sich von Gott gepackt sieht, den Weg des Volkes zu verlassen[31]. Zudem ist jetzt יד "Hand" nicht determiniert, was an
die undeterminierte Hand beim Exodus erinnert (vgl. Ex 13:3,14,16) und
die Selbstexilierung der Gemeinde wohl als Exodus deuten will.

3.3.2.   Jes 31:5-6

MT: כְּצִפֳּרִים עָפוֹת כֵּן יָגֵן יְהוָה צְבָאוֹת עַל־יְרוּשָׁלָם גָּנוֹן וְהִצִּיל פָּסֹחַ וְהִמְלִיט:[5]
[6]שׁוּבוּ לַאֲשֶׁר הֶעְמִיקוּ סָרָה בְּנֵי יִשְׂרָאֵל:

Wie einen Vogel mit ausgebreiteten Schwingen, so wird JHWH
Seba'ot Jerusalem behüten. Er behütet und befreit, verschont und rettet.
Kehrt um zu dem, von dem ihr euch weit entfernt habt, Söhne Israels!

1QJes[a]: כצפרים עפות כן יגן יהוה צבאות על־ירושלם גנון והציל ופסח והמליט:
שוביו לאשר העמיקו סרה בני ישראל:

Wie einen Vogel mit ausgebreiteten Schwingen, so wird JHWH
Seba'ot Jerusalem behüten. Er behütet und befreit *und* verschont und
rettet, *die zu ihm umkehren* von dem, von dem ihr euch weit entfernt
habt, Söhne Israels!

Die winzige Einfügung verändert den Text sehr empfindlich, denn nun
geraten die "Umkehrenden" ins Blickfeld – eine beliebte Selbstbezeichnung der Gemeinde von Qumran (CD vi 5; viii 16; 1QH ii 9; vi 6) –,
die von Gott gerettet werden.

---

[30] Pulikottil, *Transmission*, 211.
[31] Vgl. dazu 4Q174 1-2 i 14f. und die Selbstbezeichnung der Qumraner: "die den Weg
(des Volkes) verlassen haben"; dazu auch CD viii 16; xix 29.

3.3.3. Jes 2:3

MT: וְהָלְכוּ עַמִּים רַבִּים וְאָמְרוּ לְכוּ וְנַעֲלֶה אֶל־הַר־יְהוָה אֶל־בֵּית אֱלֹהֵי
יַעֲקֹב וְיֹרֵנוּ מִדְּרָכָיו

Viele Völker machen sich auf den Weg. Sie sagen: Kommt, *lasst uns
ziehen zum Berg JHWHs*, zum Haus des Gottes Jakobs. Er wird uns
seine Wege zeigen...

1QJes^a: והלכו עמים רבים ואמרו לכו ונעלה [....] אל־בית אלהי יעקב וירונו
מדרכיו

Viele Völker machen sich auf den Weg. Sie sagen: Kommt, lasst uns
ziehen zum [...] *Haus des Gottes Jakobs*. Sie werden *uns* seine Wege
zeigen...

Die wiederholt geäußerte Ansicht, den Textausfall mit einer Parablepsis
zu erklären, befriedigt nicht. Vielmehr ist ein ganz empfindliches Texte-
lement, die Fixierung der Aussage auf den Gottesberg Zion in Jerusalem,
ausgelassen. Jerusalem und der Zion sind nicht mehr Zentrum der eschatologischen Völkerwallfahrt (die Lakune im Text ist zu klein), sondern
das "Haus des Gottes Jakobs"[32]. Die Identifikation der Gruppe ("sie"),
die von nun an die Unterweisung anstelle Gottes übernehmen werden,
wird nicht geklärt. Sie legt sich aber nahe, denn hier ist eine ureigene
Aufgabe der Qumrangemeinde angesprochen, wie sie z.B. in 4QpJes^a vii
3.26-28 zum Ausdruck kommt, wo sogar der Messias seine Weisungen
aus der Gemeinde heraus erhält und auf der Basis des Gemeindegesetzes
den Völkern Recht spricht.

3.3.4. Jes 1:24-25:

MT: ^24לָכֵן נְאֻם הָאָדוֹן יְהוָה צְבָאוֹת אֲבִיר יִשְׂרָאֵל הוֹי אֶנָּחֵם מִצָּרַי וְאִנָּקְמָה
מֵאוֹיְבָי: ^25וְאָשִׁיבָה יָדִי עָלַיִךְ

Deswegen, Spruch des Herrn JHWH Seba'ot, des Starken Israels:
Wehe, ich will Rache nehmen an meinen Feinden, mich rächen
an meinen Gegnern. Und ich wende meine Hand gegen dich...

1QJes^a: לכן נאם האדון יהוה צבאות אביר ישראל הוה אנחם מצריו ואנקמה
מאובו: והשיב ידי עליך

Deswegen, Spruch des Herrn JHWH Seba'ot, [des Starken Israels]:
Wehe, ich will Rache nehmen an *seinen Feinden*, mich rächen an
seinen Gegnern. Und *er wendet* meine Hand gegen dich...

Die Änderung der Suffixe von der 1. Sg. zur 3. Sg. ist markant und weist
auf eine Gestalt, die kontextuell nur erkennbar wird, wenn man den in

---

[32] Zur positiven messianischen Konnotation "Jakobs" vgl. Num 24:17; CD vii 19; 1QM
xi 6; 4Q175,12 u.ö.

v 21 genannten "Gerechten", der in Jerusalem herrschte, personal versteht – nicht als "Gerechtigkeit" wie die EÜ – und auf den "Lehrer der
Gerechtigkeit" bezieht[33]. Dieser regierte tatsächlich einmal in Jerusalem
(Jes 1:21), aber seine Feinde – gemeint ist wohl der "Frevelpriester"
(vgl. 1QpHab viii 8ff.) – hatten ihn verdrängt.

3.3.5. Jes 14:1-2

MT:

כִּי יְרַחֵם יְהוָה אֶת־יַעֲקֹב וּבָחַר עוֹד בְּיִשְׂרָאֵל[1]

וְהִנִּיחָם עַל־אַדְמָתָם וְנִלְוָה הַגֵּר עֲלֵיהֶם וְנִסְפְּחוּ עַל־בֵּית יַעֲקֹב:

וּלְקָחוּם עַמִּים וֶהֱבִיאוּם אֶל־מְקוֹמָם וְהִתְנַחֲלוּם בֵּית־יִשְׂרָאֵל[2]

עַל אַדְמַת יְהוָה לַעֲבָדִים וְלִשְׁפָחוֹת וְהָיוּ שֹׁבִים לְשֹׁבֵיהֶם וְרָדוּ בְּנֹגְשֵׂיהֶם:

Ja, JHWH wird mit Jakob Erbarmen haben und Israel noch weiter
erwählen.
Er wird ihnen Ruhe gewähren auf ihrem Ackerboden und zugesellt
wird ihnen der Fremdling und sie schließen sich dem Haus Jakobs an.
Und Völker werden sie nehmen und sie an ihren Ort bringen und das
Haus Israel wird sie zum Erbbesitz nehmen auf dem Ackerboden
JHWHs, zu Knechten und Mägden und sie werden die gefangen
fortführen, die sie gefangen fortführten und sie werden ihre Treiber
niedertreten.

1QJes[a]:

כי ירחם יהוה את־יעקב ובחר עוד בישראל

והניחם על־אדמתם ונלוא הגר עליהם ונספחו [ע]ל־בית יעקב:

ולקחום עמים רבים והביאום אל־אדמתם ואל מקוממ והתנחלום בית־

ישראל

אל אדמת יהוה לעבדים ולשפחות והיו שובים לשוביהם ורדים בנגשיהם:

Ja, JHWH wird mit Jakob Erbarmen haben und Israel noch weiter
erwählen.
Er wird ihnen Ruhe gewähren auf ihrem Ackerboden und zugesellt
wird ihnen der Fremdling und sie schließen sich dem (?) Haus Jakobs
an.
Und *zahlreiche* Völker werden sie nehmen und sie bringen *in ihr
Land und* an ihren Ort und das Haus Israel wird sie zum Erbbesitz
nehmen *hin zum* Land JHWHs, zu Knechten und Mägden. Und sie
werden *Umkehrende sein für die, die sich ihnen zugewandt haben*
und Niedertretende ihre Treiber.

Durch die Einfügung des qumran-spezifischen Terminus רבים "viele/
alle" wird eine entscheidende Perspektive eingebracht, die den Text auf
die "Vollversammlung" der Qumrangemeinde lenkt. Es geht hier jetzt
nicht mehr darum, dass irgendwelche Völker dem Haus Jakob Migranten
aufdrücken, vielmehr geht es hier eher um ein Programm der Gemeinde

---

[33] van der Kooij, *Die alten Textzeugen des Jesajabuches*, 97.

zur Integration von Fremden. Ähnliches finden wir in den sonstigen
qumranischen Bestimmungen für den Umgang mit Fremden, ganz besonders in der Rezeption des *Qahal*-Gesetzes (Deut 23) in 4Q174 iii 2-4;
4Q394 iii 9f.; CD xiv 4f.

3.3.6. Zwischenfazit: Der Abschreiber hatte seine eigene Gegenwart
im Blick, als er den Text abschrieb. Von seiner Gegenwart gedrängt
modernisierte und ajourierte er die Sprache auf seinen zeitgenössischen
Dialekt hin. Mit z.T. minimalen Änderungen brachte er den ihm überlie-
ferten Text auf den springenden Punkt seiner Gegenwart. Indem er sich
in der Sukzession des biblischen Verfassers sah und sich wie dieser als
Autor des Textes verstand unbeschadet der Tatsache, dass in anderen
Gruppierungen des Judentums diese Texte bereits einen standardisierten
Zustand erreicht hatten, konnte er diesen Text im Blick auf die Gegenwart seiner Gemeinde umschreiben. Dazu ging er mit den geringst
möglichen Mitteln vor, beschränkte sich auf Minimal-Varianten, die
manchmal lediglich als punktuellen Anstoß dienen sollten, da er z.B.
eine einmalige Perspektiv-Änderung durch Numeruswechsel "du" –
"ihr" oder Personwechsel "ich" – "wir" sogar im laufenden Vers nicht
notwendig durchhielt. Er wollte also lediglich andeuten und ließ – wie
bei einem Anakoluth – seine Leser den erstrebten Textzustand selber
entwickeln.

Er bezog alte Prophezeiungen des Jesaja auf seine Zeit so, wie es auch
die *pešarîm* machten, allerdings verblieb er im Text selbst, während die
pešarîm ihre Aktualisierungen in einen Kommentartext stellten. Das aber
macht deutlich, dass die Charakterisierung des Schreibers als Kopist
erheblich zu kurz greift. Die hier analysierten Varianten zeigen, dass der
Jesajarolle eine Konzeption zugrunde liegt, die diesen Prophetentext mit
den sog. *jaḥad*-Texten verbinden soll.

4. Rewritten/reworked/Para- und Pseudo-Texte

4.1. Eine spezielle Art der Schriftauslegung begegnet in einer Reihe
von Handschriften, deren Bezeichnung in der Qumranforschung Kontro-
versen ausgelöst hat, an deren Klärung E. Tov und A. Lange maßgeblich
beteiligt waren. Es handelt sich um Texte, die ganz eindeutig biblischen
Texten nahe stehen, selbst aber keine solchen sind. Gemeinhin werden
sie als "Para-Texte" oder "Paraphrasen"[34] bezeichnet. A. Lange nennt

---

[34] Vgl. J. C. VanderKam, *Einführung in die Qumranforschung* (UTB 1998; Göttingen:
Vandenhoeck & Ruprecht, 1998), 76.

sie "parabiblical texts" oder im Blick auf gewisse Anachronismen in vormakkabäischer Zeit "paratextual texts"[35]. Daneben scheint sich gegenwärtig die von E. Tov vorgeschlagene Bezeichnung "Reworked oder Rewritten Bible" einzubürgern. Unter diesem Label verbergen sich nun ganz unterschiedliche Texte, die lediglich ihre Unmittelbarkeit zum Text einzelner biblischer Bücher gemeinsam haben. M.W. war es A. Lange, der eine Charakterisierung der zu dieser Großgruppe gehörenden Schriften vorgenommen hat. Dieser Unterteilung möchte ich mich hier anschließen:

4.1.1. Die eigentlichen **"rewritten texts"** sind nach G. Vermes wie folgt zu charakterisieren: "In order to anticipate questions, and to solve problems in advance, the midrashist inserts haggadic development into the biblical narrative – an exegetical process which is probably as ancient as scriptural interpretation itself"[36]. Nach S. W. Crawford[37] folgen solche Texte weitgehend dem Pentateuch, weichen dann aber plötzlich ohne jede Kennzeichnung von der Vorlage ab. Es handelt sich also um selbständige Texte, die an Bibeltexte erinnern, aber nicht im klassischen Sinne Fortschreibungen enthalten. An die Stelle der Fortschreibung ist die Neuformulierung getreten – wahrscheinlich ein Zugeständnis an das um sich greifende hellenistische Literaturverständnis.[38] Hier sind als erstes 5 Mss. zu nennen (4Q158; 4Q364-367, dazu noch 4Q422; 4Q464), die sich auf den Pentateuch beziehen und aufgrund paläographischer Erkenntnis in die späthasmonäische Zeit (frühes 1. Jh. v. Chr.) gehören. Sie stellen offensichtlich weniger eine Textsammlung, als vielmehr eine Bearbeitung pentateuchischer Texte dar und stehen interessanterweise der protosamaritanischen Textlinie nahe.[39] Nichts deutet auf eine qumranische Verfasserschaft hin. Möglicherweise steht hinter diesen Texten eine bisher unbekannte vorqumranische Pentateuchredaktion, die im

---

[35] A. Lange, "Pre-Maccabean Literature from the Qumran Library," *DSD* 13/3 (2006): 277-305, bes. 289, n. 58.

[36] G. Vermes, *Scripture and Tradition in Judaism: Haggadic Studies* (StPB 4; Leiden: Brill, 1961), 95.

[37] S. W. Crawford, "The Rewritten Bible at Qumran," in *The Bible and the Dead Sea Scrolls*. Vol. 1.: *The Hebrew Bible and Qumran* (ed. J. H. Charlesworth; N. Richland Hills, Tex.: BIBAL Press, 2000), 173-95.

[38] Vgl. M. Rösel, "Der Brief des Aristeas an Philokrates, der Tempel in Leontopolis und die Bedeutung des Religionsgeschichte Israels in hellenistischer Zeit," in *"Sieben Augen auf einem Stein" (Sach 3,9). Festschrift für Ina Willi-Plein zum 65. Geburtstag* (eds. F. Hartenstein and M. Pietsch; Neukirchen: Neukirchener Verlag, 2007), 327-44, bes. 335.

[39] E. Tov, "Rewritten Bible Compositions and Biblical Manuscripts, with Special Attention to the Samaritan Pentateuch," *DSD* 5 (1998): 334-54.

Nachgang zum priesterlichen Endredaktor des Pentateuches (R^P) zwar keine Aufnahme in den jüdischen und/oder christlichen Kanon gefunden, trotzdem aber entscheidende kanon-hermeneutische Bedeutung hat. Es sind Übereinstimmungen mit der Tempelrolle und Nähen zum Jubiläenbuch zu beobachten. Außerhalb des Pentateuches sind diverse Handschriften mit Texten aus der Chronik (4Q118) und aus Jeremia (4Q70; 4Q72) zu nennen, vor allem aber ist die Tempelrolle (11Q19) zu dieser Kategorie zu rechnen.

4.1.2. Paratextliche oder **parabiblische Texte** sind nach dieser Unterscheidung Texte, die sich eng an biblische Texte oder Themen orientieren, aber selbst keine biblischen Texte sind: es handelt sich um freie Nacherzählungen. Zu nennen ist hier das Genesis-Apokryphon (inkl. 1Q20 und 4Q538 [?]), eine interpretierende Nacherzählung von Gen 5:28-15:4 in aram. Sprache, die im Kontext ihrer Zeit den Glauben an die alleinige Macht Gottes stärken will, der einzig in der Lage ist, das Handeln der Menschen zu lenken. Paläographisch datiert die Rolle um die Zeitenwende; sie ist wahrscheinlich importiert, denn nichts deutet auf einen qumranischen Ursprung hin; sie kam aber inhaltlich dem qumranischen Interesse an den biblischen Patriarchen entgegen. – Zu nennen sind für diese Kategorie weiter: das Moses-Apokryphon (dazu 1Q29; 1Q22) und das Pentateuch-Apokryphon A (4Q368). Auch zu dieser Kategorie könnte die Tempelrolle gehören. Für den Bereich außerhalb pentateuchischer Themen sind zu nennen: das Josua-Apokryphon (4Q378-379; 4Q522; 5Q9) und 4QVisSam (4Q160). – Schließlich sind hier die Jubiläen-Texte zu nennen, die in enger Übereinstimmung mit dem Buch der Jubiläen Texte aus der Genesis nacherzählen (1Q17-18; 2Q19-20; 3Q5; 4Q216-224; 11Q12). Daneben existierte schon sehr früh eine weit ausufernde Henoch-Tradition, die sich breit in der Qumranliteratur niedergeschlagen hat (4QEn^{a-f}; 4QEnGiants^{a-f}; 4QEnAstr^{a-d}).

4.2. Pseudo-Texte sind wie die Pseudepigrapha Texte, deren Autorenzuschreibung offensichtlich nicht mit dem wirklichen Autor übereinstimmt. Zu nennen sind hier v.a. die Pseudo-Ezechiel-Texte (4Q385; 4Q388; 4Q391). Auch freie Nachgestaltungen in der Art des Jubiläen-Buches (4QpsJub^{a-c}[4Q225-227]) sind hier zu nennen. Zu dieser Kategorie sind auch die vielen Testamente zu rechnen, die in Qumran nahezu ausschließlich in aram. Sprache vorliegen und sicher aus vorqumranischer Zeit stammen: 1/4QTLevi (1Q21; 4Q213-214); 4QTJacob (4Q537); 4QTJud (4Q538); 4QTNapht (4Q215); 4QTJoseph (4Q539). Schließlich gehören dazu auch solche Texte, die sich um die Aufnahme alter Priestertraditionen kümmern (4Q542 [Qahat]; 4Q543-548 [Amram]; 4Q549 [Hur]; 11Q13 [Melchisedek]; 11Q18 [Neues Jerusalem]).

4.3. Zwischenfazit: Zusammenfassend ist darüber zu räsonieren, wie sinnvoll überhaupt eine solche Unterscheidung ist. Sie kann sich lediglich auf formale Elemente stützen und deshalb nur etwas Äußerliches konstatieren. Wichtiger jedoch ist die Tatsache, dass in Qumran überhaupt eine Rezeption biblischer Texte in breitem Umfang stattgefunden hat, wobei diese Rezeption formal durchaus unterschiedlich ausgestaltet werden konnte. Ob diese formalen Differenzen nun auch ästimativen, d.h. wertenden Charakter hatten etwa im Sinne prä-kanonischer Textautorisation, ist nicht zu erkennen. Aus der späteren „anachronistischen" Kanonperspektive gesehen ging man in Qumran mit biblischen Texten und Themen konservativ und innovativ um. Einerseits zeigt sich in vielen „biblischen" Handschriften eine immer deutlicher werdende Tendenz hin zur protomasoretische Textlinie, andererseits scheinen die Autoren und Schreiber der Qumranlinie durchaus nicht festgelegt gewesen zu sein. Es wurden eben nicht primär Texte, sondern Inhalte weitergegeben.[40] – Eine solche divergente Textrezeption ist in Qumran sehr verbreitet, aber nicht einmal für Qumran typisch. Schon im Alten Testament selbst lassen sich unterschiedliche Modi der Rezeption erkennen. Dazu vergleiche man etwa die Texte des Deuteronomistischen Geschichtswerkes mit den Büchern der Chronik. Im außerqumranischen Judentum ist an die Antiquitates von Flavius Josephus und an den Exodus bei Ezechiel Tragicus zu erinnern. Solche Neuformulierungsprozesse sind typisch für die hellenistische Zeit, sie finden sich häufig in der LXX und dokumentieren, dass die alten Überlieferungen grundsätzlich als offen für Aktualisierungen gedacht wurden, dass das Eigentliche der Texte erst durch Aktualisierungen in neue Kontexte hinein sichtbar werden konnte. "Mit der so skizzierten Offenheit hatte das hellenistische Judentum ein wesentliches Instrument zur Bewältigung der Diaspora-Situation in der Hand"[41].

5. Die Rezeption alttestamentlicher Texte in der D- und S-Literatur

In der rezenten Auslegung von 2Kor 3:16f. ist die Möglichkeit bedacht worden, im 2. Versteil einen Pesher zum 1. Versteil zu erkennen.

---

[40] Dazu vgl. man etwa das Zitat von Ez 44:15 in CD iii 21-iv 4, wo bei stringenter Beibehaltung des Sinnes der Aussage die bedeutungstragenden Vokabeln ausgetauscht worden sind.

[41] Rösel, "Der Brief des Aristeas," 336.

Christian Metzenthin[42] hat versucht aufzuzeigen, dass hier eine struktu-
relle Ähnlichkeit der Schriftinterpretation wie die in der Pesher-Interpretation in CD vi 3-10 vorliegt, dies, obwohl in beiden Fällen das cha-
rakteristische Deutewort (*pišrô* "seine Deutung ist...") nicht vorliegt:
"Der Brunnen, den die Fürsten gegraben haben,... (Num 21:18) ist das
Gesetz, und die ihn gegraben haben, sind die Umkehrenden Israels, ...".
Eine solche Auslegung besteht im Wesentlichen aus einer Identifikation. Dahinter steht die Überzeugung, dass das Numeri-Zitat sich nicht
auf die Wüstenwanderung der Israeliten bezieht, sondern eine Aussage
für die aktuelle Gegenwart der Gemeinde in Damaskus beinhaltet. Wie
bei einer allegorischen Gleichnis-Auslegung werden die Elemente des
zitierten Textes Zug um Zug in die Gegenwart des Interpreten übertra-
gen (identifizierende Nominalsätze). Ähnliche Deutungsvorgänge lassen
sich in CD iii 21-iv 4 zu Ez 44:15; CD viii 9-12 zu Deut 32:33 und
CD iv 14-19 zu Jes 24:17 (hier sogar mit dem *pišrô*-Deutewort) u.ö.
beobachten.

Im Blick auf die S-Literatur hat Sarianna Metso[43] die Technik des
Zitierens aus den alttestamentlichen Schriften untersucht. So werden in
1QS v 13f. Exod 23:7; in 1QS v 16f. Jes 2:22 und in 1QS viii 12f. Jes
40:3 zitiert. Erst ein Vergleich mit den älteren S-Handschriften aus 4Q
zeigt, dass nun die Bibelzitate als eine Art Schriftbeweis angeführt
werden, was an die Reflexionszitate beim Evangelisten Matthäus erinnert.

Die hier vorliegende Pesher-Exegese zeigt sich als die in Qumran ver-
breitete Auslegungsform, bei der Elemente aus der rezipierten Schrift-
stelle aufgenommen und ausschließlich aktualisierend gedeutet werden.
Dabei kann sowohl im rezipierten Zitat wie in der Auslegung eine
gewisse Formulierungsfreiheit vorherrschen. Dies kann – so in 2Kor
3:16f. und bes. in Gal 3:16 – so weit gehen, dass das rezipierte Zitat
kaum noch zu erkennen ist oder sogar ganz fehlen kann[44].

---

[42] C. Metzenthin, "Abraham in der Damaskusschrift und im Galaterbrief: Vergleichende
Überlegungen zur Schriftauslegung," *BN* 134 (2007): 79-103.

[43] S. Metso, "The Use of Old Testament Quotations in the Qumran Community Rule,"
in *Qumran between the Old and New Testaments* (eds. F. H. Cryer and T. L. Thompson; JSOTSup 290; Sheffield: Sheffield Academic Press, 1998), 217-31; idem, "Biblical Quotations in the Community Rule," in *The Bible as Book: The Hebrew Bible and
the Judaean Desert Discoveries* (eds. E. D. Herbert and E. Tov; London: British
Library & Oak Knoll Press in association with The Scriptorium: Center for Christian
Antiquities, 2002), 81-92.

[44] Beispiel: in CD vii 18 wird der Stern aus Amos 5:26 aufgenommen und ausgelegt,
obwohl er im Zitat von Amos 5:26 in CD vii 14 fehlt.

6. Schlussfolgerungen

Die Rezeption biblischer Texte in Qumran erfolgt also in vielfältiger Weise. Qumran hat die unterschiedlichen Arten der Rezeption nicht erfunden, sondern stand selbst bereits in einem breiten Strom von unterschiedlichen Rezeptionsmodi, deren Ursprünge sich z. T. noch bis in die Zeit der Endredaktion der biblischen Bücher zurück verfolgen ließen. Kanon-hermeneutisch von großem Interesse ist, dass für die Qumrangemeinde diese Endredaktion keineswegs als eine unveränderbare Fixierung des Textbestandes verstanden wurde. Die Texte konnten vielmehr auch weiterhin umgeschrieben oder gar fortgeschrieben werden, Kompilationen mit anderen Schriftstellen waren an der Tagesordnung. Komplette Neuformulierungen wurden den alten Texten an die Seite gestellt. Selbst das Abschreiben biblischer Texte wurde noch zur Interpretation genutzt, denn die Gemeinschaft war durchaus der Ansicht, dass die Texte für sie geschrieben waren und sich in ihrer Gemeinschaft ereigneten.

Dieser Aktualisierung diente vor allem die qumrantypische Kommentarform des Pesher, die den rezipierten Schrifttext ganz seiner ursprünglichen Bedeutung entkleidete und ihn exklusiv auf die Gegenwart der Gemeinde applizierte. Diese Fortschreibung wurde weiter entwickelt, so dass der Kommentatoren schließlich auch ohne biblisches Zitat auskommen konnten, weil sie ihre Gedanken aus dem Kopf heraus entwickelten. So wie sie die biblischen Texte im Kopf hatten, so konnten auch ihre Leser die Auslegung mit dem in ihren Köpfen gedachten Bibelzitaten oder Textanspielungen selbst verknüpfen (Aposiopese).

Dieser frische und kreative Umgang mit biblischen Texten ist nur denkbar, weil man an eine Fortdauer der Inspiration durch den Geist glaubte, eine *inspiratio continua*, die erst später durch das Außenskelett kanonischer Einschränkung verdrängt und ersetzt wurde.

THE DEAD SEA SCROLLS AND THE NEW TESTAMENT

Loren T. STUCKENBRUCK, Princeton Theological Seminary

INTRODUCTION

A straightforward comparison between the Dead Sea Scrolls and the New Testament is problematic in itself. Any discussion of article length which, of necessity, sacrifices the provision of detail and therefore cannot begin to enumerate lists of parallels is only able to attempt an assessment of the question as a whole and suggest pathways for future study. In laying the groundwork for such a discussion, I would like to note several caveats at the outset, especially in view of the casual perception of "the Dead Sea Scrolls" and "the New Testament" as "collections" of literature. Of course these designations are anachronisms that in each case can only be applied due to circumstances of history[1] and, even if

---

[1] With regard to the New Testament I have in mind the long process that led to the "canonization" of books that would comprise the New Testament as it is received today in Catholic, Protestant, and most Orthodox traditions. For all the factors that enable readers to integrate and interpret New Testament texts in relation to one another, one cannot assume that any of the authors thought they were contributing literature that would lead to inclusion within an increasingly circumscribed collection. On this there is wide agreement, despite differences concerning the coherence of the writings that would be canonized; see e.g. B. M. Metzger, *The Canon of the New Testament: Its Origins, Development and Significance* (Oxford: Clarendon Press, 1987) and L. M. McDonald, *The Biblical Canon: Its Origin, Transmission, and Authority* (3d rev. and updated ed.; Peabody, Massachusetts: Hendrickson, 2007). With regard to the Dead Sea Scrolls as a whole (even if they are delimited to inscribed materials recovered from the ruins and eleven caves nearby), to speak of a "collection" has less to do with the deliberate output of individual or groups of writers (whatever their relationship to communities that inhabited the ruins of Khirbet Qumran) than (a) with circumstances that led to their writings being placed in this or that cave and (b) with the broad yet important, still unanswered question of to what extent the different groupings of manuscripts in the caves interrelate. On this problem, see the seminal discussion by D. Dimant, "The Qumran Manuscripts: Their Content and Significance", in *Time to Prepare the Way in the Wilderness: Papers on the Qumran Scrolls by Fellows of the Institute for Advanced Studies of the Hebrew University* (eds. D. Dimant and L. H. Schiffman, STDJ 16; Leiden: Brill, 1995), 23-58 and the more recent reflections on the profiling of the literary deposits in the caves by D. Stökl Ben Ezra, "Old Caves and Young Caves: A Statistical Reevaluation of a Qumran Consensus," *DSD* 14 (2007): 313-33 (with bibliography in

regarded as discrete collections, they possess nothing less than a different character.

First, we should draw attention to a point that is often assumed yet infrequently expressed: neither the writings that constitute the New Testament nor those that are found among the Dead Sea Scrolls represent collections that align with the reasons why their authors composed their works. On the one hand, the "New Testament" consists of writings composed independently on scrolls, though within a comparatively widespread, diverse, yet remarkably coherent movement centered around conviction that associates definitive activity on the part of Israel's God with selected events pertaining to Jesus of Nazareth. These writings would eventually be gathered into various groupings – e.g. the gospels, Pauline writings – and, during the second century C.E. would begin to be brought together and arranged within single codices. Through the complicated process shaped by synodic decisions, usage in different Christian communities, responses to perceived heresies, participation in contemporary trajectories towards standardization in the Mediterranean world, an entity began to emerge in the fourth century C.E. that would increasingly be formally called "the New Testament". The "New Testament", therefore, is *not intrinsically a collection of compositions*, but rather denotes an acquired status that incrementally included some or excluded other writings to represent what would be considered "canonical".

On the other hand, the designation "Dead Sea Scrolls" is not as descriptive as it might first appear. Firstly, the expression has conventionally come to refer to written remains recovered from eleven caves in the environs of Khirbet Qumran rather than, more broadly, to all ancient repositories found in caves up and down to the west and northwest of the Dead Sea and in the Judaean wilderness (Masada, Naḥal Ḥever, Naḥal Se'elim, Wadi Murabbaʿat, Wadi ed-Daliyah, Khirbet Mird). Secondly, while one might in some cases be able to speak of collections of writings in individual caves[2] and although a number of compositions were authored within a social continuum of a Jewish movement (whether we wish, with Josephus, Philo and Pliny the Elder to call it "Essene" or, more narrowly, think of a "Yaḥad" which settled at Qumran), it is by no means clear that the fragmentary remains come from scrolls that were being

---

notes 15-16) and S. J. Pfann, "Reassessing the Judean Desert Caves: Libraries, Archives, 'Genizas' and Hiding Places," *BAIAS* 25 (2007): 147-70.

[2] E.g. the storing of writings together in single jars (so Cave 1) or, possibly, other caves in which fragmentary materials lay in a contiguous state (though this cannot be determined for those caves not initially excavated by archaeologists).

gathered and stored in a way that deliberately excluded writings composed by others – a point which is reinforced by the existence of numerous non-Yaḥad compositions copied in late-Hasmonaean and Herodian
hands after Khirbet Qumran was settled.[3] Beyond the "biblical" manuscripts, such compositions include virtually all the Aramaic works (e.g.
Genesis Apocryphon, testamentary literature, apocalyptic texts, portions
of *1 Enoch* and *Book of Giants*),[4] a large number of works preserved in
Hebrew (notably, e.g. *Jubilees, Temple Scroll, Musar le-Mevin, Book of
Mysteries*)[5] and a few remains preserved in Greek.[6] Thus to speak mean-
ingfully of "collections", since compositions in different scrolls could
not be gathered into single "books" or codices, can only be entertained
in a limited sense: (a) where it can be shown that scrolls were deposited
together in the caves (e.g. especially in jars) and (b) where single manuscripts can be shown to have contained documents composed by different authors that have been brought together, for example, as in several of
the early Enochic compositions (4Q203-204, 4Q205, 4Q206, 4Q207,
4Q212),[7] several Yaḥad works in 1Q28 (which combines 1QS, 1QSa,

---

[3] While the absence of some works composed in Greek (e.g. 1 Macc, 2 Macc, Wis) might
not be surprising, this should not be pressed too far towards the notion of a collection
that deliberately segregates along ideological lines. For example, 4Q448 (Col. B, the
song in praise of Jonathan) and the presence of parts of Ben Sira (2Q18; 11Q5 xxi-xxii)
among the caves shows, respectively, that neither anti-Hasmonaean nor anti-luni-solar
calendrical interests can be said to characterize the Scrolls as a whole. Alternatively, it
may be best to think about "collections" of materials, whether by cave or by groupings
of materials distinguishable within a cave (the latter being more difficult to determine,
beyond observations regarding codicological relationships, due to our lack of knowledge about the precise locations where the manuscripts were found within the caves).

[4] From the extensive secondary literature see e.g. the overviews by J. J. Collins, "Pseude-
pigraphy and Group Formation," in *Pseudepigraphic Perspectives: The Apocrypha &
Pseudepigrapha in Light of the Dead Sea Scrolls* (eds. E. G. Chazon and M. E. Stone;
STDJ 31; Leiden: Brill, 1999), 43-58, esp. 55-58 and D. Dimant, "Old Testament
Pseudepigrapha at Qumran," in *The Bible and the Dead Sea Scrolls* (ed. J. H. Charles-
worth; 3 vols.; Waco: Baylor University Press, 2006), 2:447-67.

[5] The specifically "Qumran"-sectarian provenance of many of the Hebrew documents cannot be assumed. For helpful discussions of criteria for more narrowly determining such
provenance, see A. Lange and H. Lichtenberger, "Qumran. Die Textfunde von Qumran,"
in *TRE* 28:45-65, 75-79; A. Lange, "Kriterien essenischer Texte", in *Qumran kontrovers: Beiträge zu den Textfunden vom Toten Meer* (eds. J. Frey and H. Stegemann; Ein-
blicke 6; Paderborn: Bonifatius, 2003), 59-69; and Ch. Hempel, "Kriterien zur Bestim-
mung 'essenischer Verfasserschaft' von Qumrantexten," *Qumran kontrovers*, 71-85.

[6] The existence of only Greek fragments in Cave 7 and some in Cave 4 warns against any
assumption that inclusion and exclusion of documents was based on linguistic alle-
giances.

[7] L.T. Stuckenbruck, "The Early Traditions Related to *1 Enoch* from the Dead Sea
Scrolls: An Overview and Assessment," in *The Early Enoch Literature* (eds. G. Boc-
caccini and J. J. Collins; Leiden: Brill, 2007), 41-63.

and 1QSb), including the *Two Spirits Treatise* (1QS iii 13-iv 26) and, of course, a number of the biblical manuscripts.

The recognition of essential differences between "the New Testament" and "the Dead Sea Scrolls" as collections is enough to demand that we be cautious about attempting to draw any direct lines of connection between or of influence from one to the other. Such lack of caution is especially apparent in comparisons which have centred on some of the following sorts of claims: (a) that this or that figure in the Dead Sea Scrolls can be identified with this or that figure in the New Testament (as proposed, for example, by Barbara Thiering[8] and Robert Eisenman[9]); (b) that this or that idea or practice of "Essenes" or "the Qumran community" gave rise to or is responded to by the same in early Christian communities (so e.g. Brian Capper,[10] Rainer Riesner,[11] Yigael Yadin,[12] and Hans Kosmala[13]); and (c) that some of the instructions in the New Testament were specifically formulated with "Qumran Essenes" in mind, whether adopting them straight out – as in Jesus' radical instructions on divorce (Mark 10:2-9)[14] and oath-taking (Matt 5:33-37)[15] – or

---

[8] So in *Jesus and the Riddle of the Scrolls: Unlocking the Secrets of His Life Story* (San Francisco: HarperCollins, 1992).

[9] Among Eisenman's many publications to this effect, see *The Dead Sea Scrolls and the First Christians* (Shaftesbury: Element, 1996) and *The New Testament Code: The Cup of the Lord, the Damascus Covenant, and the Blood of Christ* (London: Watkins, 2006).

[10] Cf. e.g. B. Capper, "Community of Goods in the Early Jerusalem Church," *ANRW* II.26.2, 1730-1774; idem, "The Palestinian Cultural Context of Earliest Christian Community of Goods", in *The Book of Acts in its Palestinian Setting* (vol. 4 of *The Book of Acts in Its First Century Setting*; ed. R. Bauckham; Carlisle and Grand Rapids: Paternoster and Eerdmans, 1995), 323-56; idem, "Essene Community Houses and Jesus' Early Community," in *Jesus and Archaeology* (ed. J. H. Charlesworth; Grand Rapids: Eerdmans, 2006), 472–502.

[11] See Rainer Risener, "Jesus, the Primitive Community, and the Essene Quarter of Jerusalem," in *Jesus and the Dead Sea Scrolls* (ed. J. H. Charlesworth; The Anchor Bible Reference Library; Garden City, New York: Doubleday, 1993), 198-234 and *Essener und Urgemeinde in Jerusalem. Neue Funde und Quellen* (2d ed.; Giessen: Brunnen, 1998).

[12] "The Dead Sea Scrolls and the Epistle to the Hebrews," in *Aspects of the Dead Sea Scrolls* (eds. C. Rabin and Y. Yadin; Scripta Hierosolymitana 4; Jerusalem: Magnes Press, 1965) 36-55

[13] H. Kosmala; *Hebräer-Essener-Christen* (Studia Post Biblica 1; Leiden: Brill, 1959).

[14] Based on analogies in strictures against polygamy in *Damascus Document* (cf. CD iv 20 – v 6) and *Temple Scroll* (11Q19 lvii 15-19, applied to the king in an elaboration of Deut 18); cf. J. A. Fitzmyer, "Divorce among First-Century Palestinian Jews," *Eretz Yisrael* 14 (1978): 103-10; and J. R. Mueller, "The Temple Scroll and the Gospel Divorce Texts," *RevQ* 10 (1979-1981): 247-75; concerning the problem of comparing the distinguishable issues of divorce with monogamy, however, D. Instone-Brewer, *Divorce and Remarriage in the Bible: The Social and Literary Context* (Grand Rapids:

rejecting them – as in Jesus' directive to love one's enemy over against those who endorse a view to love their neighbor and hate their enemy (Matt 5:43).[16] The assumption that the Dead Sea Scrolls were essentially the product of an isolated Jewish sect shaped the discussion about their relevance to early Christian ideas and practices, and the discussion of the Scrolls' significance was often framed by the question of whether or not the early Jewish-Christian movement could have had contact with the Essenes. It is along these lines – and within the framework of understanding the non-biblical and non-Aramaic scrolls as essentially products of an Essene movement – that Herbert Braun's two-volume work entitled *Qumran und das Neue Testament*[17] proceeded; Braun's careful – and minimalist – assessment of alleged parallels between the "Qumran-Funde" and New Testament texts could only go so far. To be sure, the possibility of such connections between two contemporary sectarian groups cannot be ruled out from the outset. However, the exploration of connections in these terms requires a significant degree of sociological continuity for purported influences to gain in plausibility. Frequently, the significance of tradition-historical parallels would be evaluated under the proviso that social links between persons and groups among Jesus' followers and the "Essenes" provide a likely explanation.

Now I do not wish to deny that such links existed. On the contrary, one would be misguided to rule out such a possibility. However, it is one thing to map a possible socio-religious terrain during the first century C.E. and another to establish more precisely that this is the reason for an alleged parallel. Moreover, much of the discussion about the relationship

Eerdmans, 2002), 61-72 and 175-77 (though ultimately wishing to read Mark 10:2 through Matt 19:3) and L. Doering, "Marriage and Creation in Mark 10 and CD 4-5," in *Echoes from the Caves: Qumran and the New Testament* (ed. F. García Martínez; STDJ 85; Leiden: Brill, 2009), 133-63.

[15] Initially, R. E. Murphy, *The Dead Sea Scrolls and the Bible* (Westminster, Maryland: Newman, 1956), 85 and K. Schubert, "The Sermon on the Mount and the Qumran Texts," in *The Scrolls and the New Testament* (ed. K. Stendahl; New York: Harper, 1957), 118-28 (here 126). The parallels between Jesus' complete prohibition of oaths and CD (xv 1-2 and xvi 2-6), however, break down, as the latter focuses on the prohibition as it pertains to the deity; see J. Carmignac, *Le docteur de justice et Jésus-Christ* (Paris: Éditions de l'Orante, 1957), 83-84.

[16] This is argued frequently; see e.g. E. Stauffer, *Die Botschaft Jesu: Damals und heute* (Dalp-Taschenbücher 333; Bern: Francke, 1959), 128-29; Schubert, "The Sermon on the Mount," 120-21; see H. Braun, *Qumran und das Neue Testament* (2 vols.; Tübingen: Mohr Siebeck, 1966), 1:17-18 (with further bibliography).

[17] H. Braun, *Qumran und das Neue Testament* (Tübingen: Mohr Siebeck, 1966). Braun's work provided a thoroughgoing evaluation of parallels that were being alleged by Qumran scholars to have a bearing on the interpretation of New Testament texts.

between the Dead Sea Scrolls and the New Testament from the time of
the initial discoveries until the early 1990s was engaged in a quest that
strained to get at unattainable forms of specificity. Though discussions
of this sort have continued until the present (and with some justification),
the terms for exploring the impact of Dead Sea Scrolls research on New
Testament interpretation have changed.

What accounts for such a shift, and how might it be characterized?
The publications of mostly Cave 4 materials since the end of 1990 (Dec.
30), when Emanuel Tov was appointed as Editor-in-Chief for the Dead
Sea Scrolls publication project, provided a new impetus – perhaps even
a broader basis – for assessing the scrolls' value for our understanding
of the New Testament documents. In particular, there has been an
increasing recognition that many of the documents cannot be casually
labelled as "sectarian" or, if so, they cannot be obviously traced to the
"Yaḥad" that settled at Khirbet Qumran or linked to "Yaḥad"-related
documents. While since the 1950s many scholars suspected that the
Aramaic texts from Caves 1, 2, 4, 6 and 11 were pre- or proto-Essene
and therefore did not originate at Qumran, similar considerations have
been given to a large number of texts preserved in Hebrew whose specific "Qumranic" origins cannot be demonstrated. These Hebrew documents include *Jubilees* (1Q17-18, 2Q19-20, 3Q5, 4Q176a-b, 4Q216-224,
11Q12); *Musar le-Mevin* (1Q26, 4Q415-4Q418, 4Q418a, 4Q423); *Book
of Mysteries* (1Q27, 4Q299-300, 4Q301?); *Temple Scroll* (4Q524,
11Q19-20, 11Q21?); *4QMessianic Apocalypse* (4Q521); *Apocryphon
Pentateuch* A (4Q367); *Prayer of Enosh* (4Q369); *Exhortation Based
on the Flood* (4Q370); materials related to Joshua (4Q378-379, 4Q522,
5Q9), Jeremiah (4Q383, 4Q384?, 4Q385b, 4Q387b, 4Q389a), Ezekiel
(4Q385, 4Q385c, 4Q386, 4Q388, 4Q391), Joseph (4Q371-373) and
Moses (4Q374-376, 4Q385a, 4Q87a, 4Q388a, 4Q389-390); *Ways of
Righteousness* (4Q420-421); *Ritual of Marriage* (4Q502); *Daily Prayers*
(4Q503); *Words of the Luminaries* (4Q504-506); *Songs of the Maskil*
(4Q444, 4Q510-511); *4QBeatitudes* (4Q525), *4QNon-Canonical Psalms*
A and B (4Q380-381); *11QPsalms* (11Q5-6); *11QApocryphal Psalms*
(11Q11); and the *Two Spirits Treatise* (cf. 1QS iii 13-iv 26). As a consequence, the relevance of parallels can, less than before, relate to the
question of how much influence the Yaḥad or even "Essenism" exerted
within Palestinian Judaism before 70 C.E. Instead, faced with a wider
variety of materials than had been appreciated before and with sources
that may have circulated well beyond the bounds of "Qumran Essenism"
and cannot be accounted for by appeals to a wider Essene movement,

New Testament scholars can weigh the influence of the scrolls without necessarily having to ask whether there is any relationship between early Christianity and the Essenes, even if they wish to retain a "Qumran-Essene" hypothesis in some form.

In light of these preliminary comments, a reassessment of what New Testament scholars can learn from the scrolls is in view. Whereas it is not within the scope of the present discussion to tabulate or catalogue "evidence" of New Testament texts that can arguably be illuminated by the Dead Sea Scrolls materials,[18] I propose below to draw attention to the *kinds* of contributions Scrolls research can make to our understanding of traditions that circulated through the writings of Jesus' immediate followers and early Christian communities.[19] While some of the points to be described below have been known since the beginning of Scrolls studies over sixty years ago, others shall reflect newer considerations and developments. Although a number of issues relating to New Testament study have not been included below,[20] I hope that the following list will offer a representative range of issues, illustrated by appropriate examples.

---

[18] Taking the social complexity and diverse origin of the scrolls into account, we are once again in a position, now on a different footing than what determined the work of Braun (bibliography in n. 16), to attempt a commentary on the New Testament that takes the significance of Dead Sea Scrolls research as a point of departure.

[19] Several recent publications make important contributions in suggesting ways Scrolls and New Testament studies can be placed in a constructive conversion: G. J. Brooke, *The Dead Sea Scrolls and the New Testament* (London: SPCK, 2005); J. Frey, "The Impact of the Dead Sea Scrolls on New Testament Interpretation: Proposals, Problems, and Further Perspectives," in J. H. Charlesworth, ed., *The Bible and the Dead Sea Scrolls: The Princeton Symposium on the Dead Sea Scrolls* (3 vols.; Waco: Baylor University Press, 2006), 1:407-61; and the essays edited by F. García Martínez in *Echoes from the Caves* (bibliography in n. 14). Each of these assessments, including the present one, overlaps to some extent, while reflecting distinctive perspectives on the problem.

[20] The following issues and areas of study which have received considerable attention since the discovery of the Scrolls are not treated below: the relation of the Scrolls to John the Baptist, the Scrolls' contribution to the study of Aramaic as a background for Jesus tradition, "works of the law" in the Scrolls and Pauline thought, proto-Christological epithets such as "Son of the Most High" and "anointed one(s)", cosmic dualistic thought (light versus darkness) in relation to Johannine literature, angelology in relation to the designation "holy ones" for the faithful community, and calendar. In addition to the literature cited in the previous footnote, readers may consult J. A. Fitzmyer, *The Dead Sea Scrolls and Christian Origins* (Studies in the Dead Sea Scrolls and Related Literature; Grand Rapids: Eerdmans, 2000); R. Zimmermann, *Messianische Texte aus Qumran: Königliche, priesterliche und prophetische Messiasvorstellungen in den Schriftfunden von Qumran* (WUNT II.104; Tübingen: Mohr Siebeck, 1998); and the remaining contributions to *The Bible and the Dead Sea Scrolls* edited by Charlesworth.

1. Literary- and Source-Critical Approaches

I begin with an area in which Dead Sea studies have thus far not been
sufficiently explored: the wider literary context within which to consider
source-critical work on the Synoptic Gospels. In particular, I have in
mind the way scholars have engaged in accounting for the existence of
shared traditions (sometimes word for word or with only minor changes),
while attempting to explain the sometimes obvious differences that set
them apart. Analysis has, of course, focused on explanations for (a) traditions shared by Mark, Matthew and Luke; (b) Mark and Matthew;
(c) Mark and Luke; (d) Matthew and Luke; and even (e) between one of
the Synoptics and the Gospel of John. In discussing the possible literary
and tradition-historical relationships amongst these writings, we are not at
this stage able to offer new solutions so much as to raise again fundamental questions that initially gave rise to the insights resulting from source-
criticism. In particular, not least with the Scrolls in mind, one may ask
what steps did the author or editor of one composition take to transform
traditional material into a work that bears a distinct character? At what
point does editing work on a document result in a new recension or, further, in an entirely new literary work? If we search after analogies for
differences between the gospels, several models known from the study of
ancient source materials could, of course, prove useful: (a) variants within
a continuous textual tradition (more customarily referred to as text-critical
variants); (b) the existence of different recensions to the same work (e.g.
as variously the case for Greek Daniel, Greek Tobit, *Ethiopic* or *1 Enoch*,
Slavonic or *2 Enoch*, *Joseph and Aseneth*, *Testament of Abraham*; *Prov-
erbs of Ahiqar*); and (c) the existence of common material in two distinguishable works (e.g. 1-2 Kings and 1-2 Chronicles; *Life of Adam and
Eve* and *Assumption of Moses*). There are problems, however, if one
attempts to explain changes amongst the Synoptic Gospels on the basis
of these models. A process of scribal transmission (a) can only account
for smaller or slight changes between texts, and does not begin to address
how some of the more major differences in – so (b) and (c) – could have
arisen. While a study of (b) and (c) might bear some affinity with identifiable processes of development within the Synoptic tradition, the tem-
poral proximity of the recensions (b) and documents (c) in relation to one
another remains difficult to determine; whereas the Synoptics probably
took shape within a generation of one another, it is by no means clear that
the same can be affirmed for the text examples noted under (b) and (c).
The difficulty in pinning down literary models as analogies for the growth

of the Synoptic tradition has led to a reconsideration of the role of orality as a way of explaining both a certain continuity and fluidity of tradition[21] as well as throwing light on how easily the smaller units of tradition could appear in different arrangements.[22]

Amongst the Dead Sea documents, the existence of multiple versions of documents provides material evidence for the transmission, editing, rewriting, and adaptation of textual traditions, sometimes within a newly devised framework or even document. Of particular relevance here is the observation that the Scrolls are roughly contemporaneous to one another or at least chronologically contiguous in a way that could not previously be demonstrated for the Jewish writings mentioned in the preceding paragraph. This is especially significant since the parallel Dead Sea manuscripts were recovered from caves proximate to one another, while the precise contexts in which the gospel traditions were initially conveyed and received, beyond inference and guess work, remain unknown. In other words, the Scrolls illuminate the kinds of *literary* processes that may have been at work when written traditions were circulating at an early stage.

The best examples of documents going through a process of smaller[23] or more substantive[24] changes can be observed in the following documents: *Serek ha-Yaḥad* (1QS, 4Q255-264, 5Q11); *Hodayot* (1QHᵃ, 1Q35, 4Q427-432, 4Q471b); *Serek ha-Milḥamah* (1QM, 4Q491-496; cf. 4Q471 and also the disputed status of 4Q285 par. 11Q14); *Damascus Document* (Cairo Geniza manuscripts A and B, 4Q266-273, 5Q12, 6Q15; cf. also Cairo Geniza manuscripts A and B); *Musar le-Mevin*

---

[21] As emphasized recently by James D. G. Dunn, e.g. in *Jesus Remembered* (Grand Rapids: Eerdmans, 2003), who is influenced by the focus on orality in Middle Eastern cultures advanced by Kenneth E. Bailey; see, most recently, *Jesus Through Middle Eastern Eyes: Cultural Studies in the Gospels* (Downers Grove: Intervarsity Press, 2008).

[22] So the fundamental insight developed in the form-critical studies of R. Bultmann (*Geschichte der synoptischen Tradition*, with a Forward by G. Theissen [2d ed.; FRLANT 12; Göttingen: Vandenhoeck & Ruprecht, 1995, repr. 1931] and Martin Dibelius (*Die Formgeschichte des Evangeliums. Mit einem Nachtrag von Gerhard Iber* [3d rev. ed.; ed. G. Bornkamm; Tübingen: Mohr Siebeck, 1966]). This is not to deny the possibility of oral transmission playing an important role in the production of the Gospels, but rather to stress that the process of *literary* editing and reworking of tradition could show the same degree of flexibility.

[23] Such changes involve the (a) addition, (b) omission, or (c) substitution of smaller words or phrases. Though one is able to analyze these text-critically in order to determine a more original text, they illustrate how much textual variation and the early stages of transforming a text can be construed as overlapping processes.

[24] Here one may think of (a) the development of documents into distinguishable recensions in which differences reflect identifiable tendencies, (b) the rearrangement of discrete blocks of text, and (c) rewriting that begins to produce a new literary product.

(1Q26, 4Q415-418, 4Q418a, 4Q423); *Shirot 'Olat ha-Shabbat* (4Q400-407, 11Q17, Masada ms.); and *Barki Nafshi* (4Q434-438). Beyond the level of textual readings themselves, *Serek ha-Yaḥad*, *Hodayot*, *Serek ha-Milḥamah* illustrate the growth and development of documents through additions, omissions, and rearrangements of material. Significantly, manuscripts related to both the *Hodayot* (4Q427 7 i 7-19; 1QHᵃ xxv 34-xvii 3; 4Q427 7 i 7-19; 4Q431 1-2; cf. also 4Q428 cols. lxii-lxiv and 4Q471b) and another document, possibly *Serek ha-Milḥamah* (4Q491 11 i), preserve the so-called "Self-Glorification Hymn". According to Hartmut Stegemann and Eileen Schuller, editors of the recent DJD edition of 1QHᵃ, this first person psalm is positioned in several distinct parts of the *Hodayot*: (a) towards the end of the reconstructed manuscripts of 1QHᵃ and 4Q428, (b) towards the beginning of 4Q427 at the reconstructed ii 18-v 3, and (c) at the very beginning of 4Q431 (cols i-ii). On the other hand, the hymn occurs in another manuscript (4Q491 11 i 8-18) that does not otherwise overlap with the *Hodayot* manuscripts.[25] However one determines which of the manuscripts reflects a more original collection, the shifting of discrete units of tradition in and out of a document shows how difficult it is to regard the manuscripts as belonging to the same composition without qualification. A further example may involve the incorporation and adaptation of some of the halakhic material in *Damascus Document* into the *Community Rule*, so that in the context of the latter it is transformed by its new literary setting.[26] This

---

[25] H. Stegemann and E. Schuller, *1QHodayotᵃ with Incorporation of 1QHodayotᵇ and 4QHodayotᵃ⁻ᶠ* (DJD XL; Oxford: Clarendon Press, 2009), 300-01. For different assessments of the relationship between 4Q491 and the other manuscripts, see E. Eshel, "4Q471b. 4QSelf-Glorification Hymn (= 4QHᵉ frg. 1?)", in E. Chazon et al., eds., *Qumran Cave 4: Poetical and Liturgical Texts, Part 2* (DJD XXIX; Oxford: Clarendon Press, 1999), 421-32 (another recension) and F. García Martínez, "Old Texts and Modern Mirages: The 'I' of Two Qumran Hymns", *ETL* 78 (2002): 321-39 (different documents not "genetically related").

[26] In particular, see the shared material is found in the penal code set forth in 1QS vii, on the one hand, and in 4Q266 10 ii-11//4Q267 9 vi//4Q269 11 i-ii//4Q270 7 i, on the other. See the discussions on the relationship of these texts in Ch. Hempel, "The Penal Code Reconsidered", in *Legal Texts & Legal Issues: Proceedings for the Second Meeting for the International Organization of Qumran Studies, Published in Honour of Joseph M. Baumgarten* (eds. M. Bernstein, F. García Martínez and J. Kampen; STDJ 23; Leiden: Brill, 1997), 337-48 and *The Laws of the Damascus Document: Sources, Tradition, and Redaction* (STDJ 29; Leiden: Brill, 1998), 144-48; S. Metso, "The Relationship between the Damascus Document and the Community Rule," in *The Damascus Document: A Centennial of Discovery: Proceedings of the Third International Symposium of the Orion Center for the Study of the Dead Sea Scrolls and Associated Literature 4-8 February, 1998* (eds. J. M. Baumgarten, E. G. Chazon, and A. Pinnick; STDJ 34; Leiden: Brill, 2000), 85-93.

kind of analysis, which emerges from detailed comparative studies, adds nuance to the questions that New Testament scholarship may continue to ask: against what existing models of reworking written tradition did those responsible for Q, Matthew, Luke, and even Mark understand their activities? In response, one may argue that amongst the Dead Sea Scrolls we have the best available and contemporary evidence for how the incremental growth and transformation of written tradition could take place. Comparative studies that place the relative Scrolls material in conversation with source-critical work in the Gospels hold promise and may now be considered a *desideratum*.

2. Fulfillment Hermeneutics and Memory

Here we refer to what has been known since the early stages of Dead Sea Scrolls research, but which remains worth noting on the basis of renewed reflection. The expression "fulfilment hermeneutics" describes the reading strategy of writers when they construed sacred traditions as repositories of divine promises coming to fruition in their community's recent past and more contemporary circumstances.[27] In other words, sacred tradition was not so much written for the remote past as for other times (recent past, present, future). Since the initial discoveries of *pesharim* in Cave 1 to Micah (1QpMic=1Q14), Habakkuk (1QpHab), Zephaniah (1QpZeph=1Q15) and Psalms (1QpPs=1Q16), scholars have explored the special character of this hermeneutical strategy for the Qumran Yaḥad, and it was soon after the recovery of further such texts from the remaining caves that links were being drawn to the New Testament. In one well known instance, Krister Stendahl argued that the *pesharim* illuminate the Gospel of Matthew's habit (even more so than Mark, Luke, and John) of presenting events key events surrounding Jesus' life and teaching as the fulfilment of biblical (Old Testament) texts whose authors are made to prophesy them.[28] Before qualifying Stendahl's attempt to

---

[27] For the expression "fulfillment hermeneutics", see J. H. Charlesworth, *The Pesharim and Qumran History* (Grand Rapids, Mich.: Eerdmans, 2002), 5-6.

[28] See K. Stendahl, *The School of St. Matthew, and Its Use of the Old Testament* (2d ed.; Philadelphia: Fortress Press, 1968). The passages, together with parallels in the other New Testament Gospels, are Matt 1:22-23 (Isa 7:14); 2:5-6 (Mic 5:1, 3; cf. John 7:42); 2:15 (Hos 11:1); 2:17-18 (Jer 31:15); 3:3 (Isa 40:3; cf. Mark 1:3 [with Mal 3:1], Luke 3:4-6; John 1:23); 4:6 (Ps 91:11-12); 4:14-16 (Isa 8:23-9:1); 8:17 (Isa 53:4); 11:10 (Mal 3:1; cf. Exod 23:20); 12:17-20 (Isa 42:1-4); 13:14-15 (Isa 6:9-10; cf. Mark 4:11, Luke 8:10, John 12:39-40); 13:35 (Ps 78:2); 15:7-9 (Isa 29:13); 21:4-5 (Isa 62:11, Zech 9:9; cf. John 12:15); 21:13 (Isa 56:7, Jer 7:11); 26:31 (Zech 13:7); and 27:9 (Zech 11:13, Jer 18:2-3).

regard Matthew's "formula quotations" as modelled on *pesher*, we may draw attention to several parallels.

First, while the classic *pesharim* exemplify the recent, contemporary and future fulfilment of sacred tradition, it is significant that this perspective occurs in a number of texts that fall outside the *pesher* genre and that do not in fact use the term *pesher* at all.[29] Thus Matthew (and those who made use of fulfilment quotations before him) may reflect an interpretive strategy which, though found specifically amongst the sectarian texts discovered at Qumran, was more widespread and, in any case, not confined to a particular genre.

Second, the Gospel of Matthew (in particular, though also the other New Testament gospels) and *pesharim* relate their scripture interpretation to a series of key figures known through recent events. On the side of the *pesharim*, the biblical texts are made to refer to a number of figures and groups such as the Teacher of Righteousness, Man (or Spouter) of Lies, Wicked Priest, Furious Young Lion, House of Absalom, House of Absalom, and Seekers of Smooth Things. On the side of Matthew's Gospel, biblical quotations are applied and fulfilled in relation to Jesus, the twelve disciples, the people, and Jesus' opponents (Jewish leaders, Judas Iscariot), though here, unlike the Qumran texts, proper names play a more prominent role.

Third, both the *pesharim* and Matthew relate their reading of biblical tradition to one who they believed was endowed with unique teaching authority: the Teacher of Righteousness and Jesus, respectively. In both cases, however, claims made about these key figures are bound up with the writers' interpretive strategies which cannot be confidently traced back in their preserved forms to either figure. We have, instead, primarily to do with a perspective, and cultural memory, of devotees and followers whose piety these key figures inspired. It is interesting in this regard to note that the writer of the *Habakkuk Pesher* only claims, in the third person, that in principle "all the mysteries of his [God's] servants the prophets" were revealed to the Teacher (1QpHab vii 1-5; cf. ii 1-10), though not one of the interpretations of Habakkuk given in the *pesher* itself is actually credited to the Teacher. Thus the authority of the Teacher functions as a warrant for the implicit claims made by the writer himself

---

[29] See esp. J. A. Fitzmyer, "The Use of Explicit Old Testament Quotations in Qumran Literature and in the New Testament", *NTS* 7 (1960-1961): 297-333, with its most recent republication in idem, *The Semitic Background of the New Testament* (Grand Rapids and Livonia, Mich.: Eerdmans and Dover Booksellers, 1997), 3-58.

(about whom little else is known) to apply the intention of the biblical text to recent and current events.[30] Though in the Gospel traditions, a number of teachings are explicitly ascribed to Jesus himself, the pesharist's strong hand in presenting and shaping what is remembered about the Teacher opens the way to asking whether or not, for example, the authority attributed to Jesus' teaching in Matthew's Gospel (Matt 7:29; pars. Mark 1:22, 27 and Luke 4:32) functions not only as a claim about Jesus himself (however much Jesus understood himself this way) but also, by extension, as a way of sanctioning and giving weight to the anonymous writer's own presentation of Jesus on behalf of his community of hearers and readers.[31] Thus the fulfilment hermeneutics of the Scrolls and Gospels does not so much lead to comparisons between the Teacher of Righteousness and Jesus as it throws light on the implicit claims to authoritative interpretation on the part of the pesharists, on the one hand, and the literary tradents of Jesus tradition, on the other.

To be sure, the present comparison needs to retain an awareness of several basic differences between pesharic biblical interpretation and that of the Gospel tradition. First, and obviously, unlike the Gospels (especially Matthew), none of the Qumran texts ever expressly refer to a biblical text as "fulfilled",[32] while no biblical quotation in the New Testament is ever introduced with one of the Qumran *pesher*-formulas. This basic difference is enough to underscore that one should be wary of regarding ideas expressed in the one as assumptions that were being held in the other.

Second, the formal quotations of scripture appear in a wide variety of literary contexts amongst the Qumran documents: Leaving the parabiblical compositions on prophetic figures[33] and rewritten biblical materials[34]

---

[30] See L. T. Stuckenbruck, "The Legacy of the Teacher of Righteousness in the Dead Sea Scrolls", in *New Perspectives on Old Texts: Proceedings of the Tenth International Symposium of the Orion Center for the Study of the Dead Sea Scrolls and Associated Literature 9-11 January 2005* (eds. E. G. Chazon, B. Halpern-Amaru and R. A. Clements; Leiden: Brill, 2010), 23-49 (here 25 n.3, 35-36, and 45-47).

[31] Similar, though varying, claims to authority on the part of writers may be observed at work in *1 En.* 104:10-11 and 4 Ezra 14:37-48, though in these cases, the authors are not formally anonymous, but manipulated tradition and constructed their narratives pseudepigraphically.

[32] Cf. Fitzmyer, "Old Testament Quotations", 55.

[33] So e.g. *Apocryphon of Moses* (1Q22, 1Q29, 4Q375-376, 4Q408); 4QVisSam (=4Q160); *Pseudo-Daniel* (4Q243-245); 4Qpap paraKings (4Q382); *Apocryphon of Jeremiah* (4Q383-384, 4Q385a, 4Q387, 4Q387a, 4Q388a, 4Q389-390); *Pseudo-Ezekiel* (4Q385-386, 4Q385b, 4Q388, 4Q391).

[34] See the *Temple Scroll, Jubilees* and *Reworked Pentateuch*.

aside and taking the use of *pesher* and *pesher*-like commentary as points of departure, we have the following[35]: (a) quotations followed by interpretations that reflect the order of a biblical text from the same document without a break (continous *pesharim*, e.g. 1QpHab and 4QpNah); (b) quotations plus interpretations, presented without a break, in which the lemmata from a biblical book do not always follow the textual arrangement of that book (4QpPsa[a], 4QpIsa[b], 4QpIsa[c]); (c) quotations plus interpretations from the same biblical book without following the sequential arrangement of that book and interrupted by text (4Q252); (d) quotations accompanied by interpretations from different biblical books strung together without intervening text (4Q174, 4Q177, 4Q182, 11Q13); (e) quotations accompanied from different biblical books sometimes either without formal introductions or separated by short phrases or sections of intervening text (see e.g. 4Q175, 4Q183?); (f) quotations accompanied by interpretations without use of the term *pesher* and separated by intervening text (e.g. *Damascus Document*; cf. CD A cols. vi-viii); (g) documents that present themselves as *pesher* without identifying the biblical base text (4Q180-181). Except for category (a), in which the arrangement of the received biblical tradition determines and shapes what is presented in the commentary, those writings under the other categories organise in a wide variety of ways the choice and reading of the authoritative text-traditions around particular perspectives or themes.[36] Though there may be a certain analogy between category (e) and the Gospel traditions, the latter, in the way they interpret biblical tradition, are not simply thematic, but orient *all* the material to underlining the significance of Jesus himself. Hence, the Gospel traditions are more likely than any extant Qumranic counterparts[37] to put the idea of scripture fulfilment into the mouth of Jesus himself; in this way, Jesus is presented as drawing on sacred tradition to account for the ministry of John the Baptist (Matt 11:10), his own ministry (Luke 4:21, 22:37; John 7:37-38), those

---

[35] The following categories are my own, though the writings under (b) through (g) are discussed as "commentaries on prophetic scriptures" by George J. Brooke, "Thematic Commentaries on Prophetic Scriptures", in *Biblical Interpretation at Qumran* (ed. M. Henze; Studies in the Dead Sea Scrolls and Related Literature; Grand Rapids: Eerdmans, 2005), 134-57 (here 138-55). Despite the explicit focus of his study, Brooke acknowledges that the authoritative texts chosen for comment range well beyond prophetic writings themselves (Pentateuch, historical books, Psalms).

[36] Determining the theme that guides such choices is easier in some documents (e.g. 4Q174, 4Q175) than in others (*Damascus Document*) which draw on authoritative materials (a) to focus on exhortation

[37] The pesharic fulfilment quotations are always introduced and presented as the words of the anonymous authors.

who respond positively to his teaching (John 6:45), those who oppose him (John 10:34; 13:18; 15:25), and those unable to understand his parables (Matt 13:14-15[38]).[39] While it is never formally clear from the Scrolls what interpretations of biblical tradition are openly being attributed to the Teacher of Righteousness, the Gospels are bolder in ascribing such interpretation to Jesus.

Third, unlike the *Habakkuk Pesher* (1QpHab vii 1-2), the Gospel traditions say nothing about the prophets not having the ultimate meaning of their words disclosed to them. If anything, the Gospel writers, in having Jesus reduce the importance of the Messiah being the Son of David, assumes that David understood what it meant for him to call him "Lord" (Ps 110:1; cf. Mark 12:35-38//Matt 22:41-45//Luke 20:41-45; see also cf. Acts 2:25-35). In addition, the prophet Isaiah's awareness about the opponents of Jesus is assumed in Mark 7:6-8 (par. Matt 15:7-9; cf. John 12:39-41). To the extent that the *Habakkuk Pesher* represents what was thought about the prophets' limited awareness of the meaning of their revelation, the Gospel traditions steer in a different direction. Whereas the Dead Sea sectarian texts reflect an unquestioned inner-Jewish discourse which could assume continuity with sacred tradition shared by other groups, the presentation of Jesus in Matthew's Gospel was battling against suspicions that Jesus and the movement which sprang from him had exceeded acceptable boundaries; in their references to prophetic figures such as David and Isaiah, the Gospels could not afford to undermine continuity with biblical tradition of contemporary Jews.

3. The Present: Life of the Pious Within Two Overlapping Epochs

In concert with some early Jewish apocalyptic literature, the Dead Sea Scrolls put us in a better position to appreciate how much Jesus' and early Christian understanding of existence in the present world order is indebted to Judaism. To be sure, this point in itself is uncontroversial. However, a particularly "Christian" understanding of existence is frequently contrasted with those espoused within Second Temple Jewish traditions, as if it were essentially a *novum* introduced through the teaching

---

[38] The parallels in Mark 4:12 and Luke 8:10 likewise cite Isa 6:9-10 which, however, is not explicitly introduced as fulfilled.

[39] In addition, John's Gospel is more reticent than the Synoptics in having the narrator introduce the fulfilment quotation (only 12:15, 38, 39-40; 19:24, 28, 36, 37), while fulfilment quotations are attributed also to John the Baptist (1:23), the disciples (2:17), and the crowds (6:31; 7:42; 12:13).

and activities of Jesus' and expressed by theological reflections in Paul's letters. I refer particularly here to the "eschatological tension" that is made to carry considerable weight in relation to defining characteristics of faith in the New Testament. On the one hand, Jesus proclaimed the imminent dawning of God's kingly rule while, at the same time, claimed that it was already arriving through his ministry.[40] On the other hand, for Paul the Christ-event (God's definitive act through Jesus' death and resurrection) had marked a shift away from the old era, ushering in a new age that would culminate in when things are set right in the eschaton.[41] While the perspectives of Jesus and Paul were manifestly different and while scholarly debates concerning their respective emphases persist, their similar understanding of life in the present world as one of negotiating divine presence and triumph (the "already") with ongoing evil in all its dimensions (the "not yet") has provided a nucleus around which a distinctive character of Christian faith presented in the New Testament may be articulated.

Though it is frequently recognised that tensions between fulfilment and promise could be held within the Hebrew Bible and that, to some extent, these could be at work in Second Temple apocalyptic Jewish literature, the prevailing understanding of Jewish apocalyptic thought as being essentially concerned with a "doctrine of two ages" has resulted in an underestimation of the formative significance of Jewish tradition for precisely these aspects of New Testament thinking. Here the Dead Sea Scrolls provide important evidence in supplementing what early Jewish traditions tell us about the understanding of life amongst pious Jewish within an "Already-Not Yet" scheme.

A number of documents in the Dead Sea Scrolls reflect back and develop apocalyptic traditions in *1 Enoch* and *Jubilees* that regard the

---

[40] See e.g. C. H. Dodd, *The Founder of Christianity* (New York: Macmillan, 1970); N. Perrin, *Jesus and the Language of the Kingdom: Symbol and Metaphor in New Testament Interpretation* (Philadelphia: Fortress Press, 1976), 204; J. D. G. Dunn, *Jesus and the Spirit: A Study of the Religious and Charismatic Experience of Jesus and the First Christians as Reflected in the New Testament* (London: SCM Press, 1975), 41-67; T. P. Rausch, *Who Is Jesus? An Introduction to Christology* (Collegeville, Minnesota: Liturgical Press, 2003), 77-93.

[41] Influential advocates of this reading of Paul have been W. Kümmel, "Paulus", in idem, *Heilsgeschehen und Geschichte: Gesammelte Aufsätze 1933-1964* (Marburg: Elwert, 1965), 439-56; J. C. Beker, *Paul the Apostle: The Triumph of God in Life and Thought* (Edinburgh: T. & T. Clark, 1989); and J. D. G. Dunn, e.g. in *Jesus and the Spirit*, 308 ("[t]he most characteristic feature of Christian experience") and *The Theology of St. Paul the Apostle* (Grand Rapids: Eerdmans, 1998), 461-498 (esp. 462-65, 472-77). See recently T. R. Schreiner, *New Testament Theology: Magnifying God in Christ* (Grand Rapids: Baker, 2008).

present age as a time of wickedness during which, however, active demonic forces are essentially defeated powers and can be controlled through various means. The Enochic and *Jubilees* traditions, both of which are preserved in fragments amongst the Scrolls, deal with the problem of evil in the present age by taking a myth about rebellious angelic beings as their point of departure. In *1 Enoch* 6-16 the story, which embellishes the more neutral text-tradition in Genesis 6:1-4, not only functioned to condemn questionable impositions of foreign culture (so esp. chapters 6-11),[42] but also offered an aetiology for the origin of demonic spirits (chapters 15-16) that focused primarily on the fallen angels' offspring, the giants who *inter alia* are also called "Nephilim" (*1 En.* 7:2; *Book of Giants* 4Q530 2 ii 6, 4Q531 1.2, 4Q532 2.3 cf. *Jub.* 7:22) and *mamzerim* (cf. *1 En.* 10:9, cf. 9:9).[43] Having destroyed one another (*1 En.* 10:9, 13:6, 14:6, 16:1; *Jub.* 5:7, 7:22; *Book of Giants* 4Q531 7) or having been destroyed by the Great Flood (*1 En.* 89:6; *Book of Giants* 4Q530 2 ii 6-12; cf. 4Q370 i 6, Wis 14:6; *Sib. Or.* 2:227-232, *3 Macc.* 2:4; *3 Bar.* 4:10), they could only survive as spirits that are credited with afflicting humanity and leading them astray to idolatry (*1 En.* 15:11; *Jub.* 10:11-13). Their destruction in the past signifies that, though they are active or even hold sway in the present time, their future annihilation at the final judgement is assured (*1 En.* 10:12-14; 16:1; cf. *Jub.* 10:8)[44] because royal power in the cosmos belongs to God alone (*1 En.* 9:4; 84:2-6; 4Q203 9.6).

This view, which regards the present as a period during which persistent evil is managed and negotiated with confidence in view of their defeat by God in the past, extends into a number of documents preserved amongst the Scrolls. We mention briefly three examples. The first

---

[42] For this interpretation see G. W. E. Nickelsburg, "Apocalyptic and Myth in 1 Enoch 6-11", *JBL* 96 (1977): 383-405 and *1 Enoch 1: A Commentary on the Book of 1 Enoch Chapters 1-36; 81-108* (Heremeneia; Minneapolis: Fortress Press, 2001), 170.

[43] On this tradition, see further L.T. Stuckenbruck, "Giant Mythology and Demonology: From the Ancient Near East to the Dead Sea Scrolls," in *Die Dämonen – Demons. Die Dämonologie der israelitisch-jüdischen und frühchristlichen Literatur im Kontext ihrer Umwelt* (eds. A. Lange, H. Lichtenberger and K. F. Diethard Römheld; Tübingen: Mohr Siebeck, 2003), 318-38; "The Origins of Evil in Jewish Apocalyptic Literature: Interpretation of Genesis 6:1-4 in the Second and Third Centuries BCE," in *The Fall of the Angels* (eds. C. Auffarth and L. T. Stuckenbruck; TBN 6; Leiden: Brill, 2004), 86-118; and A. T. Wright, *The Origin of Evil Spirits: The Reception of Genesis 6:1-4 in Early Jewish Literature* (WUNT II/198; Tübingen: Mohr Siebeck, 2005).

[44] This conviction fed the view that divine judgment in the past serves as the prototype for eschatological judgment; for a discussion of the relevant texts, including *1 En.* 91:5-9 and 106:19-107:1, see L. T. Stuckenbruck, *1 Enoch 91-108* (CEJL; Berlin: Walter de Gruyter, 2007), 94-95 (comment on *1 En.* 93:4c).

is preserved in the Hebrew fragments belonging to *Songs of the Maskil* (4Q444 and 4Q510-511). At several points this composition offers a list of and refers to malevolent such as "demons", Lilith, hyenas, howlers, jackals, "impure spirit(s)", spirits of destruction and *mamzerim* (cf. 4Q510 1.4-8; 4Q511 2 ii 3, 10.1-4, 35.7, 43.6, 48-49+51.2-3, 121; 182.1; cf. 4Q444 2 i 4).[45] The last-mentioned of which refers to the disembodied spirits of the giants (cf. *1 En.* 10:9). The songs, formulated as hymns of praise to God,[46] are written for a *Maskil* to recite as a way, with assuredness (cf. 4Q444 1-4.1-4; 4Q511 1.4-8, 2 i 3), to neutralize the effects of these forces during the present yet temporary "age of the dominion of wickedness" (4Q510 1.6-8; 4Q511 3.3; 10.3, 5; 35.8).[47] The second text comes from 11Q11 (=*11QApocryphal Psalms*). Here one of the demonic beings denounced in an "in]cantation" (*la]ḥaš*) is directly addressed in the second person and, if the reconstruction is correct, may be called "offspring from] Adam and from the seed of the ho[ly one]s" (11Q11 v 6), that is, a spirit remnant of the giants.[48] The series of texts reflect a certain confidence that despite these times of "humiliation" (cf. 11Q11 iv 12), demonic powers can be subdued. The third text, which has less to do with demonic powers (in the plural) than with the chief demon Belial, illustrates a similar perspective on the present age, though does not deal with it in the same way as in the previous examples The yearly liturgy of the Qumran community in *Serekh ha-Yaḥad* is formulated against the backdrop of understanding the current period as being under Belial's rule or dominion (1QS i 23-24 and ii 19; cf. further 1QM xiv 9-10 par. 4QMᵃ = 4Q491 8-10 i 6-7; cf. further 1Q177 iii 8). Like the Enoch tradition and other texts that come under its influence, Belial's dominion is regarded as temporary; in addition, like the apocalyptic traditions, the community believed it is possible to manage or neutralize demonic power in anticipation of its final destruction. Here, not exorcism but community denunciation in the form of a curse

---

[45] There is also a reference to *mamzerim* in 1QHa xxiv 12; however, it is isolated and without sufficient context to determine its precise meaning, i.e. whether it is a label applied to a class of sinners or functions as a designation for demonic beings.

[46] On the genre of "hymnic exorcisms", see A. Lange, "The Essene Position on Magic and Divination," in Bernstein, García Martínez and Kampen, *Legal Texts and Legal Issues,* 377-435 (here 383, 402-403, 430-433), who also applies this classification to 1QapGen xx 12-18, *Jub.* 10:1-14; 12:16-21.

[47] See 4Q510 1.6-7: "and you (viz. the demonic beings) have been placed in the age of the dominion of wickedness and in the periods of subjugation of the sons of ligh[t]..." (par. 4Q511 10.3-4).

[48] For a discussion of the alternative reconstructions of the lacuna, see Wright, *The Origin of Evil Spirits*, 183-184 and note 66.

is the measure appropriated against the chief demon. During the time which is essentially characterized by Belial's rule, the Aaronic blessing of Numbers 6:24-26 provides the grist of terms with which the Community formulated curses to be spoken against Belial and petitions for divine protection from evil (1QS i 16 – iii 11). This approach to evil is not based on any overwhelming anxiety that threatens to undo the piety of the community as a whole, but rather is an expression of confidence that the power of Belial is only temporary. Though unlike the Enochic tradition there is here no reference to God's past activity as a guarantor of evil's future annihilation, the community's confidence in its position of advantage reflects the claim of its members to participate in an angelic form of existence even in the present.[49] The apocalyptic traditions preserved through the Enochic literature and *Jubilees* which are more concretely reflected in practices adopted among the Dead Sea Scrolls reveal that some measures for handling evils of life were shaped by a certain "eschatological tension".

It has long been recognized that the New Testament Gospels share a similar view that the present age is dominated by personified evil (John 12:31, 14:30, and 16:11; cf. Luke 11:24-26). Not surprisingly, this shared understanding of the cosmos has been attributed to Christianity's debt to Jewish apocalyptic thought. However, the classic "two ages" scheme, which only becomes clear in later Jewish apocalypses such as 4 Ezra and 2 Baruch, has far too often supplied the foil with which "Christian" ideas are conveniently contrasted. Moreover, many New Testament scholars overlook the extent to which the measures of dealing with the present evil age in Jewish tradition also, in themselves, provide a framework within which Jesus' ministry of exorcism and claims about the Christ-event as the inauguration of a new age could develop. Once faith communities came to regard Jesus' death and resurrection as a decisive act of God, such claims provided them with further basis for dealing with persistent evil forces (through petitionary prayers,[50] exorcisms,

---

[49] For this view, see the following sectarian texts: 1QS xi 8; 1QSb iv 26; 1QH[a] xi 21-23; xiv 12-13; xix 10-14; 2.10, 14; 5.3; 10.6-7; 4Q181 1.3-4; 1QM vii 6 par. 4Q491 = 4QM[a] 1-3.10; 12.1-2, 7-9; cf. further 4Q511 8.9 and 11Q14 ii 14-15. See esp. the discussions by M. J. Davidson, *Angels at Qumran: A Comparative Study of 1 Enoch 1-36, 72-108 and Sectarian Writings from Qumran* (JSP Supplements 11; Sheffield: Sheffield Academic Press, 1993), 132-285 and K. P. Sullivan, *Wrestling with Angels. A Study of the Relationship between Angels and Humans in Ancient Jewish Literature and the New Testament* (AGAJU 55; Leiden: Brill, 2004), 147-178.

[50] See *Aramaic Levi Document* (4Q213a=4QTLevi[a] 1 i 10 par. *Jub.* 1:19-20); 11Q5 xix (esp. lines 13-16); *Jub.* 10:3-6 and 12:19-20 (cf. also 15:32; 19:28); and Tob 8:3. On these petitions for protection from demonic power, which serve as formative back-

hymns); indeed, as in the apocalyptic traditions discussed above, they could do so with renewed vigour, recognising that the eschatological defeat of these powers is assured. However, as fundamental as these convictions about God's activity in Jesus were for his followers, there was little emphasis, beyond statements of principle, that malevolent effects of evil spirits, Satan, and sin have been demonstrably wiped away. Instead, in the meantime, in joyful anticipation of eschatological justice and reward, though this time based on Christological convictions, they could address or neutralize these unrelenting problems through temporary expedients.

4. Parallels Between Jesus' Teaching and the Scrolls

A number of Dead Sea Scrolls texts compare positively with instructions attributed to Jesus. While these parallels do not require interpreters to assert a direct relationship between Jesus and the authors of those compositions, they do establish his identity as a Jew concerned with issues being contested amongst his Jewish contemporaries.[51] Among the many examples of this in the Gospels, we may note four from that have come up time and again in scholarly discussion, two which have been known for a long and two which have become known since further materials became available from Cave 4 in 1991.

First, there is Jesus' categorical stricture against divorce in Mark 10:6-9, which appeals to Genesis 1:27 (v. 6, "God created them male and female") and to Genesis 2:24 (v. 7, "a man shall leave his father and mother and cleave to his wife, and they shall become one flesh"). This instruction, which expressly refers to the way things were from creation and makes no explicit allowances for an exception, has no real

---

ground for the petitions in Mt. 6:13 (cf. 2 Thess 2:3) and John 17:15, see L. T. Stuckenbruck, "Pleas for Deliverance from the Demonic in Early Jewish Texts," in *Studies in Jewish Prayer* (eds. R. Hayward and B. Embry; JSS Supplements 17; Oxford: Oxford University Press, 2005), 55-78.

[51] The criterion of exclusively shared traditions (i.e. between Jesus in the Gospels and the Scrolls) is misleading because it tends towards a reductionism in defining Jesus' socio-religious matrix and does not give adequate room for differences that emerge when the parallels are analyzed. A similar point holds on the other side for the determination of authentic Jesus tradition: the criterion of double dissimilarity builds a portrait of Jesus who is so disengaged from his contemporaries that his views cannot be linked with those of any particular group. Just as traditions attributed to Jesus are complex, this is no less the case for any of the movements whose ideologies his are compared with.

parallel in Jewish tradition.[52] However, it can be compared with the appeal to Genesis 1:27 in the *Damascus Document* (see CD A iv 20 – v 2), in which the principle of creation (iv 21) also plays a role. There argument of the *Damascus Document* does not pertain to divorce, however, but rather is levelled specifically against polygamy. In doing so, the writer takes the law of the king in Deuteronomy 17:18-19 and, on grounds of "the foundation of creation", widens its application to anyone who is pious. The Markan Jesus does not have Deuteronomy 17 in view; instead, in specifying that God "created them male and female *from the beginning of creation*" opposes the original state of relations between man and woman to Mosaic legislation which came about "on account of your hardness of heart". To be sure, the discourse about polygamy may have implications regarding divorce; since the prohibition of simultaneous marriage to more than one woman implies that only death can make marriage to someone else possible, then it follows that divorce is not an option to begin with (cf. *Temple Scroll* at 11Q19 lvii 17-19).[53] If this holds, then the parallel between Jesus in Mark 10 and the admonition of CD A iv is at least implied. Nevertheless, the appeal to creation in both texts serves very different purposes, so much so that another text in *Damascus Document* not preserved in CD (4Q271 3 5-15) actually countenances the possibility of remarriage for a woman who has a "bad [na]me" (line 13). While scholarly debate has not settled whether or not an unsuitable woman in this passage includes a divorcee,[54] the possibility of remarriage here – nothing extant in the text mentions that this is occasioned by death – stands in relation to the stricture in CD A iv in an way that parallels the relation of Mark 10:11-12 to verses 6-9. In both documents as they stand, the way things should be is not set forth without some consideration being given to the very real question of remarriage.

---

[52] In terms of origin, Jesus' stricture in Mark 10:6-9 should be distinguished from the instruction in vv. 11-12 which presupposes that divorce has already taken place.

[53] So the argument of L. H. Schiffman, "Laws Pertaining to Women in the *Temple Scroll*," in idem, *The Courtyards of the House of the Lord: Studies on the Temple Scroll* (STDJ 75; Leiden: Brill, 2008), 519-540 (esp 527; repr. from 1992) and V. Noam, "Divorce in Qumran in Light of Early Halakah," *JJS* 56 (2005): 206-223 (here 206-210).

[54] So Vered Noam argues that this text may include a divorcee (though it would be on grounds of adultery, if one takes the phrase *la'asot ma'aseh ba-dabar* in 4Q271 3.11 as an allusion to *'erwat dabar* in Deut 24:1); see further J. Kampen, "Matthean Divorce Texts Reexamined," in *New Qumran Texts & Studies. Proceedings of the First Meeting of the International Organization for Qumran Studies, Paris 1992* (ed. G. J. Brooke; STDJ 15; Leiden: Brill, 1992), 149-168 (here 155-156).

Second, scholars have drawn attention to the prohibition of oath-taking in Matthew 5:33-37 (cf. Jas 5:12), which seems to have an important parallel with Second Temple Hebrew tradition[55] in the *Damascus Document* at CD A xv 1-2 (no parallel amongst the Dead Sea manuscripts).[56] The shared emphasis is that both texts forbid swearing by appealing to God. They do this, however, in different ways. In Matthew oaths are prohibited in relation to parts of the cosmos that are associated with God's kingly activity and presence (heaven, earth, Jerusalem), and there is no express mention of God's name; the *Damascus Document* text (CD A xv 1) is concerned with protecting the divine name by forbidding oaths sworn by the names of El (literally "*aleph* and *lamed*") and Adonai ("*aleph* and *daleth*"), as well as swearing by the "Torah of Moses" because it contains the divine name (cf. Lev 19:12). Another difference consists in what each text ultimately commends. Whereas CD qualifies the prohibition by making allowance for "the oath of the children by the curses of the covenant (*šěbu'at ha-banim ba'elot ha-běrit*)" (line 2),[57] Jesus seems to deny the value of taking oaths altogether (Matt 5:34, 37) and displays no interest in being drawn into a debate on casuistic distinctions.[58]

The third example relates to the background for the Beatitudes in the Sermon on the Mount (5:2-12). In 1965 the only real parallel that Braun could adduce for the Beatitudes from the Scrolls was the expression "humble in spirit" (1QM xiv 7 - ענוי רוח/עני).[59] As far as the form of

---

[55] There is evidence in Jewish Greek literature of suspicion towards oath taking; see Philo, *Leg.* 3.207; *Spec.* 4.40; and *Decal.* 93).

[56] E.g. K. Schubert, "The Sermon on the Mount and the Qumran Texts," in *The Scrolls and the New Testament* (ed. K. Stendahl; New York: Harper, 1957), reprinted with a foreword by J.H. Charlesworth (New York: Crossroad, 1992), 118-128 (here 126) and R. E. Murphy, *The Dead Sea Scrolls and the Bible* (Maryland: Westminster, 1957), 85 argued from this that Jesus' instruction is "Essene"; for the disparagement of oaths amongst the Essenes, see Josephus, *B.J.* 2.135 (cf. *Ant.* 15.371), though in 2.139 and 142, as in 1QS v 7-13 – see n. 57 – oaths are made compulsory for anyone joining the group.

[57] This qualified use of oaths concurs with a whole series of qualified prohibitions preserved in CD A xvi 1 – ix 1 (pars. 4Q266 8 ii 1-10; 4Q270 6 iii 13-15; 4Q271 4 ii 1-16), whereas elsewhere in sectarian texts binding oaths are enjoined on those who enter the *Yaḥad* (1QS v 7-13 and shorter pars. 4Q256 ix 6-8, 4Q258 i 5-7).

[58] It is, however, not as clear from Jesus' halakhic criticisms of the scribes and Pharisees in Matt 23:16-22 whether oath taking is being as categorically ruled out as in the Sermon on the Mount. On the latter passage as a Matthean reworking of Jesus' tradition to address post-Jesus controversies, see U. Luz, *Matthew 21-28*, (trans. J. E. Crouch; Hermeneia; Minneapolis: Fortress Press, 2005), 118-21 (though Luz ultimately regards Matt 23:16-22 as an attempt to work out the grounds on which oaths are to be rejected).

[59] Also extant already was the same expression in 1QH[a] vi 3, a text which would inform Puech's analysis (bibl. in note 62 below).

the Beatitudes is concerned, he noted that the macaristic term אשרי
"scheint in den bisher bekannten Qumran-Texten überhaupt zu fehlen".[60]
Though already mentioned by Jean Starcky in a 1954 communique (with
J. T. Milik),[61] 4Q525 did not become the focus of attention until the studies published by Émile Puech and George Brooke in the late 1980s.[62] In
relation to the Matthean Beatitudes, several parallels were quickly established in the manuscript at 4Q525 2-3 ii 1-6: (a) the text likewise contains a set of beatitudes (the beginnings of four of these are extant) introduced by אשרי (equivalent for Greek μακάριος Matt 5:3-11; cf. Ps 1:1
passim); (b) the text refers to someone who conducts activity "with a
pure heart" (2-3 ii 1) and who, if the reconstruction is correct, is declared
"blessed" for it (cf. Matt 5:8); (c) a lengthier, final beatitude is pro-
nounced on one who attains Wisdom (2-3 ii 3) and does not abandon,
forget, or loathe her when in distress but thinks of her, meditates on her
and puts her before his eyes (2-3 ii 5-7; cf. the final beatitudes in Matt
5:10 and 11-12 for those who are persecuted for their piety). Of course,
the Matthean beatitudes do not explicitly refer to "wisdom"; however,
the strong association of Jesus with Wisdom in the Gospel of Matthew
(cf. 12:28-30; cf. Sir 51:23-27) suggests that it is as Wisdom that Jesus
is uttering the beatitudes at the beginning of the Sermon on the Mount.
If this is the case, then persecution "for my sake" (Matt 5:11, an equivalent to "for righteousness' sake" in v. 10) would come close to the
emphasis in 4Q525 on continuing devotion to Wisdom despite distress.
One should beware of drawing these parallels too far: the distress in
4Q525 is not specifically explained as arising *because of* wisdom, nor is
it clear that the similarities, even when considered in the wider context,
support the dual claim that both the Matthean beatitudes (including 5:13-
16) and 4Q525 have initiation ceremonies for respective entering community members in view.[63]

[60] Braun, *Qumran und das Neue Testament*, 13-14 (here 13).
[61] In *Comptes rendus de l'Academie des Inscriptions et Belles-lettres* (Paris: Librarie
C. Klincksleck, 1954), 403-09 (408); cf. also J. Starcky, "Le Travail d'édition des
fragments manuscrits de Qumrân", *RB* 63 (1956): 49-67 (67).
[62] See É. Puech, "Un hymne essénien en partie retrouvé et les Béatitudes: 1QHª V 12-VI 18
(= col. XIII-XIV 7) et 4QBéat.", *RevQ* 13 (1988): 59-88 and G.J. Brooke, "The Wisdom
of Matthew's Beatitudes (4QBéat and Mt. 5.3-12)," *Scripture Bulletin* 19 (1988-1989):
35-41, republished in updated form as "The Wisdom of Matthew's Beatitudes," in idem,
The Dead Sea Scrolls and the New Testament, 217-34. For the official publication by
Puech of all 50 fragments of 4Q525, see *Qumran Cave 4.XVIII: Textes hébreux
(4Q521-4Q528, 4Q576-4Q579)* (DJD XXV; Oxford: Clarendon Press, 1998), 115-78.
[63] There is no positive evidence that 4Q525 should be read as a Yaḥad document. For the
argument, see Brooke, "The Wisdom of Matthew's Beatitudes," 232-233, who, based

The fourth example, well known since initial publication in 1992, illustrates how intertextuality in the New Testament with sacred tradition from the Jewish scriptures can include the reception of that tradition in the Second Temple period. In describing the eschatological activities of the Adonai, 4Q521 2 ii + 4[64] quotes Psalm 146:7-8 (line 8) and Isaiah 61:1 (line 12). Just before the citation that recognizably comes from Isaiah 61 ("he will bring good news to the afflicted"), the text adds two activities not found in either Psalm 146 or Isaiah 61: "for he will heal the wounded, and he will bring the dead to life". In the tradition shared by Luke and Matthew (Luke 7:22 par. Matt 11:5), Jesus' answers John the Baptist's disciples' question about his identity by describing his activities based on a series of allusions which include Isaiah 61: "the blind see (Ps 146:8; Isa 29:18, 35:5, 42:18) and the lame walk (cf. Isa 35:6); lepers are cleansed and the dumb hear (Isa 35:6; cf. 29:18, 42:18), and the dead are raised (cf. Isa 26:19) and the poor are having good news brought to them (Isa 61:1)". This last part of Jesus' answer, which clearly draws on Isaiah 61:1 in combination with the raising of the dead, follows precisely the order as given in 4Q521 2 ii + 4.12. Though it is possible that the reference to raising the dead in 4Q521 is an allusion to Isaiah 26:19, the occurrence of this motif within a list that draws on Isaiah 61 indicates that we more likely have to do with an adaptation of the latter. Jesus' answer, then, draws on Isaiah 61 in a form that is only found in 4Q521. This does not mean, though, that one can assert the direct influence of the Dead Sea text (not to mention of Essene ideas – 4Q521 does not make use of any sectarian terminology characteristic of the Yaḥad) on Jesus. This is for several reasons: (1) 4Q521, though referring to "his (God's) anointed one/messiah" (2 ii +4.1-2), does not do in connection with activities (lines 8, 12) that are attributed to God;

---

on similarities in phraseology, reads 4Q525 together with the entrance oaths of 1QS v 7-11 "as a reminder of Essene initiation" (233). Neither is it clear that Puech's reconstruction of 1QH[a] VI 2-7 as a lengthy beatitude that likewise is concerned with initiation.

[64] Émile Puech published the first study of the manuscript in "Un apocalypse messianique (4Q521)," *RevQ* 15 (1991/1992): 475-519. Since then, much has been written about this document and its relationship to the Gospel tradition. See esp. F. García Martínez, "Messianische Erwartungen in den Qumranschriften," *JBTh* 8 (1993): 171-208 (here 182-85); J. J. Collins, "The Works of the Messiah", *DSD* 1 (1994): 98-112; K.-W. Niebuhr, "Die Werke des eschatologischen Freudenbotes (4Q521 und die Jesusüberlieferung)," in *The Scriptures in the Gospels* (ed. Ch. M. Tuckett; BETL 131; Leuven: Leuven University Press, 1997), 637-46; and H. Kvalbein, "The Wonders of the End-Time: Metaphoric Language in 4Q521 and the Interpretation of Matthew 11.5 par.," *JSP* 18 (1998): 87-110.

by contrast, the activities referred to by Jesus are his own. (2) 4Q521 draws on traditions from Psalm 146:7-8, while no part of Jesus' answer quotes anything that is distinctive from the Psalm. (3) The list of activities attributed to Jesus is one continuous whole, while in 4Q521 the allusions to Psalm 146 and Isaiah 61 are presented separately with several lines between. What can be said, nonetheless, is that Jesus' catalogue of activities provides evidence for his messianic identity by taking up Isaianic tradition in a re-presented form that 4Q521 has also preserved. 4Q521 cannot by itself explain why it is that God's "messiah" should do these things, but it does explain that Isaianic tradition was circulating in a form well known enough that its tradents in "Q" expected their contemporaries to recognize it. In addition, one may note that the activities associated with the Lord in 4Q521 are such that could be associated with the eschatological period in which God's Messiah will be obeyed by heaven and earth (2 ii +4.1) and when the commandments of "the holy ones" (i.e. angels) will be heeded by "all t]hat is in them" (2 ii + 4.2).[65]

5. Ideas Allegedly Formulated in Opposition to Traditions in the Dead Sea Scrolls

While the contrasts between material preserved amongst the Dead Sea Scrolls and traditions in the New Testament are both numerous and obvious, there are a few which have been construed as deliberate. Here it is appropriate to mention four of the more obvious examples which are commonly listed and have attracted considerable attention.

First, in the Sermon on the Mount, Jesus is made to be critical of a tradition, "You shall love your neighbor (τὸν πλησίον σου; cf. Lev 19:18) and hate your enemy (τὸν ἐχθρόν σου)" (Matt 5:43), which is introduced by the words, "You have heard it said".[66] Jesus' response to this searches for the other extreme, namely, "love your enemies (ἀγαπᾶτε τοὺς ἐχθροὺς ὑμῶν) and pray for those who persecute you" (5:44). The introductory words suggest that we have to do with a tradition which circulated in a form that could (a) be transmitted as a teaching and (b) function as a distinct strategy for conducting socio-religious relations. In addition, the text impresses on readers the formal nature of the instruc-

---

[65] So L. Novakovic, "4Q521: The Works of the Messiah or the Signs of Messianic Times," in *Qumran Studies: New Approaches, New Questions* (eds. M. T. Davis and B. A. Strawn; Grand Rapids: Eerdmans, 2007), 208-31.
[66] I focus on Matthew's version since the Lukan parallel to Matt 5:43-48 (Luke 6:27-36) does not quote the teaching to which Jesus is opposed.

tion. We only otherwise find an explicit enjoinder to hate enemies in Jewish tradition in *Serekh ha-Yahad* at 1QS i 9-11. The text, which occurs at the beginning of the document, specifies that the work was written in order "to love all the sons of light, each one according to his lot in the plan of God and to hate all the sons of darkness, each one in accordance with his guilt in God's punishment". A subsequent passage (1QS ii 4-9) incorporates this purpose into the community's liturgy, though without expressly using the word "hate". Here the priestly members of the Yahad are told to pronounce a curse on the sons of darkness:

> Cursed are you for all your wicked and guilt-ridden deeds. May he (viz. God) hand you over to dread into the hands of all whose carrying out acts of vengeance. Cursed be you without mercy, because of the darkness of your deeds, and may you be sentenced to the gloom of everlasting fire. May God not be merciful when you entreat him, nor pardon you when you do penance for your faults. May he lift the countenance of his anger to avenge himself on you, and may there be no peace for you in the mouth of those who intercede.

The community's curse against the sons of darkness adapts wording from the Aaronic blessing of Numbers 6:24, reformulating it in a negative way.

The claim that Jesus is specifically concerned with a tradition associated with the "Essene" community at Qumran has had relatively few critics.[67] However, a straightforward co-ordination between the logion and a formalized tradition circulated in a community such as at Qumran should take the following two points into account. First, the possessive pronoun "your" is in the singular, that is, a *community* setting is not in view. One could explain the singular as providing a parallel for the singular as used in Leviticus 19. Still, if the descriptiveness of "your" is in question, how appropriate is it to identify a parallel within a community's formal activities? Second, though the Qumran text provides a better parallel, the notion of hating one's enemy could be taken for granted as emerging from the Jewish scriptures (esp. 2 Chr 19:2; Ps 5:5; 26:5; 31:6; 45:7; 97:10; 119:104, 163; 139:21-22; Hos 9:15; Amos 5:15).

Second, in a tradition only preserved in Luke's Gospel (16:1-8), Jesus' parable about a dishonest steward who wastes his master's goods culminates in a reference to "the sons of light". When the steward collects from his master's debtors half of what is owed, his master commends him for having acted shrewdly. This story leads Jesus to pronounce, "For

---

[67] For an early summary of the discussion, see Braun, *Qumran und das Neue Testament*, 17-18.

the sons of the world are more shrewd in their generation than the sons of light" (v. 8b). The story is told in order to remonstrate against those who would imitate "the sons of light" whom Jesus regards as wasteful of what they have been given. "Sons of light" is, of course, a widespread designation amongst the Dead Sea Scrolls, not only in Yaḥad texts (1QS i 9, ii 16; 1QM i 1, 3, 9, 11, xiv 17 par. 4Q491 8-10 i 14; 4Q174 1-2 i 9; 4Q177 10-11.7; 12-13 i 7, 11; 4Q266 1a-b 1; 4Q280 2.1) but also in other materials whose socio-religious context is harder to identify (1QS iii 13, 24, 25; 4Q510 1.6; esp. the Aramaic 4Q548 1 ii + 2.16).[68] Whereas "sons of light" in all the Scrolls texts denotes those who are aligned with God (so that "light" is opposed to "darkness"), Jesus' use presupposes that the designation circulated in a way that is no longer descriptive but functioned like a label or proper name.[69] Whether or not the parable has the Essenes or Qumran group in view, it remains that the most relevant background for "sons of light" is extant amongst the Scrolls.

Third, Jesus' parable of the talents (Matt 25:14-30 par. Luke 19:11-27) advises that someone entrusted with money should invest it, activity which, for example, in the Book of Tobit is treated as good financial planning (Tob 1:14; 4:1-2, 20-21; *passim*). The servant who does not take any risk at all is called by the master a "wicked and lazy servant" who "ought to have deposited my money with the bankers, and at my coming I would have received back my own with interest" (Matt 25:26-27 par. Luke 19:22-23). Though the parable is not about financial planning per se but is concerned with God's kingdom, the force of its message derives from the view taken on investment. In *Musar le-Mevin* at 4Q416 2 iii 3-5 par. 4Q418 9 there is evidence for a very different, if not opposing view: "as you have received it (money), thus give it back, and you will have joy if you are innocent from it.... If someone places it at your disposal until death, put it away and do not corrupt your spirit by it". The parable of Jesus is not engaged in a polemic against such a tradition so much as proceeding along very different lines to illustrate that those who invest what they have been given will be rewarded.

---

[68] See the helpful discussion, which further links the expression "mammon of righteousness" in Luke 16:9 with a "wealth of wickedness" amongst the Scrolls, by D. Flusser, "The Parable of the Unjust Steward: Jesus' Criticism of the Essenes," in *Jesus and the Dead Sea Scrolls* (ed. J.H. Charlesworth; Garden City: Doubleday, 1992), 176-97. Nevertheless, Flusser's conclusion that "the 'sons of light' in Jesus' parable of the unjust steward can be identified directly with the Essenes, who are the authors of the Dead Sea Scrolls" (191) is overstated.

[69] This contrasts with the more positive, descriptive function of the "children/sons of light" in John 12:36, Eph 5:8 and 1 Thess 5:5.

Fourth, the Matthean version of Jesus' healing of a man's withered hand on the Sabbath (Matt 12:9-14 par. Luke 6:6-11) has Jesus justify his action by appealing to the need to rescue one's animal on the Sabbath day if it has fallen into a pit (Matt 12:11; see the parallel in Luke 14:5). The Matthean text has Jesus say, "Who among you would not take hold of your only sheep (Luke: a child or an ox) and lift it out (ἐγερεῖ) if it falls into a pit on the Sabbath?" For a parallel in contrast, many have drawn attention to the prohibition in the *Damascus Document* at CD A xi 13-14 (par. 4Q270 6 v 18, 4Q271 5 i 8-9): "and if it (an animal) falls into a cistern or a pit, one should not lift it out on the Sabbath". Though Jesus' view is often deemed to be more "liberal" than that taken in the *Damascus Document* and, therefore, is thought to be opposing such a view,[70] one should note two problems in forging a direct connection: (1) Jesus' saying is a rhetorical question and (2) it is uttered under the presumption that his interlocutors (Matt 12:14-Pharisees; Luke 14: 3-scribes and Pharisees) that there would be agreement with this point. To suggest that the saying in its present forms in Matthew 12 and Luke 14 has the non-Qumran Essenes behind the *Damascus Document* in view is to miss the emphasis of the logion itself.

6. Tradition that Exposes Jesus' Radical Approach to Questions of Purity

Jesus' show of compassion towards the blind, deaf and lame (Matt 11:5 par. Luke 7:22; Matt 15:30-31; 21:14; Luke 14:13, 21) and his open association with "sinners" (Mark 2:15-17 par. Matt 9:10-13, Luke 5:30-32; Matt 11:19 par. Luke 7:34; Luke 15:1-2) run counter to passages in the Scrolls which exclude such people from full participation in the worshipping community (1QSa ii 5-8; CD xv 15-17 par. 4Q266 8 i 7-9; 4QMMT at 4Q394 8 iii-iv 4; 4Q491 1-3.10; cf. 4Q174 1 i 3-6; 11QTemple lxv 12-14).[71]

> No man defiled by any impurities of a man may enter into the assembly of these; and no man defiled by these should be established (in his) standing in the midst the congregation. And anyone defiled in his

[70] See J. H. Charlesworth, "The Dead Sea Scrolls and the Historical Jesus," in idem, *Jesus and the Dead Sea Scrolls*, 33-34: Jesus "may well have directed his attack against an Essene teaching on the Sabbath". See further Braun's overview of early scholarly debate in *Qumran und das Neue Testament*, 25-26.
[71] See J. D. G. Dunn, "Jesus, Table-Fellowship, and Qumran," in Charlesworth, *Jesus and the Dead Sea Scrolls*, 255-72 and idem, *Jesus Remembered* (Grand Rapids: Eerdmans, 2003), 604-05.

flesh, paralyzed at the feet or hands, lame or blind or deaf or dumb or with a defiled blemish in his flesh visible to the eyes or an unstable old man who cannot stay upright in the midst of the congregation – these shall not en[ter] to take their place [in] the midst of the congregation of the m[e]n of renown, for the angels of holiness are [in] their [congre]gation.

It is not clear that Jesus' activity is formulated in specific contrast to the Dead Sea texts. However, the latter do not provide concrete evidence from the late Second Temple period that such regulations could be in force for a pious Jewish community, while the Gospel traditions emphasize how much Jesus' liberal approach to halakhic matters stood out in sharp relief. Despite this stark contrast, Jesus' healing of those who by their illnesses and disabilities were considered "impure" shares an assumption with the Dead Sea texts and biblical tradition (cf. e.g. Lev 21:17-24) that such conditions are problematic and, therefore, are in need of healing, whether through Jesus' activity or in a spiritual or physical resurrection in the eschaton.

7. Additional Background Previously Explained by Appeal to Graeco-Roman Culture

The Scrolls may provide preserve expressions of the Jewish religious context which can be introduced into discussions which have otherwise focused on parallels to early Christian practices described in the New Testament taken from the Graeco-Roman world. Three examples, one well known and the others now emerging, may be mentioned.

The first is the sharing of goods attributed to Jesus' devotees in Jerusalem in Acts (2:44-45; 4:35-37; 5:1-4; cf. 6:1). This has been compared with the sharing of one's property required from those being initiated into the Yaḥad according to *Serekh ha-Yaḥad* (1QS i 1-13; v 2; vi 2-3, 16-25; vii 6-8; ix 21-23 par. 4Q258 iii 6; CD A xiii 11; xiv 20 par. 4Q267 9 iv 8-9).[72] Ernst Haenchen, in his commentary on Acts, played

---

[72] See the discussion in Braun, *Qumran und das Neue Testament*, 143-49; see further J. A. Fitzmyer, "Jewish Christianity in Acts in the Light of the Qumran Scrolls," in idem, *Essays on the Semitic Background of the New Testament* (SBS 5; Missoula: Society of Biblical Literature, 1974), 271-303 (301-02: "... the early Jewish Christian church was not without some influence from the Essenes. It is not unlikely... that among the 'great number of priests' (Acts 6:7) who were converted some were Essene and provided the source of Essene influence"); Charlesworth, "The Dead Sea Scrolls and the Historical Jesus," 18; and Capper, "The Palestinian Cultural Context".

down as "deceptive appearance"[73] the significance of any similarities between Qumran texts and the Jerusalem congregations, stressing a number of essential differences.[74] This comparison, however, is one-sided and presupposes that interpreters decide between the Essenes, on the one hand, and descriptions of philosophical and religious schools, on the other, as discrete alternatives. As Gregory Sterling has shown,[75] the descriptions in Acts of common life in the Jerusalem community of Jesus' adherents is best understood against the background of idealizing presentations of religio-philosophical groups preserved by ancient authors writing in Greek; significantly, this literary tradition included the reports by Josephus and Philo on the Essenes. Thus the comparison can be conducted on the basis of an *idealizing tradition of summary* that takes Acts and Josephus-Philo (and the reports of Chaemeron [on Egyptian priests first cent. C.E.], Philostratus [Egyptian sages third cent. C.E.], Arrian [Indian sages second cent. C.E.], and Iamblichus [Pythagoreans third-fourth centuries C.E.]) as the point of departure. Given the comparability of what Josephus and Philo say about Essene groups and material in the Dead Sea Scrolls – which is also ideologically shaped – one may ask whether the basis for comparison should be so limited to a Hellenistic tradition. Whatever it is that inevitably distinguishes Acts from descriptions of the Yaḥad in the Scrolls, there is no reason for the comparisons to include Scrolls texts as well.

Not insignificant, therefore, is the convergence of approximate correspondences between the language of the sectarian literature and Acts 4:32 (πλῆθος; cf. *rbym* and *rb* esp. in 1QS vi 1, 1-25 *passim*), as well as with 2:44 and 4:32 (expression of community unity: having ἅπαντα κοινά, reflecting the sense of *yaḥad* used both adverbially and as the community's self-designation). Moreover, the prominence of Levites in the Yaḥad (1QS i-ii and pars. in 4Q256 ii 3.12; iii 4; 4Q257 ii 1) has a counterpart in Acts to single out Joseph called Barnabas, a Levite, as an exemplary figure for the liquidation of his property and the distribution of the proceeds through the apostles in the community (4:36).

---

[73] E. Haenchen, *The Acts of the Apostles: A Commentary* (rev. and trans. by R. McL. Wilson; 14th ed.; Philadelphia: Westminster Press, 1971), 230-35 (234).

[74] E.g. the supposed "celibacy" of the community and that the Qumran community did not allow anyone to retain property in private (1QS i 11-12; Josephus, *B.J.* 2.122; cf. Philo, *Prob.* 77, see also 84 and 91). See further, J. A. Fitzmyer, *The Acts of the Apostles* (AB 31; Garden City: Doubleday, 1998), 270.

[75] "'Athletes of Virtue': Analysis of the Summaries in Acts (2:41-47; 4:32-35; 5:12-16)", *JBL* 113 (1994): 679-96 (here 688-96).

In view of the other considerations mentioned above, what kind of relationship between the Jerusalem and the Qumranic sectarian texts might these affinities suggest? The idealizing language of Acts and the Scrolls does not reflect back to us a straightforward report – and, in any case, cannot be expected to provide snapshots of contemporary fits within a sociological continuum in first century C.E. Judaea – so that it is difficult to find "historical" evidence for how the Qumran community really worked, on the one hand, and how the earliest Jewish Christian community organised its life in Jerusalem, on the other. To draw any connection between historically reconstructed entities behind the texts that suggest influence is almost an impossible aim to achieve in terms of probability. Regarding tradition-history, however, the parallels make it hard to discount the contextual possibility that the description of the community in Acts 2 and 4 is somehow indebted to ideals that could be articulated as such in contemporary, even antecedent Jewish tradition. Thus even if it is the "sectarian" Qumran documents that furnish the closest Jewish parallels for the sharing of goods among Jesus' followers in Jerusalem, we are not obliged – beyond the admission of possibility – to presume that here is a case of direct Essene influence on early Christianity. Instead, one may have to take seriously analogous social factors, including a strong sense of identity related to a founder, an ethical vision for coherence of a group enhanced by the interpretation of sacred tradition, and a belief that this unity would form the basis for the eschatological restoration or reconstitution of the community of God. From these considerations, then, we learn two things: (1) tradition-historical comparisons of Acts 2 and 4 in relation to the ancient Mediterranean world cannot be firmly resolved along discrete alternatives (Graeco-Roman and Jewish) and (2) such comparisons, valuable as they are, have an appropriate outlet in posing a further set of questions which focus on social conditions that make analogies among distinct communities that shared a common Jewish heritage, without requiring contact to have taken place between them, possible.[76]

---

[76] For studies that move the questions and analysis in this direction, see E. Regev, *Sectarianism in Qumran: A Cross-Cultural Perspective* (Religion and Society 45; Berlin: Walter de Gruyter, 2007); idem, "Wealth and Sectarianism: Comparing Qumranic and Early Christian Social Approaches," in F. García Martínez, *Echoes from the Caves*; and the essays by D. J. Chalcraft in idem, ed., *Sectarianism in Early Judaism: Sociological Advances* (London: Equinox, 2007), 25-51 ("The Development of Weber's Sociology of Sects: Encouraging a New Fascination"), 52-73 ("Weber's Treatment of Sects in 'Ancient Judaism': The Pharisees and the Essenes"), and 74-111 ("Towards a Weberian Sociology of the Qumran Sects"). For a note of caution on a sociological

The second example comes to attention through recent indepth studies of *Musar le-Mevin*, a Hebrew composition which did not become available for study until the early 1990's and was published in the DJD series in 1998.[77] The significance of this composition has not gone lost on scholarship, especially since its publication,[78] and this is not least true in relation to New Testament study.[79]

Until very recently, one area on whose Graeco-Roman background there has been nearly unanimous agreement is the so-called "household codes" (or *Haustafeln*) found in a number of New Testament epistles (Col 3:18-4:1; Eph 5:21-6:9; Titus 2:1-10; 1 Pet 2:18-3:7). These codes, which provide short memorable instructions to members of the household (husbands, wives, fathers, mothers, children, slaves), have been anchored in influences traceable to Aristotle or Stoic ethics which circulated in the Mediterranean world and came to New Testament writers through Hellenistic Jewish writings.[80] Those who acknowledge the

approach towards Qumran sectarianism, see J. Jokiranta, "'Sectarianism' of the Qumran 'Sect': Sociological Notes," *RevQ* 78 (2001): 223-239.

[77] J. Strugnell and D. Harrington, eds., *Qumran Cave 4.XXIV. Sapiential Texts, Part 2: 4QInstruction (Musar le Mevin): 4Q415ff. with a Re-edition of 1Q26* (DJD XXXIV; Oxford: Clarendon Press, 1999).

[78] The work has figured prominently in several collections of essays, for example, *Wisdom Texts from Qumran and the Development of Sapiential Thought* (eds. Ch. Hempel, A. Lange and H. Lichtenberger BETL 159; Leuven: Leuven University Press and Peeters, 2002); *Wisdom and Apocalypticism in the Dead Sea Scrolls and in the Biblical Tradition* (ed. F. García Martínez; BETL 168; Leuven: Leuven University Press and Peeters, 2003); and *Sapiential Perspectives: Wisdom Literature in Light of the Dead Sea Scrolls. Proceedings of the Sixth International Symposium of the Orion Center for the Study of the Dead Sea Scrolls* (eds. J. J. Collins, G. E. Sterling, and R. A. Clements; STDJ 51; Leiden: Brill, 2004). In addition, it has been the focus of sustained study in several monographs: D. F. Jeffries, *Wisdom at Qumran: A Form-Critical Analysis of the Admonitions in 4QInstruction* (Piscataway: Gorgias Press, 2001); E. J. C. Tigchelaar, *To Increase Learning for the Understanding Ones: Reading and Reconstructing the Fragmentary Early Jewish Sapiental Text 4QInstruction* (STDJ 44; Leiden: Brill, 2001) ; M. J. Goff, *The Worldly and Heavenly Wisdom in 4Q Instruction* (STDJ 50; Leiden: Brill, 2003); B. G. Wold, *Women, Men, and Angels: The Qumran Wisdom Document Musar lᵉMevin and Its Allusions to Genesis Creation Traditions* (WUNT 2.201; Tübingen: Mohr Siebeck, 2005); and J.-S. Rey, *4QInstruction: Sagesse et eschatologie* (STDJ 81; Leiden: Brill, 2009).

[79] There is insufficient space here to discuss the blending of sapiential and apocalyptic traditions in *Musar le-Mevin* and its implications, for example, for the way "Q" studies have often based their reconstructions on the growth of the tradition on distinctions that could not be reconciled at any given level; see M. J. Goff, "Discerning Trajectories: 4QInstruction and the Sapiential Background of the Sayings Source Q," *JBL* 124 (2005): 657-73.

[80] So early on by M. Dibelius, *An die Kolosser, Epheser, an Philemon* (HNT 12; Tübingen: Mohr Siebeck, 1912), who argued for a Stoic background and, more recently, by D. E. Balch, *Let Wives Be Submissive: The Domestic Code in 1 Peter* (SBLMS 26;

possibility of Jewish mediation of more widespread domestic codes have not countenanced the possibility that formulaic regulations governing family relationships are preserved in Hebrew or Aramaic sources.

In this connection, however, Jean-Sébastian Rey has demonstrated the importance of *Musar le-Mevin* as a new conversation partner.[81] In focusing on Ephesians 5:21-6:9, he chooses the most convenient fit to themes found in *Musar*, especially in material which author of Ephesians adapted (and changed or augmented) from Colossians.[82] Though earlier studies drew attention to a surprising number of words, expressions, short phrases and themes in Ephesians that are exclusively shared with the Qumran sectarian texts,[83] no such connections had as yet been adduced for the household codes in the epistle.[84] The comparison, in particular, centres around instructions on the husband and wife relationship (Eph 5:21-33) and on honouring one's parents (6:1-4).

According to Rey, *Musar* at 4Q416 2 iii 20-iv 13 (par. 4Q418 10.5-10) treats husband-wife relations that resonates with Ephesians in at least four

---

Chico: Scholars Press, 1981), 21-62 who emphasizes household management traditions in the Mediterranean world; cf. also *Families in the New Testament World: Households and House Churches* (eds. D. Balch and C. Osieck; Louisville: Westminster John Knox, 1997) and A. T. Lincoln, "The Household Code and Wisdom Mode of Colossians", *JSNT* 74 (1999): 93-112, who refers to this as "the consensus view" (100). For the emphasis on Hellenistic Jewish literature, see J. E. Crouch, *The Origin and Intention of the Colossian Haustafeln* (FRLANT 109; Göttingen: Vandenhoeck & Ruprecht, 1971).

[81] "Family Relationships in *4QInstruction* and in Eph 5:21-6:4," in *Echoes from the Caves*, 231-55. Rey's study works out some of the ideas already suggested by Wold in *Women, Men, and Angels*, 237-39 and esp. "Family Ethics in *4QInstruction* and the New Testament," *NovT* 50 (2008): 286-300.

[82] Despite the parallels adduced for e.g. Col 1:12-14 from the Dead Sea Scrolls, the relationship between Colossians and the Scrolls may be examined along different lines. Most attention has focused instead on extent to which the so-called heretics attacked in the epistle espoused ideas are explicable on the basis of Jewish traditions extant in the Scrolls (or, alternatively, a form of proto-Gnostic thought); for a summary of the problems, see R. McL. Wilson, *A Critical and Exegetical Commentary on Colossians and Ephesians* (ICC; Edinburgh: T. & T. Clark, 2005), 35-57.

[83] In the volume edited by J. Murphy O'Connor, reprinted with a foreword by J. H. Charlesworth, *Paul and the Dead Sea Scrolls* (New York: Crossroad, 1990, orig. London: Geoffrey Chapman, 1968), several contributions, originally published elsewhere highlight the indebtedness of the language of Ephesians to Qumran language and ideas nowhere found in the Old Testament: P. Benoit, "Qumran and the New Testament," 1-30 (16-18); K. G. Kuhn, "The Epistle to the Ephesians in the Light of the Qumran Texts," 115-31; J. Coppens, "'Mystery' in the Theology of Saint Paul and Its Parallels at Qumran," 132-58 (134, 146-56); F. Mussner, "Contributions Made by Qumran to the Understanding of the Epistle to the Ephesians," 159-78.

[84] As illustrated in Braun, *Qumran und das Neue Testament*, 215-25. Until *Musar le-Mevin* became available for study, this state of comparison and analysis did not progress further.

ways. First, the text stresses the unity within the marriage through repeated allusions to Genesis 2:24 (4Q418 2 iii 20; iv 1, 3-4, 5) where, as in Ephesians 5:31 (and *contra* 1 Cor 6:16) "flesh" and the verb "unite" (iii 21) do not simply a reference to the sexual bond but, more broadly, embrace the couple's relationship as a whole. Second, there is the emphasis on understanding the wife as her husband's flesh (4Q416 2 iv 5-6: "you will be one with the wife of your bosom, for she is the flesh of [your] na[kedness"; cf. Gen 2:23, "flesh of my flesh") which, as in Ephesians 5:28-30 (cf. 5:23, 25), strengthens the force of the instructions to the husband.[85] Third, the sage of the *Musar* defines the husband's relationship to the wife in terms of domination: "over her spirit he has given you dominion" (4Q416 iv 6-7; cf. Gen 3:16, Num 30:7-9), while the father no longer has dominion over her (iv 6). With a different language directed at wives, Ephesians does not mention "rule" or "having dominion" but exhorts, within a framework of mutual submission (*contra* Col 3:17-18 which applies the imperative "submit" to women alone), to place themselves under their husbands as they would Christ (Eph 5:21-22). As in the *Musar*, the shared emphasis on the husband's superiority is grounded in the context of the strong bonds of unity (i.e. not confined to sexual relations). The author of Ephesians draws out the implications of this further than the *Musar* by exhorting husbands to "love" their wives (5:25, 28, 33; cf. Col 3:19). Fourth, the instruction to the husband is further grounded in what the *Musar* calls "the mystery of existence" (*raz nihyeh*; 4Q416 2 iii 21), while the writer of Ephesians, having quoted Genesis 2:24, declares, "This is a great mystery, and I am applying it to Christ and the church"; cf. 5:31-32). The "mystery" in *Musar* is not personified, but it does function in the document as a fundamental principle on which the cosmos and human social actions rest; although it has in some sense been disclosed to the one addressed (4Q416 2 iii 17-18) and there are some who already understand it (4Q418 123 ii 4), the addressee is nevertheless exhorted throughout to investigate, observe, meditate on and understand this "mystery" (4Q416 2 i 5; 2 iii 14; 4Q417 2 i 2, 18, 25; 4Q418 43-45 i 4 – "your mysteries"). For both Ephesians and *Musar*, it is "mystery" that provides the cosmological point of departure for reflections on everything else; in Ephesians it is correlated the divine will, whether Christ or the relationships for which Christology provides a warrant (see Eph 1:9, 3:3-5, 5:32; 6:19). Moreover, while the instructions in 4Q416 iii 20-iv 13 are, unlike Ephesians 5:21-33, *all* directed at the

---

[85] Cf. Wold, "Family Ethics in *4QInstruction* and the New Testament," 298-99.

husband, it should be noted that in one passage, only preserved in broken text, the writer of *Musar* also addresses instruction on husband-wife relationships to a woman (4Q415 2 ii 1, "honour him as a father... "); such an address is singular in ancient Jewish literature.

In the immediately preceding passage, *Musar* (4Q416 2 iii 15-19 par. 4Q418 9+9a-c 17-18 + 10a-b 1-2) offers instructions on parent-child relations which elaborate on the text traditions in Exodus 20:12 ("honour your father and mother so that your days may be long..." NRSV; cf. Deut 5:16). Significantly, as Ephesians 6:1-4 where, not only quotes the fifth commandment from the Decalogue but also refers to the function of parents as teachers for their children (4Q416 2 iii 17, "for they are the crucible which taught you"; cf. Eph 6:4b, to fathers: "bring them up in the discipline and instruction of the Lord"[86] NSRV). Again, as in the passage on husband-wife relations that follows, the *Musar* correlates obedience to parents and its favourable consequences with "the mystery of existence" that has been revealed (4Q416 2 iii 17-18).

The juxtaposition in both *Musar* and Ephesians of the instructions to husbands and wives, on the one hand, and to children in relation to parents, on the other, cannot be explained by a dependence of the latter on the former; indeed, the structure of Ephesians adheres to that of its predecessor in Colossians 3:18-21. While more analysis that also takes the Graeco-Roman context into account is needed, Rey's conclusion that "the differences between Eph 5:21-6:4 and Col 3:18-21 have parallels in the text of *4QInstruction*"[87] offers a thesis that puts the study of household codes in Ephesians, and perhaps even the New Testament, on a new footing. The sapiential tradition of *Musar le-Mevin* does not preserve any identifiers of Qumran authorship or, generally, of a sectarian group. However, if there is anything to be made of other parallels noted between the language of Ephesians and sectarian *Yaḥad* texts, not too much should be inferred from the *Musar*'s non-Qumranic and apparently non-sectarian origin that group's ideas would have enjoyed a wider circulation than those held by the Qumran group. Whatever the actual dissemination of traditions found in the Dead Sea texts, the existences of reports about Essenes living in relative isolation (e.g. by Pliny the Elder and Josephus) at least indicate that peculiarity and separatism could, ironically, lead to the preservation and distribution of their ideas.

---

[86] The corresponding passage in Col 3:20-21 has neither a quotation from the Decalogue, nor does it say anything about parental instruction of children.

[87] Rey, "Family Relationships in *4QInstruction* and in Eph 5:21-6:4," 254.

The third example which illustrates how the Dead Sea texts are shifting the balance of New Testament interpretation from Graeco-Roman ideas (whether non-Jewish pagan or Hellenistic Jewish sources) to a Hebrew or Aramaic speaking Jewish matrix relates to theological anthropology. In a series of recent studies, Jörg Frey, drawing initial inspiration from colleagues working on the emerging sapiential materials from Qumran in Tübingen and taking note of previous Pauline scholarship,[88] has addressed the background to Paul's use of the term "flesh" as a part of the human being primarily associated with sin (cf. Gal 5:3, 17, 19 and Rom 8:5-8 in which "flesh" and "spirit" are categorically opposed to one another).[89] Frey argues that neither בשר in the Hebrew Bible, nor the use of σάρξ in Wisdom of Solomon (7:1; 12:5; 19:21), Philo (throughout, with few exceptions, e.g. *de Gig.* 5, 7-8) and non-Jewish Hellenistic or gnostic traditions adequately explain Paul's usage. More similar usage can be found for "flesh" in the *Hodayot* (1QHᵃ v 30-33, vii 34-35, and xii 30-31) and *Serekh ha-Yahad* (cf. 1QS xi 7, 9-10, 11-12). Analogous to the previous example on the household codes, Frey maintains that *Musar* provides further evidence for a negative valuation of "flesh". According to *Musar* the wicked are called "(all) spirits of flesh" which will be shaken or demolished on the day of judgment (4Q416 1.10-13; cf. 4Q417 2 i 17, 1 i 15-18 and 4Q418 81.2).[90] For them there is no

---

[88] Esp. R. Jewett, *Paul's Anthropological Terms: A Study of Their Use in Context Settings* (AGJU 10; Leiden: Brill, 1971), 49-94.

[89] See Frey, "Different Patterns of Dualistic Thought in the Qumran Library: Reflections on their Background and History," in Bernstein, García Martínez and Kampen, *Legal Texts and Legal Issues*, 275-335; "Flesh and Spirit in the Palestinian Jewish Sapiential Tradition and in the Qumran Texts: An Inquiry into the Background of Pauline Usage," in *Wisdom Texts*, 367-404 (here 385-97); see also Frey, "The Notion of 'Flesh' in 4QInstruction and the Background of Pauline Usage," in *Sapiential, Liturgical and Poetical Texts from Qumran: Proceedings of the Third Meeting of the International Organization for Qumran Studies, Oslo 1998* (eds. D. Falk et al.; STDJ 35; Leiden: Brill, 2000), 197-226; idem, "Die paulinische Antithese von 'Fleisch' und 'Geist' und die palästinisch-jüdische Weisheitstradition", ZNW 90 (1999): 45-77; and idem, "The Impact of the Dead Sea Scrolls on New Testament Interpretation," 451-58.

[90] While the expression *rwḥ bśr* is collective in the reference in 4Q417 (where it is contrasted with "a spiritual people"), its meaning in the form *k(w)l rwḥ* in 4Q416 and 4Q418 seems less obvious. In 4Q416 the collective meaning is suggested by an implied contrast between this expression and "all the sons of his truth" (*kl bny 'mtw*; frg. 1, 10), so that the meaning of *kwl* is "all". In 4Q418 the collective meaning is likewise implied, though less clear-cut, because the expression is followed up by two parallel phrases: (1) *kwl 'šr śn'*, which may mean either "everything which he (God) hates" (which would then refer to evil deeds associated with the "spirit of flesh") or "all whom he hates" (which could refer to the wicked as a whole); and (2) *kwl t'bwt npš*[, that is "every/all abomination(s) of the soul", which suggests that human deeds or inclinations are in view and thus does not seem to denote those who are wicked *per se*.

possibility of meditation (*hgwy*; cf. 4Q417 2 i 14b-18a). Thus, although "flesh" in *Musar* retains the range of meanings associated with it in the Hebrew Bible, these texts demonstrate that on several occasions it functions as a qualifier for "inclination" and "spirit" and, as such, carries a negative connotation. Taken together with the other Dead Sea texts, a portrait of "flesh" emerges as a dimension of human existence that obstructs understanding, so that, for example, "the spirit of flesh" cannot know the difference between good and evil (4Q417 2 i 17-18). Moreover, the one addressed in 4Q418 fragment 81 is told that, in his special position "as a holy of holies" in the land and among the *elim* (line 4), God "has separated" him "from every spirit of flesh" (lines 1-2). Finally, "every spirit of flesh" will be shaken up in eschatological judgment (4Q416 1.12).

Frey's argument that the term "flesh" in the Dead Sea texts has acquired a negative connotation and therefore provides an important background for Pauline language is, I think, convincing. However, one may question whether Frey is right in concluding that *Musar*, in providing evidence for the opposition between "spirit of flesh" and "people of spirit" (see (4Q417 1 i 15-18), "is the earliest parallel to the later Pauline antithesis between 'flesh' and 'spirit'".[91] Though Frey recognises that use of "spirit" in *Musar* is varied, his wish to see an implied antithesis of this sort is misleading. Too much emphasis can be placed on "flesh" when it is the *nomen rectum*. More than drawing a contrast between "spirit" versus "flesh", the authors of the *Musar*, the *Hodayoth*, and the final hymn in 1QS seem just as concerned with something Paul does not do: *distinguishing one kind of "spirit" from another*, that is, one that corresponds to the human's obedience and submission to God and one that is "depraved", iniquitous, and conditioned by the "flesh". Indeed, one might consider the following inference: If there is a spirit of flesh – which can be dispensed with as part of the ideal human being in *Musar* – then there may, by contrast, be a "spirit of holiness" or "holy spirit" that characterises the chosen or understanding one. To be certain, *Musar* does refer several times to the "spirit" of the addressee, and is able to designate this as a "holy spirit" (*rwḥ qwdškh*; see esp. 4Q416 2

[91] As slightly overstated by Frey, "Flesh and Spirit in the Palestinian Jewish Sapiential Tradition," 396. Frey seems to modify this claim in his conclusion on pages 403-404: while admitting that the opposition between "flesh" and "spirit" is not yet "fixed semantically", he cautiously states that "if Paul knew about the negative usage of *bśr* or σάρξ from the Jewish tradition, he could, then, form such an opposition drawing on his own experience of the life-giving spirit in his vision near Damascus".

ii 6,17; iii 6). However, this spirit does not provide an opposite to the negative connotation of "flesh". This spirit is vulnerable in that it is subject to corruption (4Q416 2 iii 6 – *wrwḥkh 'l tḥbl*), and it is morally neutral, capable of being directed by the human will this way or that. Thus, if there is an opposition between "the spirit of flesh" and "a spiritual people" (4Q417 1 i 15-18), it is not given anything more than contextual expression by the text. In the end, what to Frey looks like an inceptive anthropological dualism in *Musar*, may in fact still be no more than an ethical dualism which, though broaching the question of human nature, has not formalised itself into fixed anthropological language.[92] Formative background should not be mistaken for precise conceptual matches. This open-ended language of *Musar* could, then, be a stepping-stone in the direction of two different dualities: (1) what *later* becomes an antithesis between "spirit" and "flesh" and (2) what becomes the antithesis between one kind of spirit and another.[93]

CONCLUSION

At the close of this discussion, it is appropriate to offer reflections that relate to (1) the general issues of language, (2) the place of the Dead Sea Scrolls within New Testament study, and (3) the wider context that frames it.

First, while the New Testament writings were, in their present form, all composed in Greek, the Dead Sea Scrolls are mostly preserved in Hebrew and Aramaic, with a small number of texts in Greek (4Q119-122, 4Q126-127, 7Q1-19). While Jesus taught and spoke with his contemporaries in both Aramaic and Hebrew and many of his sayings circulated in these languages, the presence of Greek in Judea and Galilee was also making an impact on Jewish culture, at least since the conquests of Alexander the Great. The multi-lingualism that characterized many parts of the Roman East meant that ideas could undergo linguistic

---

[92] Frey, "Flesh and Spirit in the Palestinian Jewish Sapiential Tradition," 396 and 403.

[93] For a more thorough, forthcoming treatment of the question of theological anthropology in *Musar* in comparison with Ben Sira, *1 Enoch* 91-105 and the Treatise on the Two Spirits in 1QS, see L. T. Stuckenbruck, "The Interiorisation of Dualism Within the Human Being in Second Temple Judaism: 1QS III:13-IV:26 in its Tradition-Historical Context," in *Light Against Darkness: Dualism in Ancient Mediterranean Religion and the Contemporary World* (ed. E. Meyers, A. Lange, B. H. Reynolds and R. Styers; JAJ Supp.; Göttingen: Vandenhoeck & Ruprecht, 2010), 159-84.

and conceptual change as they were disseminated, whether from Hebrew or Aramaic into Greek, or even the other way around. Without being able to track the complex issues here, we may reflect on how the Scrolls have contributed to our understanding of the multi-lingual context within and in relation to which the early followers of Jesus cultivated their identity.

The Dead Sea texts have furnished a large body of evidence that is both antecedent to and contemporary with the New Testament. Predictably, this has fed the sometimes enthusiastic discussion of verbal, linguistic, phraseological and conceptual parallels around which theories about the relationship between ancient Judaism and early Christianity have been constructed. Some of these have been discussed above. Emerging from this, several general points, often taken for granted, are worth noting here: (a) The common, or comparable language – even where alleged "parallels" are not exact – render Jewish ideas transmitted amongst the Scrolls in Hebrew and Aramaic as a significant resource for interpretation, not least because they expose the variety of traditions that existed *in these languages* during the Second Temple period. Thus we have to reckon with the increasing possibility that some, if not much, of the diversity of early Christian ideas can be traced back to a diversity – whether well-developed or in embryonic stages – that already existed in some measure among Jewish circles during the Second Temple period. The Scrolls have expanded the horizon of this diversity in the direction of Hebrew and Aramaic. (b) The Dead Sea materials have provided close parallels for Greek New Testament. To the extent that any parallels are meaningful, we have to do with significant cross-currents of tradition taking place within a vibrant multi-lingual socio-lingual context in which Palestinian Judaism participated during the Second Temple period. (c) We know a lot more about Hebrew and Aramaic as developing languages during the late Second Temple period. Future studies can be expected to result in further insight regarding the impact shifts in linguistic and social mediums made on Jewish and Christian ideas, practices, and identity.

Second, in the foregoing discussion I have considered a number of ways in which the Dead Sea documents are contributing to a better understanding of the New Testament. This understanding, on the one hand, is shaped through shared traditions that are exclusively shared by both groups of writings and through instances in which practices, ideas or compositional processes in the Scrolls should arguably feature in exegetical work among New Testament scholars interested in tradition history. The identification of commonalities, however, is only the beginning of study. More profoundly, it is by exploring *perspectives* conveyed by the literature on religious life, cosmology, time and theological anthropology where a tradition-historical stimulus for reinvigorating the discipline can be found. Today, most New Testament studies concerned with Jewish tradition cannot ignore the Scrolls without cutting out what has become both an essential source of information and launching ground for new and refocused questions. Thus the significance of the Scrolls does not depend on arguments, sometimes unnecessarily specific, that concentrate on establishing direct social links between Essenes and early Christian communities. Nor should the extent of their significance derive from a straightforward identification of anonymous figures in the texts with named characters mentioned in the New Testament and other contemporary sources.

The third and final point, we do well to strike a note of caution: an essay on the significance of the Dead Sea Scrolls for New Testament interpretation can reflect or even encourage a certain myopia, however unintentional that may be. The benefit of the Scrolls for New Testament research and exegesis is best seen when, as an area for study, it is placed alongside other areas that also merit attention if one wishes to establish ways Judaism gave rise to and continued to shape early Christianity and convictions: Philo and the New Testament, Josephus and the New Testament, philosophical schools and the New Testament, non-Jewish religions in the Mediterranean world and the New Testament, Jewish literature composed in Greek and the New Testament, "apocrypha" and "pseudepigrapha" and the New Testament, and so forth. Each of these areas should not be overlooked for what they contribute to the growth and vitality of non-Christian forms of Judaism. There is a growing recognition that Dead Sea Scrolls studies are not a discrete sphere of scholarly activity that can be segregated from contiguous fields of inquiry. And so, it is only now, with the near completion of the publication of the Scrolls, thanks in large part to the oversight of Emanuel Tov, that we hopefully find ourselves in an improved position to assess them in relation to their *relative value* for understanding the degree to which Jesus and the movements that grew out of his influence remained within a Jewish matrix of discourse. In this respect, the most important work on the Scrolls' contribution to Christian beginnings lies ahead, a contribution that will require increasing numbers of scholars who specialize in both areas.

SELECTED INDEX OF SOURCES

Contributions to Biblical Exegesis and Theology

34. L.J. Lietaert Peerbolte, *Paul the Missionary*, Leuven, 2003
35. L.M. Teugels, *Bible and midrash. The Story of 'The Wooing of Rebekah'* (Gen. 24), Leuven, 2004
36. H.W. Shin, *Textual Criticism and the Synoptic Problem in Historical Jesus Research. The Search for Valid Criteria*, Leuven, 2004
37. A. Volgers, C. Zamagni (eds.), *Erotapokriseis. Early Christian Question-and-Answer Literature in Context*, Leuven, 2004
38. L.E. Galloway, *Freedom in the Gospel. Paul's Exemplum in 1 Cor 9 in Conversation with the Discourses of Epictetus and Philo*, Leuven, 2004
39. C. Houtman, K. Spronk, *Ein Held des Glaubens? Rezeptionsgeschichtliche Studien zu den Simson-Erzählungen*, Leuven, 2004
40. H. Kahana, Esther. *Juxtaposition of the Septuagint Translation with the Hebrew Text*, Leuven, 2005
41. V.A. Pizzuto, *A Cosmic Leap of Faith. An Authorial, Structural, and Theological Investigation of the Cosmic Christology in Col 1:15-20*, Leuven, 2005
42. B.J. Koet, *Dreams and Scripture in Luke-Acts. Collected Essays*, Leuven, 2006
43. P.C Beentjes. *"Happy the One Who Meditates on Wisdom" (SIR. 14,20). Collected Essays on the Book of Ben Sira*, Leuven, 2006
44. R. Roukema, L.J. Lietaert Peerbolte, K. Spronk, J.W. Wesselius (eds.), *The Interpretation of Exodus. Studies in Honour of Cornelis Houtman*, Leuven, 2006
45. G. van Oyen, T. Shepherd (eds.), *The Trial and Death of Jesus. Essays on the Passion Narrative in Mark*, Leuven, 2006
46. B. Thettayil, *In Spirit and Truth. An Exegetical Study of John 4:19-26 and a Theological Investigation of the Replacement Theme in the Fourth Gospel*, Leuven, 2007
47. T.A.W. van der Louw, *Transformations in the Septuagint. Towards an Interaction of Septuagint Studies and Translation Studies*, Leuven, 2007
48. W. Hilbrands, *Heilige oder Hure? Die Rezeptionsgeschichte von Juda und Tamar (Genesis 38) von der Antike bis zur Reformationszeit*, Leuven, 2007
49. J. Joosten, P.J. Tomson (eds.), *Voces Biblicae. Septuagint Greek and its Significance for the New Testament*, Leuven, 2007
50. A. Aejmelaeus, *On the Trail of the Septuagint Translators. Collected Essays*, Leuven, 2007
51. S. Janse, *"You are My Son". The Reception History of Psalm 2 in Early Judaism and the Early Church*, Leuven, 2009
52. K. De Troyer, A. Lange, L.L. Schulte (eds.), *Prophecy after the Prophets? The Contribution of the Dead Sea Scrolls to the Understanding of Biblical and Extra-Biblical Prophecy*, Leuven, 2009
53. C.M. Tuckett (ed.), *Feasts and Festivals*, Leuven, 2009
54. M. Labahn, O. Lehtipuu (eds.), *Anthropology in the New Testament and its Ancient Context*, Leuven, 2010
55. A. van der Kooij, M. van der Meer (eds.), *The Old Greek of Asaiah: Issues and Perspectives*, Leuven, 2010

PRINTED ON PERMANENT PAPER • IMPRIME SUR PAPIER PERMANENT • GEDRUKT OP DUURZAAM PAPIER - ISO 9706

N.V. PEETERS S.A., WAROTSTRAAT 50, B-3020 HERENT